JESUS LAND

A MEMOIR

+ + +

JULIA SCHEERES

COUNTERPOINT

A MEMBER OF THE PERSEUS BOOKS GROUP

NEW YORK

Published by Counterpoint
A Member of the Perseus Books Group

Books published by Counterpoint are available at special discounts for bulk
purchases in the United States by corporations, institutions, and other
organizations. For more information, please contact the Special Markets
Department at the Perseus Books Group, 11 Cambridge Center, Cambridge,
MA 02142, or special.markets@perseusbooks.com.

Library of Congress Cataloging-in-Publication Data

Scheeres, Julia.
    Jesus land : a memoir / Julia Scheeres.
        p. cm.
    ISBN-13: 978-1-58243-338-7 (hardcover : alk. paper)
    ISBN-10: 1-58243-338-0 (hardcover : alk. paper) 1. Escuela Caribe
(Dominican Republic) 2. Scheeres, Julia—Childhood and youth. 3. Escuela
Caribe (Dominican Republic)—Students—Biography. 4. Problem children—
Education—Dominican Republic. 5. Christian education—Dominican
Republic. I. Title.
    LE17.D65S34 2005
    373.7293—dc22
                                                                    2005014816

05 06 07 08 / 10 9 8 7 6 5 4 3 2 1

FOR DAVID

"And ye shall know the truth,
and the truth shall make you free."

—JOHN 8:32, ESCUELA CARIBE HANDBOOK

CONTENTS

AUTHOR'S NOTE

The events in this book took place a long time ago, and involve many people with whom I no longer have contact. In the interest of protecting their privacy, especially that of people who were minors at the time, I have changed names and, in some cases, identifying details.

The time element is compressed for the sake of narrative flow, but the events portrayed herein are true.

PART ONE

+   +   +

IN GOD WE TRUST

CHAPTER 1

THE HEARTLAND

It's just after three o'clock when we hit County Road 50. The temperature has swelled past ninety and the sun scorches our backs as we swerve our bikes around pools of bubbling tar.

A quarter of a mile downwind from Hanke's Dairy, the stench of cow shit slams up our noses, and we rise in unison, stomping on the pedals and gasping toward the cornfield on the other side.

It's been two weeks since we moved to the country, and this is our first foray into the wilderness beyond our backyard. Our destination is a cemetery we spotted during a drive last Sunday that Mother insisted on taking after church. While David and I sat in the back of the van glaring out opposite windows, she coasted down dirt lanes, chattering about edible corn fungus, pig manure fertilizer, and other gruesome factoids she'd gleaned from her recent subscription to *Country Living* magazine.

David nudged me when we drove by the graveyard. It was set back from the road a bit, filled with brambles and surrounded by one of those pointy black fences that circle haunted houses in children's books, usually with a large KEEP OUT sign on the gate. This fence bore no such sign. We looked at the tombstones jutting sideways from the ground like crooked teeth, and knew we had to return.

We have a thing for bone yards, as we do for all things death-related. It's part of our religion, the topic of countless sermons: *Where will YOU spend ETERNITY? THE AFTERLIFE: Endless BLISS or Endless TORTURE?* We are haunted by these questions. If we die tomorrow, will we join the choir of angels or slow roast in Hell? We're not sure of the answer. So we are drawn to graveyards, where we can be close to the dead and ponder their fate as well as our own.

Once we pass Hanke's Dairy, we sit back down onto our bike seats. Along the length of the cornfield, a series of plywood squares nailed to stakes bear a hand-scrawled message:

Sinners go to:
HELL

Rightchuss go to:
HEAVEN

The end is neer:
REPENT

This here is:
JESUS LAND

You see such signs posted throughout the countryside: farmers using the extra snippet of land between their property and the road to advertise Jesus Christ. Mother approves. She says the best thing you can do in life is die for Jesus Christ as a missionary martyr, but posting signs by the side of the road can't hurt either.

"Anything to spread the Good News," she says.

It was her idea to move to the country. She grew up in rural South Dakota and had been threatening to drag us back to the boonies for years. Dad finally caved in. His drive to Lafayette Surgical Clinic, where he's a surgeon, is half an hour longer, but now he's also gotten into the country act, donning his new overalls to drive his new tractor around our fifteen acres.

Our three older siblings escaped this upheaval by leaving for college, so that leaves my parents, my two adopted black brothers, and me.

Jerome, our seventeen-year-old brother, hightailed it out of this 4-H fairground a few nights after we landed. He got into a fight with Dad, stole the keys to the Corolla, and drove off. Hasn't been seen or heard from since, which is fine by me, since Jerome is nothing but trouble anyhow.

So basically it's me and David, our ten-speeds, and the open road. And while the country graveyard is puny compared to the one by our old house—Grand View Cemetery, which we visited often in search of fresh graves—it still contains dead people, and that's what interests us.

It takes us five minutes to pedal past the cornstalks, standing higher than a man's head, to a cluster of double-wide trailers on the other side. They're anchored in a half circle, with an assortment of plastic flamingos and gutted vehicles strewn on the bald clay before them. The irritating twang of country music leaks from the trailer nearest the road, and as we sail by, a heap of orange cats lounging in the engine compartment of a rusted station wagon scatters into the dry weeds.

I curse myself for wearing a dark T-shirt in this booming heat. We haven't seen another human since we walked outside and would have stayed indoors ourselves if boredom hadn't driven us into the farmland.

"Watch for heatstroke," Mother, a nurse, warned us before we left. "If you get cramps or diarrhea or start to hallucinate, walk your bikes."

Sweat drips into my eyes, warping the landscape, and I lift my T-shirt to wipe my face, flashing my bra at the empty world. Ahead of me, David rides shirtless, his scrawny torso gleaming like melting chocolate. He's draped his T-shirt over his head and tied it under his chin like a bonnet. Like a girl. As if he didn't look dorky enough with those black athletic glasses belted to his head with that elastic band. If anyone from Harrison sees us, we're doomed.

William Henry Harrison is our new school; Hick High, the townspeople call it. There will be 362 people in our class, compared to twelve at Lafayette Christian, our old school, and we don't know a single one of them. These are farm kids who've known each other since they were knee-high to a rooster, kids who've probably never seen a real live black person before. Kids who worry us a lot.

I stand up and stomp on my bike pedals, trying to catch up with David and tell him to put his shirt back on, but he's on his second wind and flying over the crumbling pavement at enormous speeds. I yell at him and he rolls to a stop in the shade of an oak tree, turns and grins as I glide up beside him. I stand over my bike, panting, and point at his head.

"What's up with that?"

"Keeps the sweat outta my eyes."

"Looks queer."

He shrugs and pushes his glasses up his nose.

"Come on, take it off. Someone might see you."

"So?"

"Do you want people to think you're some kind of weirdo?"

He shrugs again and stares across the road at a herd of cows trying to cram themselves into the shade of a small crabapple tree. His jaw is set; once David's brain has clamped onto a notion, there's no unclamping it.

I shake my head and reach into the grocery sack strapped to his bike frame for a can of strawberry pop. When I yank off the metal tab, warm red froth bubbles over my fingers.

"Gosh darn it!"

I hand the can to David.

"Go on and drink your half."

We're saving the other can for the graveyard. I lick the sugar from my fingers and watch a cow, this one with a black body and white face, plod after the shadow of a small cloud that drifts across the pasture. When the shadow slips over the fence, the cow halts, lifts its tail, and spills a brown torrent onto the ground. I wrinkle my nose and turn to David.

"Remember when we used to ride to Kingston pool to swim every day?"

He stops drinking and peers at me sideways. His face is dry while mine drips sweat; maybe there's something to his bonnet notion after all.

"'Course I remember, dufus. That was just last summer."

"Point is, we never knew how good we had it, compared to this." I swipe my arm across the landscape: corn, cows, barns. More corn.

"Could be worse," David says, giving me the pop can.

"How's that?"

"We could be dead."

"Well, yes. But this has gotta be the next best thing."

He snorts, and I drain the can and drop it back into the sack.

We push off and are just gaining momentum when a long red car with a jacked-up rear end barrels around the corner ahead of us. It races in our direction, the thrum of the motor getting louder and faster. Suddenly, it lurches into our lane.

We swerve down a small embankment into a cornfield, crashing hard into the bony stalks and paper leaves. The car blurs by amid hoots of laughter.

David untangles himself from his bike and offers me a hand up. I charge up the embankment to the road.

"Stupid hicks!" I scream after the car, as it evaporates into the horizon. "Frickin' hillbillies!"

David walks over to stand beside me.

"They must be bored too," he says. He shakes his head at the blank horizon and reties his bonnet. He always takes things calmer than I do.

We've seen the country kids before as we've traveled back and forth to town for church or supplies. We've seen them slouched against pickup trucks, sharing round tins of spit tobacco. Lounging on plastic chairs in front yards, watching cars go by. Maneuvering giant machines through the fields, their bodies dwarfed by metal.

They are alien to us, as we must be to them.

So much for the famous 'Hoosier hospitality.' When we moved to our new house, no one stopped by with strawberry rhubarb pie or warm wishes. Our neighbors must have taken one look at David and Jerome and locked their doors—and minds—against us.

David and I shove back onto County Road 50, determined not to waste our journey. We clear a small rise and spot the cemetery a quarter mile ahead.

"Race you!" David shouts.

We crouch behind our handlebars, and David gets there first, as always. We lean our bikes against the fence, which is coated with a fine layer of orange rust, and walk around to the gate. It creaks as I push it open. David rushes past me to a gray block of marble just inside the fence that is roped with briars. He tramples down the vines and squats before it.

"Here lies Mabel Rose Creely," he reads as I peer over his shoulder. "Born April 18, 1837, dyed November 9, 1870."

He looks up at me with a smug grin.

"They spelled 'died' wrong."

"Like, duh."

I pick my way through the brambles and crooked tombstones to a large tablet set off by itself in a corner and tap it with my shoe to flake off the mud plastering its surface.

"Check it out!" I call to David. "Enus Godlove Phelon! He's got your same birthday, June 2, 1851! Died October something . . . I can't make it out."

"What's that name again?"

"Enus Godlove Phelon."

"Anus?"

"No, Enus! With an 'E.'"

"What kinda name is that?"

"A redneck name, for sure!"

We snicker and kick about for more stones. As I crouch to read them, I try to put the car out of my head and focus on the dead people beneath our feet. This is serious business, and I've got serious questions.

First, there's the appearance of the folks in the boxes. Do maggots fester in their eye holes like in horror movies, or do they stay pickled like the frogs in Biology class? David thinks it takes about two hundred years for a person pumped full of formaldehyde to turn into a skeleton, but I'm not so sure . . .

Then there's the Afterlife question. Where is the soul of the person I'm standing on right now—Heaven or Hell? Were they satisfied with their lives, or did they want more? If they could go back and do it all over again, what would they change? Is Heaven all it's cracked up to be?

As I'm contemplating all this, I detect a movement out of the corner of my eye and raise my head. The red car. It prowls noiselessly along the cemetery's edge and rolls to a stop beside our bikes. I look at David, who's bent over a marble cross, cracking up over some dead woman named "Bessie Lou."

"David."

". . . better name for a cow, don't you think?"

"David, stop it!"

His head shoots up at the alarm in my voice, and he follows my gaze to the car—four white bodies emerge from its interior—before standing to untie his T-shirt and slip it over his narrow shoulders.

They're farm boys, our age. Bare-chested and wearing cut-off jeans and baseball caps. You can tell they're farmers by their sunburns: their faces, necks and arms are crimson but their torsos are pasty, as if they're wearing white T-shirts. If you looked up "redneck" in the dictionary, they'd be there to illustrate, and I'd say as much to David if they weren't marching toward us with tight faces.

They halt in a row behind the fence. I glance at David. Behind his smudged glasses, his eyes are wide with fear.

"Whatch y'all doing?" the tallest one asks as a cow moos in the distance. He takes off his Caterpillar cap and fans his face with it.

"Just looking!" I say breezily, as if this was Montgomery Ward's and these boys were salesmen come to check on us.

"This here's the final resting place of my great-great-grand-daddy!" yells a boy with a Snap-On Tools cap.

The tallest boy tugs a piece of field grass from the ground and sticks the end in his mouth. He chews it slowly and saws his eyes back and forth between David and me.

David's mouth is gaping. I step between him and the farm boys, still grinning.

"We just moved out here from town and . . . "

"Obviously y'alls ain't from around here, else you wouldn't be in there," says a third boy—this one in an International Harvester cap.

The runt of the litter, an acne-scarred boy in a Budweiser hat, grabs the fence in his fists and shakes it violently, rattling our bikes. Behind the tall iron grate, his stumpy body heaving back and forth in anger, he looks like a caged monkey having a tantrum.

"This here's an American cemetery!" he shouts. "Only Americans are allowed in there! It's the law!"

I take a deep breath and look back at David, who's now gaping at the trampled brambles at his feet. *Close your mouth.*

"That's fine," I say, shrugging. "We'll just leave, then."

I move toward the gate, and the human fence behind it, listening for the rustle of David's footsteps at my back. *Move.*

"What's wrong with blacky?" the runt asks. "Cat got his tongue?"

He lifts his Bud cap and orange hair falls to his neck. I ignore him, keeping my eyes on the road beyond him, the road that will lead us to safety. He moves aside at the last moment to let me push open the gate. I'm on a hair trigger. If they so much as breathe on us, I'll bloody their eardrums with my screams. I stop and wait for David to walk through the gate, then follow him to our bikes.

The farmers are at our heels.

"That darkie your boyfriend?" one of them asks to a burst of snickers. I pull my bike upright and wheel it forward so David can get his.

"No, he's my brother."

They crowd around us.

"What, your momma git knocked up by some Detroit nigger?"

There's a shuffle of dirty laughter and the runt leans forward, his pimpled jaw working up and down. He hawks a glob of chew into the dirt, narrowly missing David's sneakers. I glare at him and he throws his shoulders back and grins proudly, a string of spittle stretching from his pink face to the dust. David contemplates the lump of brown slime at his feet with knitted eyebrows, as if it were the saddest thing he'd ever seen. *Don't you freeze up on me. Don't!*

"Let's go," I order David, elbowing him in the ribs.

"Yeah, you'd best skedaddle," the tall one says.

As we mount our bikes, they watch with crossed arms and slit eyes. We've got enough fear ricocheting through us to propel ourselves all the way home without stopping. We ride in silence, cringing and waiting for the gunning motor, the flash of red behind us.

Only when we bump down the gravel lane to our house do I notice the trembling cottonwoods, the frenzied chirruping of sparrows, the dirt devils churning across the back field. On the horizon, heat lightning dances along a column of towering thunderheads. The air is suddenly sweet and cool, refreshing. It's perfect weather for a tornado.

Down in the basement, I fling myself belly-down on the cot and stare out the window at the trees pawing the green air. David's out there somewhere, walking Lecka before supper.

Neither of us uttered a word about what happened. We never do. But I can't smudge it from my mind. The farm boys' sneering red faces. The runt shaking the fence. The brown lump of spit tobacco. The anguish in David's eyes. They don't know the first thing about us; they just hate us because we're black.

The first time I felt surrounded by such hate was in 1977, when we were ten. We were driving down to St. Simons Island, Georgia, for vacation and stopped at a roadside diner in Birmingham for supper. David and I were cranky with hunger because we'd stuffed the liverwurst and lettuce sandwiches Mother passed out for lunch under our seat cushions in the van.

Dad led us to a round table at the back of the restaurant that was big enough for the eight of us, then David and I busied ourselves with the game on our placemats as we waited for the waitress to take our order. This was in our dill pickle stage, and while we looked for animals hidden in a jungle on our placemats, we debated whether to share a side of the crunchy sour disks or order a bowl each. We knew Mother's rule: we had to finish whatever we ordered, or eat it for breakfast the next day. We decided breakfast pickles wouldn't be half bad and to order a side each.

After a while, we noticed a silence and looked up. Our parents and older siblings—Deb, Dan, Laura and Jerome—sat like statues, and beyond this familiar circle, the other diners glared at us with disgust stamped on their faces.

I was used to the curious looks and occasional frowns David and I gathered as we walked down the streets of Lafayette—I assumed people were as perplexed by my brother's skin color as I was when I first saw him—but I'd never seen anything akin to the contempt reflected in the eyes of those Alabama folks.

Mother gazed down at her place setting with a clenched jaw, and my father's cheeks burned red as he watched the waitress refill the coffee cups of the patrons at surrounding tables. David and I put down our crayons and focused on our parents, waiting for them to show us what to do.

After several minutes of this silence, Father pushed back his chair and stood up. He nodded curtly at Mother, who swept her arms upward like the choir director signaling us to stand, then bustled us out the door.

As we drove from the parking lot, I looked back at the diner. Through the window, I saw the waitress scrubbing our unused table with a rag and a spray bottle. No one mentioned what happened—not that night as we sat in the van, silent and hungry and searching for a drive-through—or ever afterward.

"Learn to leave things be," Mother likes to say when bad things happen. "Turn the other cheek."

And that's what we try to do. Pretend these things don't happen. But they do, again and again.

Outside, the sky has dimmed to olive, and I hear Lecka bark playfully. David's home safe again.

I wonder what would have happened that night in Alabama, if, instead of walking out in defeat, our father had stood up and rebuked those people for treating a God-fearing family in such a shameful fashion. Our family was hungry just like they were. Didn't we have a right to eat? Weren't we all equal in the eyes of Jesus Christ? How dare they deny small children food? This was America after all, a country founded on the principles of Christian love and harmony!

Maybe he felt the same way we did this afternoon—outnumbered and out-hated. Maybe it is better to turn the other cheek in certain situations.

Reverend Dykstra often tells us that this world is not our home.

"This place is merely a proving ground," he says. "Our suffering shall be rewarded in Heaven."

But sometimes I think that I'd rather have less suffering now, even if it meant less glory in Heaven.

The basement door opens and the brass bell clangs. Supper. I drag myself off the cot and climb the dark stairway. Mother's in the galley kitchen, stirring a large pot on the stove as Rejoice Radio plays Christian pop music over the intercom. At her back, the long windows cast a murky light over the hardwood floor of the great room. The new, L-shaped sectional lurks in semidarkness in one corner of the large room, the television and card table in another. A couple of boxes listing next to the stairwell—marked "winter gear"—wait to be carried downstairs and unpacked.

As I walk behind Mother toward the dining table—where David sits with back to me—I inhale the sour steam billowing off the pot on the stove and grimace. Garbage Soup, again. I slide into the chair across from David, silently grabbing my neck as if I were choking. He smirks his agreement.

Garbage Soup is Mother's name for it, not ours. She makes it from old vegetables and plate-scrapings—flaccid celery and carrot sticks, chicken bones, potato skins, cheese rinds—that she collects in a mayonnaise jar and freezes. When the jar is full, she stews the contents in salted water for two hours, strains the broth, adds hamburger, and le voilà, Garbage Soup! She says it's loaded with vitamins, one of the most nutritious meals ever. But it tastes just like its name, sour and dirty and old. It's summertime, the air con is off to save energy, and I'm damp with sweat, but the mayo jar was full, so it's Garbage Soup for supper. Waste not, want not.

Mother grew up poor and takes pride in her penny-pinching talents, which include an apple pie made entirely from saltine crackers that costs only three cents a serving. We eat this stuff despite our sprawling ranch house and the Porsche Dad drives to work every day.

"You forgot the beverage," Mother says wearily to David as she sets the rust-colored soup on the table. She stoops her shoulders as she ladles the broth into our bowls, making herself look more frail than she already is. Steam billows onto her glasses and into the tight light brown curls of her hair. I wait for her to raise her head and look at me, but she doesn't.

David returns with a pitcher of Carnation instant milk, which he pours into the glasses. As it swirls watery gray into mine, he smirks at me again.

After Mother blesses the food, we eat in silence as she leafs through *Christianity Today* magazine at her end of the table. She's in one of her moods; we knew it as soon as we returned from our bike ride. She was in the kitchen, ripping coupons from the newspaper, her lips smashed into a hard little line. She didn't say hello and neither did we. We took one look at her and went downstairs; it's best to fall under her radar when she gets like this.

The wind moans against the side of the house *woo woo!* and rushes through the open windows, fluttering the napkins in their stand. Outside, the trees dance at the edge of the back field as Sandi Patti sings "Yes, God Is Real" on Rejoice Radio. Mother lifts her spoon and blows across it without taking her eyes from the magazine. I stare at her and wonder what set her off this time. Maybe she got news of Jerome. Or she's peeved that Dad's late for the third night in a row. She glances up to see me staring and draws the magazine closer to her face, blocking me out completely. I look at David, and he shrugs *whadda ya gonna do about it?* Sometimes it seems the smallest signs of our existence—our laughter bubbling up from the basement, a book left on the couch—irritate her. She often tells us that she looks forward to the day we all leave home.

"God will be my family then," she'll say.

God and her missionaries. She's got missionaries around the globe. Sends them letters and packages, birthday cards, chewing gum, $10 bills. Pins their photos to the bulletin board over her desk. White couples, posing with mud huts and dark children, their locations jotted on the back of each picture: *"Loving the Lord in Laos." "Coming to Christ in Colombia." "Giving God to Ghana."* It all sounds vaguely pornographic to me, although I know they're working hard to save souls.

She and Dad go on medical mission trips from which she returns giddy with enthusiasm. They make us sit through slide shows that document their god squad adventures. Look at this football-sized tumor. Here's a gangrenous spear wound. We brought these loin-clothed pagans to Jesus, healing bodies and souls at the same time.

"Such gratitude for Christ, such a hankering for The Word!" Mother will gasp, shaking her head at the wonder of it.

Sometimes they show movies about missionary martyrs after Vespers, projecting the film onto the back of the church while we sit in folding chairs in the parking lot, drinking Kool-Aid. Mother holds these people in high esteem. Says she would have been a missionary herself if it weren't for meeting our father.

I used to wish she'd show the same enthusiasm for us, pin our family photographs to her bulletin board. When I was in third grade, I poked all her missionaries' eyes out with a thumbtack in a fit of jealousy. She paddled me for it.

I excuse myself to fetch the salt shaker from the kitchen and glance down at her magazine as I walk behind her chair. "God Is Everything" is the title of the article she's reading. When I sit down again, David crosses his eyes and bares his teeth at me. I roll mine. *Dweeb.* He hooks his front teeth over his bottom lip and slits the corners of his eyes like a Chinaman. I shake my head

and trace figure eights in the pool of fat skimming my soup, ignoring him. He knows I'm in a foul mood after the run-in with
the farmers and is trying to cheer me up.

He wriggles his fingers in front of his bowl, insistently, and I
lift my head. He flares his nostrils and pokes out his lips like
those Africans you see in *Cartoon Classics*s, the ones with the
bones in their noses who dance around boiling cauldrons of
white tourists. I snort despite myself—I don't like it when he
pokes fun of his features, but he's trying so hard to distract
me—and Mother lowers her magazine. Her bifocals flash as we
quickly spoon soup into our mouths. When she lifts her magazine again, David flips up his eyelids, exposing the pink under-
sides, and rolls his pupils skyward so it looks like he's got white
marbles for eyes. He taps his fingers along the edge of the table,
a blind man, finds his spoon and jabs it at his soup bowl. *Ting!* It
collides with his milk glass instead.

"What in Heaven's name?!" Mother exclaims.

David slowly turns his marble eyes in her direction as I tug
on my milk, trying not to laugh.

"That's ridiculous!" she sputters. "David! Put your eyes back,
now!" Milk sprays out of my mouth and across the table.

"Julia!"

And then David's doubled over and I'm doubled over and
we're both convulsing in our high-backed chairs. And we can't
stop no matter how much Mother shouts for us to stop or
threatens to tell Father or bangs the table.

For a few moments, there's nothing but us and our laughter,
the soaring joy of our laughter, our laughter crashing through us
like tidal waves and raining down our cheeks as tears.

+   +   +

My parents didn't set out to adopt two black boys.

They wanted the white kid on my sister's pediatric ward. Laura was born with spina bifida, and she spent much of her childhood in hospitals, being repaired and recuperating from repairs. During one month-long stay, she met an orphaned white boy, and they became fast friends. In the desperate manner of lonesome, suffering children, they clung to each other like family. My parents inquired after adopting him, only to learn he was taken.

But the adoption agency persisted. There were scads of other children who needed homes, they said: black children.

It was 1970, and America was scarred by racial violence. Civil rights leaders had been gunned down in the streets, and communities across the nation were smarting from race riots. My parents' own state, Indiana, had once been a stronghold of the Ku Klux Klan, and was still a haven for backwater bigots.

To reject a black baby would have been un-Christian, a sin. God was testing them. This was a chance to bear witness for Jesus Christ, to show the world that their God was not prejudiced and neither were they. Red and yellow, black and white, they're all precious in His sight, Jesus loves the little children of the world. They would take a black baby home and call him son.

Such was the theory.

Years later, I learned that the first time my mother touched David, she feared "the black would rub off on her hands."

Later still, I learned the miracle of my brother's beginnings. That David was born to a thirteen-year-old girl, three months premature and weighing two pounds—less than a bottle of Jack Daniels. That machines and heat lamps kept him breathing during his first crucial months. That he was placed with a succession of foster families that gave him different names and collected their government checks and shut doors so they wouldn't hear him cry. They weren't paid to love the fragile baby with the liquid brown eyes, they were paid to keep him alive.

My parents would keep him alive and save his soul.

CHAPTER 2

FRIENDS & NEIGHBORS

David's in okra and I'm in snow peas. We kneel in parallel rows killing Japanese beetles as the sun bores down on us. We each have different methods of doing this. David plucks the beetles off the leaves with gloved fingers, squeezes them until they pop, then tosses them over his shoulder. I find this repulsive. The ground behind him is littered with their mangled metallic green and copper bodies. My method is to bat them off the plants with a trowel, then press them into the dirt with the blade, where I won't see their insides squirt out. Sometimes I whack off leaves or vegetables in the process, but at least I don't see the beetles die. Secretly, I think they're beautiful.

I pause to swipe my dripping forehead with the back of my arm and look up at the house. A grackle squawks overhead and lands on the clothesline, its purple-black body gleaming in the sun like spilled motor oil. At the end of the driveway, our mutt Lecka lies panting in the shade of her doghouse. Her name means "sweet" in Dutch. Our family tree reaches back to Holland on both parents' sides, and we attend a Dutch Calvinist church in town where people slap bumper stickers on their cars that proclaim "If you're not Dutch, you're not much." Until this year, we attended a Dutch Calvinist school as well, where all the kids were blond and lanky like me—all the kids except Jerome and David, of course.

Through the dark glass of the upstairs window, I can just make out Mother sitting in the recliner, feet up, a glass in one hand, a Russian-language book in the other. The ceiling fan spins lazily above her. She's learning Russian because the Communists are persecuting Christians, and there's a great need for people to smuggle Bibles behind the Iron Curtain to these clandestine congregations. She wants to be prepared should the Lord call her on that mission.

"What if the Commies catch you?" I recently asked her, although I already knew her answer: The best thing you can do in life is die for Jesus Christ.

But I'm not too scared of her being martyred. According to the page marked in her textbook, *Take Off in Russian,* she's still learning to ask directions to the toilet and say "I prefer cream in my coffee." She's got a long way to go before she can pass herself off as a *babushka*.

The telephone jingles as I start down a row of cauliflower, and I look up to see Mother rise to answer it, disappearing into the shadows where light from the great room windows doesn't reach.

Our new house is what they call "ranch style." There are three bedrooms upstairs—the master suite, my room, a guest room—and one in the basement for the boys. They share it, just like they did in the basement of our old house.

The entire house, bathrooms included, is wired with an intercom system, and every morning at eight Mother blares Rejoice Radio over the speakers to wake us up. It took a while to get used to this. At first I would jackknife awake, panicked that I'd fallen asleep in church. Now when the organ music starts, I thrust my pillow over my head and try to refill my ears with the sweet syrup of sleep until Mother comes pounding on the door.

"Idle hands are the devil's workshop!" she'll call through the wood. It's her favorite saying, along with "Cleanliness is next to Godliness" and "Honor thy father and thy mother."

The intercom has another important function: spying. Control panels in the kitchen and master bedroom have a black switch that can be flipped to "listen" or "talk." You can tell when Mother's eavesdropping because the speakers crackle, but we can't turn the volume down or off because we get in trouble if we don't hear her call us.

When David and I need to speak privately, we go outside. We spend most of our time there anyway. Mother's got romantic notions about toiling the land—or mostly, about her children toiling the land. And with fifteen acres, there's always something that needs toiling with.

The garden gets the thrust of our attentions. We try to get at it early, before the vegetation perspires in the heat, sending up a dizzying haze that can sting your eyes. We work on our hands and knees, ripping out crabgrass and pennyworts, killing Japanese beetles and cabbage loopers, aerating and fertilizing, all the while swatting at the horse flies and sweat bees that buzz around us.

Although we complain about our chores, there *is* a satisfaction to poking an itty-bitty tomato seed into the dirt and watching it resurrect and snake into a six-foot vine. David and I take a certain pride in our work, marveling at the two-foot zucchinis and the baskets of ruby red strawberries our hands help produce. Our garden is so bountiful that Mother fills grocery sacks with the surplus to bring to the soup kitchen downtown.

"I bet there's no Japanese beetles in Florida!" David says, pitching a crushed bug over his shoulder; it lands in the pink and orange zinnias bordering the garden.

"Nope, only geckos." I pinch off a snow pea and bite through the shell into the sweet green balls inside. "And jellyfish."

Florida! That's where David and I are moving when we turn eighteen. Things are different in Florida. Until three years ago, our family drove there every August to a timeshare condo on Sanibel Island. David and I would spend the week running around barefoot and unsupervised. There was a group of secular kids at the complex who hung out with us despite our skin color. Florida's the place where I first got drunk, first made out with a boy, first got my heart ripped to shreds.

Did it all on our last trip with Alex Garcia, a seventeen-year-old local who lounged around the complex pool in tight white bathing trunks. We flirted all week, and the night before we left, he convinced me to meet him on the beach at midnight. I wore my clothes to bed—carefully pulling the sheet around my neck so my older sister Laura wouldn't notice—and watched the alarm clock for two hours, my heart racing. When I slipped out to our designated meeting place, Alex held beer cans to my thirteen-year-old face until I passed out. When I came to, he was lying on top of me, his tongue rammed down my throat. I pushed him off and ran away.

"You're so immature!" he yelled after me.

The next morning I woke with bruises circling my mouth, but despite this, I loved Alex. He was beautiful with his caramel skin and those white trunks. But as we were driving out of the complex to return home, I saw him by the pool, frenching a twenty-two-year-old who'd just arrived that morning. I cried all the way back to Indiana.

"Too bad Jerome screwed everything up for us," David says, rocking back on his haunches and scowling at me over the broccoli. His glasses are powdered with dust.

"Yeah, we'd be there right now if it weren't for him," I say, popping another snow pea into my mouth. I wonder who Alex is kissing this summer.

"I can't believe Jerome was so dumb," David says. "I mean, our parents aren't *completely* dense."

I nod and wave away a sweat bee that's trying to land on my face. Our parents put an end to Florida when Jerome showed up one evening reeking of beer, too drunk to remember to gargle and spray himself with Glade. David doesn't know what I did with Alex. No one does; it's my secret, one that both shames and thrills me.

A bead of sweat runs down the back of my neck and I glance at my watch. It's two o'clock, just about peak heat time, and we still have to do the squash, the beans, the carrots. An hour ago, the back door thermometer was already pushing ninety-three degrees, and that was under the eaves. The sky is covered with a low cloud quilt, the sun reduced to a white pinhole. It's the usual, year-round Indiana sky, always a pearly glare. Sometimes the heat and humidity are so intense that the quarter-mile walk down the lane to check the mailbox seems like an epic journey through hot Jell-O.

"I need a drink," I say, lurching up on legs bloodless and wobbly from being bent. I look at the upstairs window; the recliner's still empty. She must be in the study, corresponding with her missionaries, scribbling churchy news onto onion paper in her loopy cursive. I peeked at some of her letters last week when she went into town for groceries; they were tucked into unsealed envelopes destined to countries around the world.

> We took a collection to renovate the narthex. Lord willing, we'll have enough for new carpeting and new paint as well. The Grounds Committee hasn't decided whether the best paint color would be pale blue or eggshell. . . . The Ladies Aide Society is holding a potluck next week before Vespers to welcome new church members. We will open our arms to receive them even as Jesus opens his arms to the sinners and the fallen. . . . Please join us in prayer for President Reagan as he leads the country toward The Light. We are blessed to have a Christian leader in the White House, and must support his efforts to reinstate school prayer and overturn abortion "rights." . . . In HIS name, Mrs. Jacob W. Scheeres.

"Hey, space cadet!"

David rubs a glove over his gleaming forehead, leaving a chalky smear.

"What?"

"I said, what are you going to be in Florida?"

"I dunno," I shrug, reaching over to the next row to pull a slender carrot from the dirt and toss it into my basket. It's best to harvest vegetables while they're young and sweet, Mother says. "Maybe I'll make jewelry from shells and sell it on the beach. You?"

"Haven't figured it out, yet. But it'd be way cool to work on one of those deep-sea fishing boats—I could put a pole in myself, and we'd eat fresh fish every night—grouper, snapper, maybe even shark!"

I scowl at him.

"You'd reek of fish guts. I'd have to hose you down with Lysol every night when you got home."

As he contemplates this thought, frowning, I walk to the pipe jutting from the ground in the middle of the garden and twist open the faucet. After a couple of burps, the water flows into the attached green hose. I grip the end in my fist, letting the water gurgle over my hand like a fountain, and hold it up to my mouth. It's well water, warm and weedy-tasting. It thuds into the dust at my bare feet, splattering my legs with muddy droplets.

"Want some?" I hold out my arm to David.

He stands and trudges over. When his face is a few inches from my hand, I slip my thumb over the hose tip and the water jets upward, bouncing off his nose and glasses. It's an old trick.

"Hey!!"

He reels away and I drop the hose and hurdle rows of vegetables. Before I reach the garden's edge, water pounds my back. I swerve to dodge the spray while David charges after me. He runs the length of the rubber hose and snaps backward like a yo-yo, falling onto the potatoes, hose still in hand. Water rains down on him, sparkling like shredded sunlight, and I flop belly-down in warm grass, laughing.

Our play is interrupted by a sharp rapping of knuckles on glass, and we look up at the house. A faint figure stands behind the upstairs window, hands on hips. Mother.

After the bone yard incident, David and I stay close to home; we're not in a hurry to cross paths with the farmers again. We don't discuss it, we just don't turn right on County Road 50. We stay out of the deep country.

Jerome returned the Corolla one night while everyone was asleep—probably fearing our parents would report it stolen and sic the cops on him—and then took off again. Mother says we can't use the car for "frivolous driving," though, which, in her mind, is all the driving we want to do.

So we've spent most of these last few weeks before school playing H-O-R-S-E and P-I-G on the small basketball court next to the pole barn; hiking through the nearby woods and cornfields with Lecka, hoping to stir up pheasants or deer or box turtles; taking turns dangling a bamboo rod rigged with bologna over a fishing hole at the back of our property; playing foosball and ping-pong in the basement. Anything to relieve the boredom and unease that constantly gnaw at us.

But all we catch is junk fish in the fishing hole, slimy carp that are too small to eat. David yanks the hook from their bloody mouths to toss them back into the water as I scream at him not to hurt them. The only thing we've kicked up during our hikes was a dead raccoon. And it's way too hot for sports.

Sometimes we lay on lawn chairs in the backyard in the late afternoon and watch thunderheads churn toward us. We'll see a breeze riffle the Browns' cornfield across the lane and lift our faces expectantly to the cool, metal-smelling air and we'll know we're in for a good squall. We'll stay reclined in our chairs as the dark clouds seethe and flicker with lightning, until the cold hard raindrops pelt us, competing to see who can withstand the storm the longest before sprinting under the eaves.

But those are the exciting afternoons. Most times, it's a devil wind riffling the Browns' cornfield, and it blasts over us like a hair dryer, pelting us with the smell of dirt and onion grass and manure, and offering no refreshment at all. But we stubbornly remain in our lawn chairs as the overcast sky fades into deeper shades of gray and Mother finally rings the supper bell, because there's nothing better to do.

As we watch the sky, we talk about things that would make country living easier. For David, that would be a BMX bike. He says he could build a ramp behind the garden and do all these tricks where you flip upside down and land perfectly centered on the fat rubber tires. Says he's seen it done in magazines. Me, I'd get a horse. A golden palomino that I'd ride bareback through the fields, all the way back to town.

Sometimes we discuss Harrison.

"Do you think all the kids will be like those farm boys?" David will ask, his eyebrows creasing with worry.

"Nah, they can't all be that ignorant," I'll respond. "Some of them have got to be normal."

Usually he lets it go at that, sitting back in his lawnchair with a sigh, but sometimes he persists.

"But what if they *are* all like that?" David asks one afternoon as we watch the darkening sky. "Ronnie Wiersma told me they hate black people at Harrison and call them names, you know, like the 'N' word."

Ronnie is a know-it-all at our church, Lafayette Christian Reformed. He went to Lafayette Christian School too, same as all the church kids do, and graduated two grades ahead of us.

"What does Ronnie know? He's at West Side."

"His older brother went to Harrison."

"Yeah, but that was a long time ago, like three years."

The subject of Harrison always puts me in a foul mood. School starts in a week, and we still don't have any friends, or any answers to our question. *What will it be like?* I try to reassure David that everything will be okay.

"Those farmers were just being stupid that day," I tell him. "We caught them off-guard is all. Now that they know who we are, they won't bother us."

All I can do is hope this is true. We often hear them in the distance as we garden: the whine of their dirt bikes banging over homemade tracks, the blare of their car radios as they tear between cornfields, the explosions of their guns as they shoot cans or grackles or squirrels, silencing the world for a long moment afterward.

Jerome, David and I walk into Harrison on the first day of school sporting matching Afros that envelop our heads like giant black cotton balls. As we stride down the entrance corridor bobbing and grinning like J.J. on *Good Times,* our classmates recoil in horror.

No.

This will not happen.

This is a nightmare.

I will myself awake and stare at the wind-up alarm clock on the bedside stand. It's almost six. I stare at it until the black minute hand jerks over the red alarm hand and the clock rattles to life, jittering over the wood surface. I wait until the nightmare dissipates completely, then I slap it quiet.

It's the Tuesday before classes start and swim team tryouts are in thirty minutes; the coach wants to make sure people can handle the early-morning workouts once school starts. I figure it might be a good way to meet potential friends.

I hear Mother rumbling around in the kitchen, opening and closing drawers and cupboards, but by the time I walk into the great room, pulling my hair into a tight pony tail, she's gone. I stand at the kitchen counter, gulping down coffee and generic granola doused with powdered milk. The sky is pink outside the great room windows, the orchard and garden wrapped in pink mist.

It's a mile and a half to Harrison, a right on County Road 650 and a left on County Road 50. I had Mother measure it with the van's odometer last Sunday after church.

After brushing my teeth, I wheel my ten-speed from the garage onto the gravel driveway. Lecka hears me and crawls from her doghouse, yawning and batting her tail in furious circles. She strains against her collar, whining, and I walk my bike over to her.

"Wish me luck, girl," I say, tugging on her ears.

As I turn to mount my bike, the venetian blinds in the master bedroom window clap shut. Mother?

I shrug and mount the bike, standing on the pedals to force the Schwinn's tires over the slippery gravel lane until I reach County Road 650. As I cruise by the Browns' white clapboard house, a dog barks in the dark interior. Opposite the Browns', a red barn slowly collapses into overgrown weeds. Next to it, a pair of meadowlarks trill in a sugar maple. Then there's an alfalfa field, bright with yellow blossoms. I inhale the sweet air and am seized by a sudden joy at the beauty around me. It's still early, and life hasn't acquired its sharp edges.

The road dips over a small creek before passing a double-wide trailer mounted on railroad ties. Pink gingham curtains hang daintily in the windows, and the muted voice of a news announcer floats through the ripped screen door along with the smell of percolating coffee.

At the intersection of County Road 650 and County Road 50 is a small brick building where farmers met in the days before telephones to discuss business. I turn left onto the ragged asphalt ribbon of County Road 50, which bisects cornfields and dairies until it reaches town, ten miles away. As I pedal up a small rise, the concrete expanse of William Henry Harrison High School swoops into view, sprouting mushroom-like between fields.

My early-morning joy slams into stomach-grinding fear. I glance at my watch—6:25—before shifting my bike into tenth gear and crouching low behind the handlebars, racing toward my new school. *Bring it on.*

As I ride closer, I notice tire tracks have ripped donuts into the front lawn. Across from the school, a cow barn is covered in graffiti. "HARRISON KICKS ASS!" "RAIDERS ROCK!" "WESTSIDE IS CRUISIN' FOR A BRUISIN'!" West Side. That's where our three older siblings went to school; it's Lafayette's smart high school, where the Purdue professors send their kids.

I swerve into the driveway and pedal to the back of the building, remembering the location of the gym from our orientation tour. There they are, about twenty girls, clumped around the back door, bags dumped at their feet. A few sit on the curb, smoking. They look up at me with sullen faces when I coast into view. I am relieved that this look is common to all teenage girls and not just me, as Mother believes.

"What's wrong with you?" she'll ask, scowling. "Why don't you smile more?"

She's one to talk.

The bike racks are located across from the gym entrance, and as I unwind my bike chain from under the seat, I sneak peaks at the girls. A couple of the smokers I've seen before, a fat girl with blond pigtails and a girl in a Tab Cola shirt.

The day after we moved in, Jerome, David and I were so bored that we rode five miles along the shoulder of Highway 65 to a Kwik Mart. A group of girls, stuffed into cut-offs and tube tops, their eyes raccoonish with black eyeliner, were leaning against the shaded wall of the cement shack. They sucked on popsicles and cigarettes and jutted out their hips at the trucks and jacked-up Camaros that pulled in for gas.

They tittered when we glided into the station, panting and sweat-stained. It was a scorcher, one of those days where the heat feels likely to peel your skin right off. Jerome stopped beside the gas pumps and gawked at the girls while David and I propped our bikes against the building.

"Better watch out, Rose Marie," one of them shouted. "I think he likes you."

Rose Marie twisted her dirty blond pigtail around a finger, staring at Jerome and sliding her grape popsicle in and out of her mouth real slow. Her friends squawked with laughter, then poked their fingers in their mouths and made gagging noises.

Jerome grinned at Rose Marie and tucked his fists under his biceps to make the muscles pop out, Totally Clueless. Seeing this exchange, I ran into the Kwik Mart and bought an orange push-up before racing away on my bike. I didn't want to be seen with the boys at that moment.

"What'd you take off for?" David asked when he caught up to me, an ice cream sandwich melting in his hand. Jerome was farther behind him.

"The smell of gasoline makes me sick," I lied.

After threading the bike chain between the front tire and the rack, I click the combination lock shut and stand to face the crowd.

Dozens of eyes land on my face, then slide away. It's a small community. They know who I am. I'm the girl from that new family, the one with the blacks. Sure enough, Rose Marie elbows the Tab girl and they both stare at me, smirking. I unzip my backpack and pretend to dig around in it for something important as I cut a wide circle around them.

There's a girl sitting alone against the wall and I walk in her direction. She's dark-haired and olive-skinned, blatantly foreign to these parts as well. We belong together, she and I; we're both outsiders. She watches me approach, but looks away when I stop and lean against the wall a few feet away from her.

I look at my watch. 6:37.

"So the coach is late?" I ask, trying to sound casual as I zip my backpack closed.

"Seems that way," she says without looking at me. She plucks a dandelion from the ground and flicks its head off between her index finger and thumb. *Mary had a baby and its head popped off* . . . Her shoulder-length black hair is feathered about her face, Farrah Fawcett—style, just like mine and every other girl's here.

"You nervous?" I ask, a bit loudly.

She shrugs.

Across the road, a row of cows plods single file toward the graffitied barn. "EAT, SHIT, AND DIE!" someone wrote over the wide entrance.

"So, what's your name?" I ask her, sitting in the grass. *Talk to me, please.* Finally she looks at me, her black bangs skimming her dark eyes like a frayed curtain.

She says something in a foreign language.

"What?"

"You can call me Mary."

"What country are you from?"

"Arcana," she says.

"Where's that at?"

"'Bout two hours east of here."

"Oh," I laugh, embarrassed. "I'm Julia. Guess we're both new."

She nods, and plucks another dandelion from the ground.

Squeals pierce the air and we turn to watch a group of girls surging around a boy who's standing over a bicycle, across from the gym entrance. He's shirtless despite the chill air, wearing only light blue satin running shorts. He thrusts out his chest— tan, broad—and a few of the girls grope it as he laughs.

They scatter when a black Camaro roars into the parking lot. It screeches to a stop slantways across two spaces, and a man in aviator sunglasses jumps out.

"There he is," Mary says. "Coach Shultz."

The shirtless boy pedals away, and we stand and move toward the other girls. Coach Schultz comes at us with swooping arms.

"Everyone inside! We're late!"

"No, you are," someone mutters.

He jingles a key into the door and holds it open, sizing up bodies as they flow into the building. I thrust back my shoulders as I walk by him, hoping to make a good impression.

In the dank locker room, Mary and I migrate silently to a corner. I try to keep my eyes to myself as I quickly strip off my shorts and T-shirt and snap into my Speedo, but can't help but notice when the big-chested girl next to me unhooks her bra and her boobs fall down like half-filled water balloons. My own boobs are still little-girl pointy—I'm what people call a "late bloomer." At sixteen and a half, I haven't gotten my period yet and am still cursed with a boyish, narrow-hipped body.

The door cracks open and there's a whistle blast.

"Enough lollygagging, girls!"

Coach Schultz orders us to pair up for warm-up exercises, and everyone immediately nabs a partner, leaving Mary and me for each other. I walk over to her. We do ten minutes of stretching on the tile floor next to the pool, and then the real competition begins.

The coach has us swim fifty yards, freestyle. Some of the girls claw through the water like cats, barely reaching the halfway flag before wheezing to a stop. Coach Schultz orders them out of the pool, and among them I see Rose Marie, sucking in air through her smoker's mouth and coughing. I grin; the process of elimination has begun.

When my turn comes, I knife through water, happy to deafen the murmuring around me. Twelve strokes to the deep end, flip turn at the black T painted on the bottom, twelve strokes back. This is one thing I do well.

David and I learned to swim at the YMCA when we were six. After I learned to float, my favorite thing to do was to scissor my arms and legs into the middle of the deep end while the other kids huddled at the ledge, terrified of letting go of the tile lip.

"Come back!" David would squeal, twisting his head around to look at me with huge eyes. "Don't go there!" But the feeling of being alone and hard to reach enthralled me, and I went from polliwog to shark in record time.

Coach Schultz blows his whistle and orders the girls who made the first cut to do continuous laps, alternating between breaststroke, backstroke, and the crawl. I lick the fog from my goggles and press them back to my face, pushing them against my cheekbones until they suck lightly on my eyeballs. At the end of my eighteenth lap, I notice a forest of legs in a corner of the pool. There's a whistle burst and I rise to the surface along with a handful of other girls, including Mary.

"There's my A-team, right there," Coach Schultz shouts, leaning against the lifeguard tower with a clipboard. We call our names to him, and he writes them down.

In the locker room, everyone hustles back into their clothes in hunched silence. I exchange a smile with Mary and pull my shorts over my suit before fleeing the sour gloom, fearing that one mean look will puncture my high spirits. As I bike back up County Road 50 in the swelling heat, carloads of girls with wet hair pass me. Sweat trickles down my face and pastes my Speedo to my body, but I'm elated. I've made the swim team *and* found a friend.

We go to Kmart for our annual trek to buy school clothes, and I hole up in a dressing room with a mound of clothes, hoping to find something that doesn't look like it was bought at Kmart. This is tricky. I choose a few pastel oxfords and polo shirts—although these have swan icons instead of the trendy alligators and horses—and a pair of plastic penny loafers. A pair of fitted paint-splattered jeans gets nixed by Mother when I walk out to model them for her.

"What do you want people staring at your butt crack for?" she asks loudly, causing several shoppers to turn in our direction. She walks to a rack of dark denim, grabs two pairs of baggy jeans and throws them into our cart as I look away, tears stinging my eyes.

None of the kids I know would be caught dead in the Kmart parking lot, but Mother views blue-light specials as manna from Heaven. *Polyester slacks, two pairs for $10? We can outfit the entire family! Reduced-for-quick-sale toothpaste? We'll stock up for the next five years!* Our family shops at Kmart for the same reason we drink instant milk and eat Garbage Soup and use dish detergent for bubble bath: we're cheap.

Mother still hasn't gotten over the Great Depression. I know that if I complain about my school clothes, I'll be subjected to stories about how her family was forced to eat withered apples from her father's general store in Corsica, and how she left for college with only two flour sack dresses to her name. *Shame on you! You don't know how good you have it!* I'd just as soon stick my hand in a vat of boiling oil than hear it once more.

Mother says money we save by being frugal helps the cause of missionaries around the world, but it certainly doesn't help mine. Once again, I'll be Dorky Girl at school. My only hope is to find more baby-sitting jobs, so I can acquire enough money to go shopping at Tippecanoe Mall like a normal person.

In the men's department, David greets us cradling an armload of satin basketball jerseys emblazoned with Big Ten logos. Purdue. Michigan. Notre Dame.

He looks at Mother with a wide-eyed mixture of hope and apprehension, and she shakes her head and strides to a table piled with T-shirts. Colored Hanes, $2.99! Mother scoops several into the shopping cart.

David hugs the shimmering jerseys to his chest.

"What's wrong with these?" he asks, alarm rising in his face.

I look at him and roll my eyes.

+   +   +

I was three years old when my mother told me I was getting a baby brother.

When she said "your baby brother," I assumed he'd be mine and mine alone, and swelled with self-importance. I would no longer be the baby of the family; I, too, would have someone to boss around.

A crib was placed in an upstairs bedroom and I'd check it several times a day, peering between the slats to see if my baby had arrived. Time after time, I was heartbroken by the empty mattress.

"Baby here today?" I'd ask Mother.

"Soon," was always the reply.

The day he arrived, on March 17, 1970, I was in the basement, lost in Mister Rogers' Neighborhood; *the older kids were at school. After the show ended, I went to the kitchen for a butter-and-sugar sandwich and Mother hushed me. My baby brother was sleeping, she said, and I was not to disturb him.*

I waited until she started washing the dishes before creeping upstairs on my hands and knees. The door to his room was closed, and I paused on the threshold, listening to pots banging against the sink, before pushing the door inward.

The sun streamed through yellow curtains as I approached the crib on tiptoes, breathing hard. Finally. Inside it was my baby doll, asleep. I stared in awe at his molasses-colored skin; nobody told me that my baby would be brown.

I pressed my face between the slats and marveled at him, at the chalky trails of dried tears crisscrossing his face, at his size. He looked much smaller than I was, although he was only four months younger.

He was my baby, and I had to touch him. I reached between the slats and poked his arm with a finger. Too hard. His eyes flipped open, big and brown and watery scared, and I snatched my hand back. His bottom lip started to quiver.

"Shh, baby, shh," I whispered. "Don't cry."

I glanced behind me at the open door; Mother would paddle me if she caught me disobeying.

But my baby didn't make a noise, he just watched me with those big brown eyes, waiting to see what I'd do next. I reached back into the crib and touched the black fuzz on his head, gently this time.

"It's okay, baby," I whispered.

I kept my hand on him until the long fringes of his eyelids drifted shut and he fell back to sleep.

CHAPTER 3

EDUCATION

I'm fully awake and staring into the moon face of the alarm clock when it starts to clatter at 5:30. Acid surges up my esophagus. This is It. The Day That Will Determine Everything. Whether we are Winners or Losers. Predators or Scavengers. Rejects or Normal. It's the first day of school.

Through the bedroom window, dawn reddens the horizon. I jump up to turn on the ceiling light and sway momentarily in the blinding whiteness. In the dresser mirror, I examine my face— no new zits, Thank You, Jesus—before thrusting myself into a blue Kmart polo shirt that matches my eyes and a pair of baggy jeans. I tried baking them in the dryer for six hours while Mother was at work, but they refused to shrink.

In the bathroom, I lay out the tools of beauty—curling iron, ultra-hold Final Net, frosted pink lipstick—on the counter and tape a picture of Farrah Fawcett to the mirror. I ripped it out of a magazine at my dad's office and have locked

myself in the bathroom every night for the past week to practice her hair, her eyes, her smile.

After I finish painting my face and crimping my hair, I shellac
my head with haispray and step back to survey the results. I look
at Farrah, I look at me. I look nothing like Farrah. My eyes are
too small, my mouth too large, my hair too limp. But we're
wearing the same shade of turquoise eye shadow, and I suppose
that counts for something.

I've decided to make a party impression at Harrison. Party
hardy. That shy girl who barely raised her head at Lafayette
Christian is gone. The new Julia will throw back her head and
laugh as if she didn't have a care in the world. And this laughter
and happiness will make her attractive to people and win her admiration and friends.

But first I must get into a party mood. I lock my bedroom
door and pull a mayonnaise jar swirling with amber liquid from
a box of sweaters in my closet. Southern Comfort. It helps my
parents laugh when they stir it into their bedtime cocktails, so I
figure it should help me too. I've been siphoning it from the bottle bit by bit whenever Mother forgets to lock the pantry.

I tilt the jar against my lips and the booze blazes down my
throat like hot sauce. I've been practicing this as well, and now
know the first swigs are always the hardest. I plug my nose and
hop from foot to foot until the fire subsides, and after the fourth
swallow my taste buds are numbed enough that I can dump it
down like water.

When I bend to slip on my plastic Kmart shoes, I lose my
balance and fall giggling against the closet door, my insides
warm with the boozy embrace. The intercom crackles.

"The bus leaves in thirty minutes," Mother says. "You miss it,
you walk."

"I'm getting ready already!" I yell at the speaker.

Good morning to you, too. I take another swig of Comfort. *Not a care in the world.*

At the breakfast table, David sits over a bowl of cereal as Rejoice Radio—the soundtrack of our family life—blares in the background. He's also gone to special lengths for the Big Day. He's hot-picked his Brillo pad hair into a soft halo. Wiped the smears from his glasses. And traded in his usual T-shirt and jeans for a short-sleeved white oxford and khaki slacks—an outfit demanding respect.

"I see you busted out the 'No Mo' Nappy' this morning," I say, sliding into the chair across from him. He gives me a grim look and goes back to staring into his cereal.

For some reason it's okay for him and Jerome to tease each other about their hair ointments, but if I join in, they get huffy. I tried one of their products myself in seventh grade, lured by the label's promise of "tresses that glow with the silky sheen of Africa." Queen of Sheba Conditioner it was called, and I caked it on. It made me look like I'd dipped my head in bacon fat, and I was able to rid myself of it only after a week of scrubbing my hair with dish soap and baking soda. The boys called me grease ball for months afterward.

I fill my bowl with generic bran flakes. I can feel the alcohol spread through my body as I chew the cardboard flakes. A hymn I recognize comes over the intercom:

> *Asleep in Jesus! Blessed sleep,*
> *From which none ever wakes to weep;*
> *A calm and undisturbed repose,*
> *Unbroken by the last of foes.*

I wag my spoon over my bowl like a conductor's baton and David raises his head.

"What's your problem?" he says.

"Great tune."

"It's about death."

"Yeah," I shrug. "But it's got rhythm."

He cocks his head and stares at me.

"Somebody punch you in the face or something?"

"What?"

"Your eyes are all bruised."

"It's called eye shadow, goof ball."

"Oh. Is it supposed to be attractive?" he asks, before cracking a smile. "Just kidding!"

"Ha ha," I say, smiling back at him. At least he's joking around; this means he's not totally freaked. This is good.

"Meet you out back in ten," he says, standing to gather up his breakfast things.

"Alrighty."

After breakfast, I gulp down more Comfort, brush my teeth, and slide bubblegum lip gloss over my mouth. In the mirror, I am a collage of yellow, pink, blue. I practice my Farrah smile, head back, teeth bared. *Not a care in the world.*

Mist hovers over the back field, and we trudge in silence through the knee-high prairie grass, which brushes our pant legs with dew and tiny seeds; Dad hasn't had time to mow it. The bus stop is at the end of the lane. My head is spacey and light, like when David and I were little and spent hours spinning in circles with outstretched arms for the simple rush of falling down in a dizzy, laughing heap. I wish we both had that feeling now, I think, looking at David as he worries his bottom lip.

On the gravel lane, a killdeer limps ahead of us, dragging a wing and crying pitifully, trying to distract us from the four speckled eggs laying camouflaged at the roadside. I glance at David—he's scowling at his feet, ignoring the bird—then look away from him, not wanting his anxiety to contaminate my numbness. *Not a care in the world.* Think Farrah. Think laughing, happy, beautiful people. Think shampoo commercials.

The lane ends in an abrupt T at County Road 650, and I drop my backpack on the ground next to a bank of plastic mailboxes and lean against them. David busies himself plucking hitchhikers from his slacks.

A rooster crows in the distance and a breeze, perfumed with fresh-cut hay, flits over us. I turn my face into it, breathing deeply, and close my eyes.

Several minutes pass. There's a faint clatter that grows louder and I open my eyes to see headlights tunneling toward us through the mist. David stiffens before recognizing the unmistakable rattle of a tractor, then goes back to pacing the road.

When the giant machine clanks into view, the farmer riding it lifts his arm at a right angle to his body as if he were swearing on the Good Book, and I wave back grandiosely, with both hands, as if I were the Queen of the Rose parade. Party Hardy.

After the farmer chugs by, David walks to the middle of the road, crosses his arms, and squints into the mist.

"You in a hurry to go somewheres?" I yell over the tractor's wake. He doesn't answer, and I laugh and it comes out as a belch, and I laugh again.

As I'm practicing a hip-thrusting dance move I saw watching *American Bandstand* while Mother was at work, the low roar of a diesel engine rises over the fields.

David backs up to the side of the road, and I pick up my backpack and stand beside him.

"Relax," I tell him.

"Easy for you to say," he says, giving me a knowing—and disapproving—look. So he knows I've been drinking. So what. He's always been such a goody-two-shoes.

We both turn to watch the headlights grow brighter. It's the school bus, No. 26, just like it said in the letter. The yellow tube shudders to a stop ten feet past us, and as we walk around it, I keep my eyes on the ground. We're at the end of the route, and it's full of kids by now, all staring down at us through the windows, sizing us up. *Not a care in the world.*

The door folds open with a bang.

"There's s'posed to be three kids at this stop! Where's the third one at?" shouts the driver, a fat woman in a purple pantsuit. The ceiling light above her seat makes her white bouffant glow like a sunlit cloud. She studies the clipboard in her hands as I climb the short stairway.

"Name, first and last."

"Hello, my name is Julia," I say brightly. "Julia Scheeres."

She crosses my name off her list and looks up as I step aside for David. Her mouth drops open when she sees him, and she turns back to me.

"Who's that?" she asks.

"I'm David Scheeres," he answers quietly.

Her eyes dart between David and me.

"He's my brother," I say impatiently, aware of a murmuring behind us.

"Brother, huh?" she says flatly, as if I were lying.

"Brother, yes." I bend to find his name on her list and tap on it. "Right there. David Scheeres."

She crosses out his name, shaking her head. *Why does this have to happen today, of all days? Can't we please be normal just for once?* My heart crimps despite my fuzzy-headedness.

"And where's the third kid?" she asks, lifting her list to her face, frowning.

"That would be Jerome Scheeres. He won't be joining us today."

She arches her stenciled eyebrows.

"Jerome, huh?" She grunts and scribbles something next to his name before scooping a hand toward the innards of the bus. "Go find yerselves a seat."

I swivel around; rows of white faces point in our direction. A pocket of space materializes at the back of the bus and I throw my head back, put on my Farrah smile, and I sashay down the narrow plank of the aisle, carefully avoiding protruding limbs. *Not a care in the world.*

Two rows before we reach the empty bench, a black boot slams down in front of me, heel first. My eyes sweep over it and up the jean-clad leg and the United Methodist T-shirt to the orange hair of the boy wearing it. It's one of them. One of the graveyard boys. Beside him sits a smaller, orange-haired kid with the same pug nose; they must be kin. Brothers.

The graveyard boy glares up at me, his eyes sparking. A corner of his mouth jerks upward like a growling dog.

"Nigger lover," he snarls. There's spit tobacco stuck in his gums. I stare at his mouth.

My Farrah smile collapses and hatred wells up in me, too, matching his hatred ounce for ounce, but there's also fear kicking at my ribcage. The bus lurches forward and I stumble over his leg and fall onto the empty bench. When I look up, David's swaying in the middle of the aisle, gawking down at the boot.

I stand. "David!"

He gingerly lifts his foot over the boot and when he's midstride, the boot rockets up and slams into his crotch. Laughter clatters around us, and the graveyard boy joins in as he retracts his leg. David twists his mouth into a sick smile and shakes his head, as if he were dealing with a mischievous child.

I grab his wrist to pull him to the bench, pushing him into the spot next to the window. For the duration of the ride to Harrison, as ripe cornfields whisk past the bus windows, David keeps his head bent and his eyes clamped shut. I try to pray, too, but my mind goes blank after the "Dear God."

The bus rumbles up Harrison's curved driveway and stops at the end of a long line of yellow buses. We wait until all the other kids drain out to join the throng of bodies moving up the sidewalk before standing. The driver watches us walk up the aisle in the rearview mirror, but turns her head when she sees me glaring at her. *Witch.*

At the school entrance, two middle-aged men in dark suits, Principal Day and Assistant Principal May—we were warned during orientation that yelling "May Day!" would get us an automatic detention—stand on opposite sides of the doorway, greeting students.

"Welcome back!" Principal Day says to me as we cross the threshold. Assistant Principal May looks blankly at David, who glances at him then looks away.

As we walk side by side over the foyer's gold linoleum floor, I try to catch David's eye, but he's scanning the crush of white faces, searching—as I've been—for a sign. A nod. A smile. A kind look. A potential friend. Instead, there's a lot of staring, a lot of whispering. A lot of eyes darting back and forth between us, and Dear God, I could use some Comfort now.

The foyer dead-ends in a cafeteria with a barnlike peaked ceiling. We wind through round blue tables in the center of the room to avoid a row of boys in baseball caps slumped against the wall.

"Woah, nice udders!" one of them shouts to a girl strolling by them. She presses her books to her chest and quickens her pace; they laugh at her.

Before we turn down separate hallways to our lockers, I grab David's arm. He turns to me with wide eyes.

"Remember Florida," I say. *Remember there's a better place than this.*

He nods solemnly. I step away from him, and a moment later he's engulfed by a wave of white bodies.

I locate my locker along the long gray wall of lockers and consult the palm of my hand, where I wrote the combination in permanent ink last night. After two tries, the door wobbles open and I dump the textbooks for my afternoon classes in the bottom of the narrow cavity. The first hour warning buzzer sounds over the hallway speakers, and the dim corridor reverberates with the sound of hundreds of lockers slamming shut. First hour starts in two minutes; get caught in the hallways after it starts, automatic detention.

I follow the stampede up a trash-strewn stairway to the second floor. As luck would have it, my first period is Algebra. Math, my worst subject. Most of the seats are already taken when I walk through the classroom door. The Preppies, all pink and green Izods and Sperry topsiders, have claimed the back rows, setting their backpacks on the chairs in front of them to wall themselves off from everyone else. Next to the window are the Hoods, in their black jeans and hooded sweatshirts. In the front rows are kids with pencils and calculators aligned on their desktops: the Nerds. The middle of the room is sprinkled with kids who don't appear to fit into any of these cliques, the Unclassifiable Outsiders. This is where I sit.

The second warning buzzer sounds. It's eight A.M. and there's no teacher. I look out the corner of my eye at the girl sitting next to me. Her kinky red hair cascades down her back in a giant ponytail and she's wearing hot pink leg warmers under a ruffled gray miniskirt. I've seen such getups on the pages of *Glamour* magazine, but never on the streets of Lafayette. She must be new, from some place big, a city. She's bending over her notebook in absolute concentration, sketching. As I lean forward to get a closer look—tiger, a very good one—a man in a white shirt and blue tie strides to the front of the room and bangs his fist on the metal desk. The preppies stop chattering and everyone looks up, except the girl beside me.

"I'm Mr. An-der-son, and this is Al-ge-bra 1," he says slowly, enunciating every syllable. He glances at the clock at the back of the room. "The time is 8:03. If you did-n't sign up for Al-ge-bra 1, leave now. If you did sign up for Al-ge-bra 1, take out your text-book, face the front of the room, and shut up. Let's make this as pain-less as pos-si-ble for ev-er-y-bo-dy."

He speaks so slowly that I wonder whether we're the idiots or he is. I dig *Algebra for Life* out of my backpack and set it on my desk along with a notebook and two sharpened pencils.

Mr. Anderson leans his broad shoulders against the blackboard and crosses his arms over his chest, surveying the room. He must have been a hunk, I think, before he developed man breasts and a gut.

"Hey you," he calls to the girl sitting beside me. She continues doodling.

"Yoo-hoo!" he yells in a high voice. There's laughter, and the girl looks up, startled, and slides an arm over her notebook. Her eyes are ringed in thick black liner. Mr. Anderson waves both hands at her.

"Who are you?" he asks.

"Elaine Goldstein," the girl says, pronouncing it as Goldstine.

Mr. Anderson rubs his chin.

"Jew name, isn't it?"

Elaine looks at him without responding as snickers spill from the back of the room.

"How do you spell that word, Goldstein?" Mr. Anderson asks. He pronounces it as if it ended in "stain." Gold-stain.

"G-O-L-D-S-T-E-I-N," Elaine spells, as Mr. Anderson writes it on the blackboard in capital letters.

"Miss Goldstain, kindly pay attention in my class." He erases her name with a broad swipe of the eraser, then starts tapping out an equation.

"O-kay, peop-le, o-pen your text-books to Chap-ter One."

Elaine's arm drifts back to her notebook, where she draws two long fangs in the tiger's mouth. A sabertooth. I drum my fingertips on the side of my desk nearest her, and she scowls over at me, her cheeks scorched with humiliation. I turn my head to stick my tongue out at Mr. Anderson—who's still writing out the equation—then look back at her.

She smiles.

I look for David in the frantic crush between classes, but don't see him.

I walk into each new classroom with a pounding heart, looking for a girl who's sitting alone and glancing about as uncomfortably as I am, someone who's also new to this circus. But by the time I locate each new room in the dark rambling hallways and rush inside with my Farrah smile, the desks are packed and I have to make do with a seat in or behind the nerd section.

By lunchtime, I still haven't spoken to a single person. Mademoiselle Smith is standing in front of French class grunting "répétez: é È, eu, eau" in a constipated voice when the noon buzzer rings and kids launch themselves from the room without waiting for her to finish her sentence.

I ignore the mass exodus and slowly copy the homework assignment into my notebook, putting off for as long as possible the moment I've been dreading all day. When I finish, I zip up my backpack and stand, the last student in the room.

"Bon appétit," Mademoiselle Smith calls to me as I walk out the door.

I find a bathroom and check myself in the mirror. My Farrah curls have unraveled and my Farrah eye shadow lies in turquoise pools under my bottom lashes. I squirt liquid soap onto a paper towel and scrub it off over the sink.

In the hallway, lunchtime noise rises from the first floor like the drone of a hornet's nest. I walk past a drinking fountain clogged with spit tobacco to the stairwell, walk down it, and observe the cafeteria through the small window in the metal door. On the far side of the room, there's a job fair. Tables have been pushed together and a banner is taped to the wall: "EXCITING career OPPORTUNITIES with Lafayette's LEADING employers: Caterpillar, Taco Bell, Alcoa. Get a Head Start on Life!"

Most of the round blue tables are filled, and a food line winds along one wall. I open the door, my stomach sour with nerves and whiskey, and stride purposefully toward it, as if someone were waiting for me, holding a space.

At the round blue tables I again recognize a seating arrangement: The center of the room belongs to the Jocks and the Preppies—the popular kids—and surrounding them are the lower orders—the Nerds, the Hoods, the Farmers, the Unclassifiable Outsiders.

As an unsmiling row of ladies in hairnets and aprons take turns spooning food into the compartments of my lunch tray—creamed spinach, tuna casserole, butterscotch pudding—I scan the room for David. He's nowhere in sight. Neither are Elaine or Mary.

I hand the cashier the $2 Mother gave me and face the room.

A girl with a side ponytail and stirrup pants stands a few feet away from me, also holding a tray and looking around. Maybe she's new, too. Maybe I should talk to her. But what would I say? *Hi, are you new, too? That sounds so dorky!* As I ponder this, a girl at a center table jumps up and yells "Christie!" and she rushes away.

The aroma of warm mayonnaise and dill pickles from the steaming casserole is making my mouth water. *Where should I sit? What group should I join? Where do I belong?* There doesn't appear to be a table for Unclassifiable Outsiders. I search the room for someone, anyone, sitting alone, and my eyes drag across the orange-haired boy. He's sitting with a bunch of farmers along the back wall, facing my direction. He hasn't noticed me yet. I watch him fork spinach into his hateful mouth, then I walk to a conveyor belt jerking dirty trays behind a wall and set my lunch on it.

There's a vending machine in the basement, next to the gymnasium. I buy a pack of Boppers and a Tab. I try the locker room door, but it's locked. So is the gym. Through the glass doors, the wood floor gleams in the pale light cast by the high windows, and the empty bleachers await the next event. A large clock on the far wall says 12:50. Fourth hour starts in ten minutes.

I find a girls' bathroom down the hallway and try the door. This one's open. I walk into a stall, slide the metal latch closed, and sit down to eat.

I'm the first to board bus No. 26 after school. The driver motions to the seat behind her when I climb in.

"Y'all sit here for the meanwhiles," she says, studying her three-inch-long nails, which are painted the same shade of purple as her pantsuit. I slide onto the bench and pretend to read my French book as kids erupt from the school building, yelling and laughing and chasing each other down the sidewalk. As the bus fills, I worry that the driver will leave without David. I stick my French book into my backpack, preparing to get off when she starts the engine if he isn't here. I'll find him and we'll walk home together.

As the driver fiddles the radio to some whiny country music station, I see David rushing down the sidewalk, head down, hands clasping the shoulder straps of his backpack.

"There's that nigger," I hear a male voice say behind me.

David stomps up the stairs with a tense face, and presses his lips together as the driver loudly informs him about our reserved seat.

"Scaredy-cat!" a boy calls as David sits down next to me. "Wuss!" David doesn't look at me.

On County Road 50, the bus gets stuck behind a combine that crawls down the road like a giant metal stink bug. I stare out the windshield, willing it to pull over and let us by. When the driver jerks to a stop beside the bank of mailboxes at the end of our lane, we're already standing, trying to get out.

I turn to David when we're halfway across the back field. The Indian summer air is thick with dirt and pollen, the afternoon still but for the lone grackle cawing atop the clothesline.

"What'd you do for lunch?" I ask him. He shrugs and looks at the ground.

"You?"

"I ate some candy."

He nods, and we walk the rest of the way to the back door in silence, because there's nothing more we want to say.

After a few days, things settle into a routine. I chug Comfort each morning, not to conjure a party attitude, but to numb myself to the snickering that breaks out when David and I slide into our reserved bus seat.

After hearing "nigger lover" and "there goes nigger and his sister" hurled at our backs too many times, I stop walking into school with him.

Seems we can never just be brother and sister like in other families. Our whole lives, people have felt an urge to make up special names for what we are. At Lafayette Christian, we were the "Oreo twins" or "Kimberly and Arnold" after the characters on *Diff'rent Strokes*. And while those nicknames bugged us, they were certainly preferable to what they call us at Harrison.

"See ya later!" I tell David when the bus door flaps open in front of Harrison. As I rush down the sidewalk ahead of him, I feel a pinch of guilt, but a greater relief as I melt into the sea of white bodies. Alone, I am part of the crowd. Together, we invite notice and ridicule. Why do I always have to be the "black boy's sister" anyway? Why can't I be my own person? It's not fair. This is a new school, and I want a fresh start.

Besides, people will think David's a sissy if he's always hanging around me. It's best for him, too. We're sixteen, and it's time we struck out on our own.

Sometimes I run into him between classes, always alone, always rushing and looking straight ahead, his face a blank mask. He's easy enough to spot because he's the only black kid at Harrison. A couple of times, he's rushed right by me without seeing me—I must have been just another white face to him, blurring by. Once I almost reached out a hand to touch him and say his name, but then thought better of it. It's better for both of us like this.

During Algebra, I'm tipsy enough to start making small talk with Elaine. One day I compliment her white hoop earrings. The next, I ask to borrow her eraser. Then I run into her while I'm buying lunch from the basement vending machine.

She's crouched outside the glass door leading to the parking lot, her body hidden but her unmistakable red hair blowing sideways across the glass. I buy an extra can of Tab.

She jumps up when she hears the door open and chucks something into the grass before whipping around to face me.

"Jesus Christ, don't sneak up on people like that!"

I wince at this blasphemy as she bends to search for whatever it is she threw into the grass. Today she's wearing a pink-and-black striped top that slumps off one shoulder, a jean miniskirt, and ankle boots that have these lacey white baby socks frothing out of them. She looks like that whorish new singer, Madonna. I've heard preppy girls poke fun at her behind her back and call her a slut, but Elaine doesn't seem to care whether she fits in at Harrison or not. I admire her for it.

She straightens, a lit cigarette in her hand. "Sorry, I'm a little on edge," she says. "How'd you find me?"

"It's alright," I say. "I was just buying some food and saw your hair in the window."

She gathers it to the side of her neck with her free hand and laughs. "Oh damn. Didn't think of that."

I stand awkwardly holding the two cans and a Snickers bar as she sucks at her cigarette and squints at a pile of dark clouds on the horizon. *I've never met a Jew before. Didn't know there were any in Lafayette, or Indiana for that matter. Jesus-killers, we called them at Lafayette Christian. But Elaine doesn't seem like a bad person.* A gust of wind tugs at our hair.

"Want some pop?" I finally ask her, holding out a can.

"Sure," she says, taking it from me. "Thanks."

Maybe I could invite her to church one Sunday. I could convert her, introduce her to Jesus. Maybe she secretly hankers for Him like those Third World heathens.

A cow moos loudly across the road, and we turn to watch it plod into the mouth of the graffiti barn, which was raided last weekend by Westsiders. "Harrison Hicks Suck Dick" it says in big red letters.

"Where you from?" I ask her.

She takes a sip before answering.

"Chicago," she says, looking at me. "Ever been?"

She is from a big city; I knew it!

"Yeah, in seventh grade," I say nonchalantly. "We went on this field trip to the Museum of Science and Industry."

I don't tell her that our bus driver got lost in the ghetto and a policeman took pity on us and escorted us to the museum.

"My dad was hired as a chemist at Eli Lilly, so that's why we had to move here," Elaine says.

The wind shifts, blowing the stench of fresh cow manure over us, and she wrinkles her nose and tells me how sorely she misses "civilization."

"Did you know that the very word *Hoosier* means country bumpkin?" she fumes, stubbing out her cigarette on the heel of her ankle boot. "Don't believe me? Go look it up in the dictionary. Hoosier, it says. Synonymous for hick, hillbilly, back-ass-ward."

I feel insulted, but bite my tongue. I'm in no position to be choosy about friends. We drink our pops and watch cows lug themselves into the dark barn one by one. The buzzer rings inside the building, signaling the end of lunch, the beginning of rejection, again.

"Will you be here tomorrow?" I ask Elaine, trying to control the desperation in my voice.

"Maybe," she says, shrugging. "You?"

"Probably."

"See you then," she says.

As I turn to walk through the glass door, happiness bubbles through me. I've got someone to eat lunch with; I'm not a complete reject after all.

We meet at the cafeteria snack bar, loading up on Tab and Baffy Taffy and Funyuns before going outside.

Elaine prefers to talk, and I prefer to listen, so we get along great. As we eat our junk food picnic on the sidewalk outside the gym, she tells me about Chicago—the Water Tower mall, the Cubs baseball games, the Lincoln Park Zoo—and explains why everything is bigger and better there than in Lafayette.

One day we're walking toward the stairwell with our food when a figure emerges from the boys' bathroom ahead of us. It's David. He ambles up the hallway, head down, kicking at a piece of balled-up trash.

I fight an urge to call out to him and ask him where he's going and why he isn't eating. I can't be my brother's keeper forever.

"See that black boy?" Elaine whispers, slowing down. "He'd be better off in Chicago."

I nod and watch David disappear around a corner, then hold out my bag of Funyuns to her.

"Tell me about that shopping mall again," I ask her as she dips her fingers into the yellow foil. "The one with the seven floors."

Mary joins us. I spot her one day while we're standing in line at the snack bar. There's a commotion in the middle of the cafeteria, and we turn to see a pair of jocks in muscle shirts wrestling across the floor. They bump up against the cheerleaders' table, and the cheerleaders shriek with delight; this is a show put on for their benefit. When the lunchroom monitor— a grumpy, man-like woman who sometimes works the snack bar—blows her whistle, the boys tumble apart and the cheer-leaders stand in unison, clapping their hands in rhythm and chanting.

"Those are some fucked-up mating rituals," Elaine sneers.

As I nod my agreement, I glimpse a lone figure in a yellow shirt at the far end of the cafeteria. David? He was wearing yellow today. I squint. No, it's Mary.

"I'll be right back," I tell Elaine.

She's sitting alone hiding behind her long bangs, but she smiles as I walk toward her.

"Where you been at?" I ask her.

"I had strep throat," Mary says, "but I'm not infectious now."

I point toward the snack bar. "Me and this other girl are gonna eat outside, wanna come?"

She wraps her cheeseburger in a napkin and follows me across the cafeteria. As we wind through the blue tables, I spot David sitting in a corner with Kenny Mudd, a nerd from my Algebra class. Everyone calls him Casper because he's albino; his skin is translucent, and his buzzed hair and eyebrows platinum blond. He wears bottle-thick glasses that make his red eyes bug out, and he's brilliant. Sitting across from each other, David and Kenny look like each other's photographic negative.

I watch David pick up a French fry and cock his head to one side as he listens to Kenny talk. He's not looking in my direction, but I grin at him anyway. He's eating proper and he's found a friend, even if that friend is Kenny Mudd. The lunch monitor frowns at me as we walk by her, and I smile at her, too, happy that this big grumpy woman is watching over my brother.

We're okay, we both are.

+   +   +

We organized a "welcome home" party in the basement. Debra put David on the couch and Herb Alpert on the turntable, and while the rest of us boogied across the carpet, David screeched and bounced on the cushions.

Mother raced downstairs and turned off the music.

"No dancing for David," she scolded. "It's too much for him."

He was almost three years old, but he couldn't walk, and he couldn't talk. He scooted around on his hands and knees. Such was the legacy of his foster-care "families." When he wanted something, he'd point at it and scream. If we didn't understand him, he'd hurl himself to the floor in shrieking frustration, and he'd do the same if he didn't get what he wanted.

He had other residue from his family services days. He'd bang his head against his crib board and fall asleep in his high chair, face-planting in his oatmeal.

I appointed myself his warden and his keeper. I pulled him around by his arms until he took his first teetering steps alone, and clapped my hand over his mouth until he learned to pronounce the names of the objects he wanted.

My name was too difficult for him. He followed me around chanting "Ju-la-la," and I called him "Baby Boo-Boo" because he was constantly tripping and falling and scraping his skin. I'd kiss away his pain and hush his cries.

He was my baby.

CHAPTER 4

HOME

"Jerome's back."

David informs me of this as we cross the back field after school. I'm studying the cover of the September issue of *Glamour*, which I pulled from the mailbox after we got off the bus. The perfection of the cover model, dark-haired in a pink argyle sweater, knifes me with envy. Anyone that beautiful *must* be happy.

Debra got me a subscription for my sixteenth birthday.

"Filth, fornication and vanity!" Mother seethed when the first issue came. She threatened to ban it from the house, and I've been mindful to keep it out of her sight ever since, hiding it under my mattress just as Jerome used to hide his dirty magazines in the basement ceiling. When Dad found his porn stash, he burned them in the backyard—I watched from my window as the dark smoke and ash rose into the hot afternoon sky—before marching Jerome to the pole barn. When Jerome started hollering, I turned up my radio.

"Did you hear me? I said Jerome's back," David says, louder.

"Yeah, I heard you."

"He knocked on the window in the middle of the night, scared the crap out of me. He had a key, but figured they'd changed the alarm on him."

"Oh," I say, scanning an article called "Eat Your Way to Perfect Nails." The photo illustration shows long blue nails gripping a cantaloupe.

"Boy, is he gonna get it when Dad gets home." He pauses before adding in a dramatic voice: "In the country, no one can hear you scream."

I roll my eyes; it's a phrase he's parroted ever since we moved out here and he saw Dad's belt hung on the pole barn wall. He stole it from that *Alien* movie: *In Space, No One Can Hear You Scream*.

At the side of the house, Lecka barks and strains at her chain, shivering with excitement at our arrival, and David jogs ahead of me to play with her.

I imagine the morning's scenario. Mother would have found Jerome at some point and called Dad at the clinic to recount Jerome's look and smell and sneering answers to her questions. He'd been gone for three weeks and they didn't try to find him. Instead, they changed the alarm code, fearing he'd sneak back during the day when the house was empty and burglarize it. Jerome has had a stealing problem ever since he was adopted. When he was little, he stole keys and change from Mother's purse. Now he steals anything he can get his hands on.

Over the past year, he's clashed frequently with Father and has taken to leaving for days at a time, staying with friends until their parents throw him out.

There will be hell to pay, now that he's come home again. Our parents' child-rearing philosophy is etched into twin paddles that hang on the basement wall: "Spare the Rod," and "And Spoil the Child." Proverbs 13:24.

David waits for me by the back door. I stuff the *Glamour* into my backpack and we go inside together. "Holy! Holy! Holy!" plays loudly on the rec room intercom.

The door to the boys' room is shut. David walks to it and twists the knob. It's locked. He shrugs and we go upstairs, where "Holy! Holy! Holy!" booms off the walls and windows. Mother's at the dining room table with the Bible opened in front of her. Her head is in her hands and her glasses lie on the plastic tablecloth. David looks at me and raises his eyebrows before tiptoeing to the cookie jar.

The ceramic lid clinks just as the music fades, and he freezes, hand in the jar. Mother looks up sharply, a tissue clutched in her hand.

"Oh, hi," she says in a weak voice. "Was . . ."

Her words are drowned out by opening chords of the next hymn, and I reach to turn down the intercom volume.

"Pardon me?" I ask.

"Was there any mail?" Her voice is brusque now, back to normal. She puts on her glasses.

"Some," I respond. I walk to her and lay a sheaf of envelopes next to the Bible. It's open to Psalm 23: *The Lord is my shepherd, I shall not be in want. He makes me lie down in green pastures, he leads me beside quiet waters, he restores my soul. . . . I will fear no evil, for You are with me, Your rod and Your staff, they comfort me.* We had to memorize it in fifth grade. It's a good passage to read to yourself, Reverend Dykstra says, whenever you feel troubled.

When Mother lifts her head to study an envelope, I notice her eyes are red.

David pours grape Kool-Aid into two glasses and brings one to me.

"So, Jerome's back?" he asks casually.

Mother's jaw tightens as she shuffles through the rest of the envelopes, separating the junk mail from the bills.

"I'd prefer not to talk about it," she says, drawing her elbows into her sides, clamping up.

David and I are both standing next to her, over her.

"Does Dad know?" I ask. I want her to look up so I can see if she was crying. I've never seen her cry before . . . if that's what she was doing. . . . I thought she was too strong for that.

"Of course he knows!" she says in an irritated voice.

"Do you want any help with supper or anything?" I persist. If she really is crying, I'd feel bad for her.

"What I want is some peace and quiet!" she says, shaking an electric bill in her hand, and still refusing to look up at us. "Don't you kids have homework to do?"

David elbows me and nods toward the basement door. I hesitate—not wanting to see Jerome, but curiosity getting the better of me—before following him downstairs. The door is still locked, and there's no answer when David knocks. In the kitchen, Mother turns the volume up on Rejoice Radio. The hymn is "Blessed Assurance."

"Jerome. Open up," David calls. Nothing. He kicks the door with his sneaker.

Silence.

"Open the door!" he shouts, pounding the wood slab with both fists. The door implodes, sucking David into the room. Jerome stands there, tall and glowering in the shadows. He has turned off the intercom, and the blinds are shut. The room smells sour, like dirty laundry. I follow David inside, and Jerome locks the door behind me. He's several shades darker than David, almost coal-colored. No one would confuse them for brothers.

David sits on his bed and I walk to the far wall and open the blinds and window to let in fresh air. The popped-out screen still leans against the wall beneath the window frame.

"So . . . where you been?" David says.

"Around," Jerome says, turning to squint at the bright window; his left eye is swollen shut.

"What happened to your face?" I ask.

He sneers.

"You should see the other guy."

"What'd you come back for?" David asks. "When Dad gets home . . ."

"To fulfill some basic needs."

Jerome keeps his one good eye on me. I turn my back to him and lean out the open window, my cheeks flaming. Why didn't he stay away? It would be better for everyone if he just disappeared once and for all. A flock of grackles falls onto the fruit trees in the back field.

"I got tired of eating beer and potato chips," Jerome continues. "I really missed our mama's delicious home cookin'."

David snickers. I turn back around as Jerome stretches out on the narrow bed next to me, his size-14 feet poking over the end of the mattress. He leers at me, and I walk over to the door and lean against it.

David swivels his legs over the side of his bed to face Jerome.

"Seriously, what are you going to do when Dad gets home?"

Jerome draws his arms behind his head and yawns. His T-shirt is ripped at the neckline, as if someone had yanked on it.

"Yell real loud and act scared," Jerome says, staring at the ceiling. "But then again, maybe tonight will be different. Maybe tonight I'll give the good doctor a taste of his own medicine."

"As if you could!" David erupts, looking at me in alarm.

"Could? Or would?" Jerome snarls. "In case you haven't noticed, I'm a lot bigger than the old fart, and a lot stronger."

"But he's our dad," David interjects, half angry, half pleading.
"You can't do that."

Jerome leaps to his feet.

"Our *dad*? You looked at yourself in a mirror lately, boy? If he
was your real dad, do you think he'd get such pleasure out of
whipping your sorry black ass?"

He jabs a finger at me.

"He's not our dad, he's her dad. Why do you think she
gets spared? Because this family thing is bullshit, figure it out
already!"

David stares at him with an open mouth, and I chew on my
thumbnail. Above us, Mother walks across the great room toward the hallway, her footsteps creaking the wood floor.

Jerome collapses back onto his bed, stomach-down. "Now let
me sleep," he says.

We've never heard Jerome talk like this before. As I gnaw on
my nail and contemplate the stains in the brown carpet at my
feet, I feel both my brothers turn to look at me, and the weight
of their stares makes me shudder.

As we eat our frozen potpies, Rejoice Radio drones in the background, and Dad's imminent arrival hangs over the supper table
like a sledgehammer. Mother reads *Guideposts* at her end of the
table and Jerome sits next to David, smirking to himself and shaking his head, as if he were remembering something funny. David
and I wolf down our food and excuse ourselves, leaving Jerome to
linger at the table with Mother. He'll try, as always, to sweet-talk
his way out of punishment, telling her how good the food tastes or
complimenting her embroidered Mexican housedress or asking if
he can fetch her more ice cream. But it won't work. It never does.

I go to my bedroom and tune my radio to WAZY 96.5. Blazin' Lafayette's Hottest Music, turning up the volume so I can hear Stevie Nicks' "Edge of Seventeen" above the strains of "Great Is Thy Faithfulness" playing over the intercom. A news report comes on about the Korean airline that was shot down.

"The body count is now official," the announcer says. "Two hundred and sixty-nine people were killed on Korean Air Flight KAL-007 when the Soviets launched a missile at it. In a speech today, President Reagan called it a massacre."

There's a static-filled pause before the president's stern yet soothing voice flows over the speakers.

"This is a crime against humanity that must never be forgotten," the president says, and I shut my eyes.

"Dear God, please keep us safe from Yuri Andropov and the Commies," I pray.

If there's a nuclear war, Mother says we have enough provisions to survive for two weeks. The basement cold cellar doubles as a bomb shelter; it's got concrete walls and a reinforced steel door that are supposed to withstand an atomic blast if it's over three miles away. The shelves are lined with canned tuna, homemade preserves, bottled water and flashlights. In the vegetable bins are blankets and trash bags, which can double as toilets in an emergency.

"What happens after two weeks?" I asked Mother as she was stocking it.

"We pray," she said.

In the kitchen I hear the sharp slap of plates being piled together. Jerome must be emptying the dishwasher, still trying to butter up Mother. Dad will be home any minute, exhausted from a day spent bent over operating tables.

I imagine his frustration deepening as he drives toward our house, the bright streetlights of town giving way to the dark isolation of the country, as he heads toward yet another emergency—his family.

On the weekends he's not on call, he likes to be left alone to tinker with cars in the pole barn or putt around our property on one of his new tractors. He planted a field of soybeans across from the house and puts on his overalls and snap-on baseball cap to inspect the crop. Sometimes I see him bending over the rows from the dining room window—his tall, narrow-shouldered frame lingering over a plant, no doubt trying to determine its state of health, same as he does all day long with his patients—and think about going out there to keep him company, but don't know what we'd talk about.

He wasn't always so distant. When we were little, he used to be playful, tugging on my pigtails as if they were horse reins or sticking David and me in the tiny backseats of his Porsche and zigzagging up the road to make us giggle. But somewhere along the line he dropped out of our lives. He founded Lafayette Surgical Clinic, managing the business affairs in addition to handling a full load of patients, and spent less and less time at home. He became a stranger to us, a stranger who comes around to mete out punishment. A stranger whose presence we've come to resent.

I'm in bed reading *Glamour,* "Bring Out the He-Man in Him!", when his Porsche growls into the driveway. I turn my radio down.

I hear the mudroom door swing open and heavy footsteps cross the great room. There's murmuring, and then heavy footsteps descending the stairs and banging on the boys' door. Incoherent shouting. Shrieks of pain. I turn off my bed stand light and press the radio to my ear under the pillow, filling my head with "Sweet Dreams" by The Eurythmics.

+   +   +

On Saturday, I rush through my chores and bike to my sister Debra's place in town. Swim practice starts Monday and I've started jogging and going for long bike rides after school to build muscle.

David doesn't ride with me anymore—he's taken up Dungeons and Dragons with Kenny Mudd. He tried to explain how it's played to me, but I didn't get it—there's no game board, just dice, paper, a pen and "imagination," he said. When he's not playing it with Kenny, he's studying the "Dungeon Master's Guide" in his room, learning to cast new spells.

Deb is twenty-three and lives on the outskirts of West Lafayette, a thirty-minute ride from our house, in an apartment complex overlooking the sluggish brown belt of the Wabash River. She works as an accountant and has a Catholic boyfriend, which irritates Mother.

Mother calls Catholics idol worshippers. All those saint statues they keep in their cathedrals are graven images, she says, and she doesn't understand why Debra would want to go out with one of them when our French Huguenot ancestors fled to Holland precisely to get away from Catholic persecution in the sixteenth century.

Despite all this, Debra has not dropped Tom, whom she started dating in high school and plans to marry. She recently started going to his cathedral instead of our church, and at the moment, Mother's not talking to her. I lied and told Mother I was visiting some made-up friend rather than see her get lathered up about Catholics again.

Deb answers the door in a red bikini that Mother would not approve of. She's seven years older than me, but anyone can tell we're sisters; we've got the same fine long blond hair, the same hipless bodies, the same snorting laugh.

"Come on in, I was just pouring some lemonade," she says, smiling and swinging the door open.

Going to Deb's is a taste of what life will be like after eighteen, a preview of freedom. When I visit, she treats me special, preparing gourmet food from her French cookbook, letting me sip small glasses of wine or sit in her living room watching that new music channel, MTV.

We spend the afternoon lounging beside the complex's kidney-shaped pool, sipping hand-squeezed lemonade with mint leaves, listening to Christopher Cross, reading fashion magazines and diving into the pool whenever the sun starts to prick our skin. I wish I could stay with her forever.

As we paint each other's nails Cinnamon Vixen, I consider telling her how bad things are at home. After she and Dan and Laura left for college, everything got worse. Mother's mood swings, Dad's violence, the name-calling at school. But I don't want to break the magic spell of the afternoon by bringing up home—I'll have to go back there soon enough.

Deb fries vegetables in beer batter for our supper. We eat wrapped in our towels in her tiny kitchen as the late-afternoon sun falls over the table, warming a handful of marigolds she's stuck in a chipped blue glass. James Galway plays on the stereo, reminding me of the nights she practiced flute at our old house. Her room was directly above mine, and as I lay in bed, her melodies fluttered down to me in the darkness, easing me into a peaceful sleep. It was angel music.

"I wish you were still home," I tell her, my eyes stinging with tears. I stare down at the marigolds to avoid her gaze.

She laughs with a soft snort and reaches behind her for the glass pitcher on the counter.

"I'm glad I'm not," she says. "More lemonade?"

When I turn onto Indian Meadow Lane, the twilight air is still soupy with heat and moisture. Lightning flashes along the chalky gray horizon; maybe there'll be a good thunderstorm tonight, a real gully washer. We're overdue. On the basketball court beside the pole barn, three figures bob and leap in the half darkness: Jerome, David and a stranger. Their sneakers scuff the cement as they perform their grunting ballet.

They don't notice me as I glide into the driveway and stop on the concrete rectangle in front of the garage. I turn to watch them as the floodlights attached to the pole barn and house snap on, revealing the mystery player. It's the boy with the blue satin shorts who was there on the morning of swim team tryouts; he's wearing the same shorts tonight. "Scottie the hottie," girls call him at school. He's a football player, and I've seen him at the tables of both the Jocks and the Hoods in the school cafeteria. He seems to get along with everyone. They say his mother's Asian—his father's war bride—and that's where he gets his toasted skin and tilted eyes.

His torso gleams in the floodlights as he swerves between my brothers, and four black arms strain after him as he plunges the ball through the low net. The three of them reel back—Jerome standing a head taller than the other two boys—and David rebounds. He tussles with Jerome as Scott walks to the side of the court and spits into the weeds. As he turns to watch my brothers play, I take in the broad T of his shoulders and the curves of his chest and arms. He's short, but studly.

The basketball bounces off the court in my direction and I turn to walk my bike to the garage.

"Hey, little sister!" Jerome shouts. "Wanna see some ball-handling?"

Everything sounds dirty with him. I keep walking.

"Hey Julia, come meet our neighbor!" David yells.

Neighbor?! "Just a sec," I mutter, leaning my bike against the garage door.

Glamour says to act casual when you're introduced to a handsome man, as if he were only a valet, or a delivery boy. But I've never even met a valet or a delivery boy.

Scott dribbles the ball and muscles ripple up and down his entire body. As I saunter toward him, he flings the ball to David and strides to meet me, stopping a few inches from my face, a spicy musk rushing off him. His wavy black hair is cut short over his ears but falls to the base of his neck in the back in a mullet. He's my height, or a little shorter.

"Julia, right?" he says, smiling, hands on his hips.

"Nice to meet you," I say, sticking my hand out. My voice doesn't sound casual, it sounds high-pitched and little girly. "What was your name again?"

He wraps his hand around mine and gives it a hot squeeze.

"Scott Cooper. I live about a mile away, up on County Road 50."

"Right or left?"

"What?"

"Which way on County Road 50 from here?"

"North. Um, right."

The dangerous side of County Road 50.

"You don't take the bus?"

"Nah, I got wheels." He jerks a thumb at a scooter parked in front of the pole barn.

"Oh."

I smile and nod and throw out my hip, not knowing what else to say. His eyes, rootbeer brown, hold mine for a few seconds before my cheeks flush and I drop my gaze, letting it slide down his chest to his abdomen to his satin shorts. When I look him in the face again, the corner of his mouth is pulled back in a sly smile; he thinks I was checking him out. I *was* checking him out.

"It's nice to meet a neighbor kid finally," I say, stumbling over the words. "Okay, then. You boys have a nice game."

Jeez, I'm such a dork. Behind him, David and Jerome mock my hip-out stance and crossed arms.

"Actually, I was just leaving," Scott says. He reaches a curvy arm behind his head and shakes his fingers through his hair. A bead of sweat hits my lower lip. I lick it off without thinking.

"Dudes, call me when you're ready to play some serious ball," he says, walking toward his scooter. "No more of this sissy shit, okay?"

He hops on the bike and kick-starts the engine.

"Oh yeah?" Jerome shouts. "How about we play on a regulation court next time, shrimp!"

Scott flips him off, grinning, before laying a long track in the gravel, rocks and dust spitting into the air. Jerome watches him disappear before peeling off his T-shirt and mopping his face with it.

David scoops up the basketball from where it rolled into the weeds and lobs it at the net with one hand, whacking the backboard, and Jerome rebounds it, then plants himself at the far end of the court for a free throw. The floodlights shine down on his back like a spotlight, and I cringe. Fat welts lace his skin like red leeches. Dad put them there last night with a belt, as punishment for running away and stealing the Corolla. *Spare the rod and spoil the child.*

Both boys' backs are riddled with welts, the fresh ones red, the old ones mottled gray, the deeper ones hardened into jagged scars. They avoid taking off their shirts in public, and seeing their bare backs always makes my throat thicken, makes it hard to breathe.

When their wounds are fresh, their allegiances change, and it's no longer children against parents. It's blacks against whites, and I'm one of the enemy. David snubs me to hang out with Jerome, the two of them bonding over their beatings.

Jerome is right. I don't get whipped like they do when I talk back or get caught in a lie. I get grounded. I'm spared the rod, and it's a dirty privilege that makes me feel guilty. I hate sharing genes with the man who hurts them, our father.

Our father, who heals the sick and dying by day, and causes injury at night.

The sound of metal grating on metal is barely audible over the cicadas at first. I wake with a start, clenching my teeth, recognizing the noise.

It's the sound of a fingernail scissors, teasing the flimsy button lock of my bedroom door. Mother doesn't like me to lock it—*what are you hiding?*—but I started again after Jerome returned. Not that it will stop it from happening. But it's an objection just the same, a small plea to stop.

I could tell by the way Jerome looked me over earlier that he'd be coming tonight, by the way he'd smirked and stared, as if we shared a secret.

We do.

It started in grade school, when I was eleven and he was twelve. That's when he began to collect the dirty magazines that blew against the guardrail on Happy Hollow Road. We'd glimpse them as we raced down the steep hill toward Kingston swimming pool, flashes of skin and hair, smeared and torn by the elements. For years, we paid no mind. Then one day, Jerome stopped his bike, bent over, and rolled one into his towel. A few days later, on a Sunday afternoon, he tried to get me to look at it. I was curled up in a beanbag under a basement window, reading Nancy Drew. Upstairs, Mother was playing hymns on the piano, accompanying herself with her warbling soprano voice.

Jerome thrust a mildewed picture of a woman with blond hair over my book. She was naked, gagged, and tied to a chair. Straps were wound tightly around the base of her breasts, making them stick out like fleshy missiles, and her blue eyes were wide with pain or fear. I stared at her in horror.

"She looks like you," Jerome said. "Except you don't have these yet." He touched the woman's strangled breasts and then my flat chest. I jumped up, Nancy Drew spilling to the floor.

"Leave me alone!" I shouted.

When David poked his head around the corner, Jerome sauntered away, hiding the magazine under his shirt.

But he didn't leave me alone.

One evening a few days later, I was in my bedroom playing with my teddy bear hamsters when Jerome knocked on the door holding Mousetrap, my favorite game.

We played laying on the floor, facing each other across the cardboard square as the rest of the family watched *Mutual of Omaha's Wild Kingdom* in the family room. I tossed the dice and it shot across the board, bumping to stop against Jerome's stomach. As I reached for it, I noticed his penis spilling from the slit of his pajama pants like a rotten banana. When I looked at his face, he was frowning in concentration at his yellow mouse, as if he were contemplating his next move. I was embarrassed for him, believing it had fallen out by accident, and he hadn't realized it. We played like that, him with his dick hanging out, me averting my eyes, until the television show ended and it was time to go to bed.

But it kept happening. I'd be peeling potatoes or practicing piano and he'd walk by with his penis poking out. I didn't understand why he did it, and pretended not to notice.

A few days after my twelfth birthday, he tried to kiss me. I was on the balcony off my bedroom, setting out apple slices for the raccoons that lived in the woods behind our house; they climbed the balcony's support posts at night, and I liked to watch them eat through the glass door. As I crouched down, arranging the fruit on a dish, Jerome tapped me on the shoulder.

"You're not really my sister," he said when I stood up. At thirteen, he was already a good six inches taller than me, and a whole lot stronger. He grabbed my shoulders and tried to smash his mouth onto mine, but I averted my face and his chapped lips grazed my forehead instead. I walked out of my bedroom and locked myself in the bathroom, afraid, creeped out, not knowing what to do.

"Please God, make him stop," I prayed.

Jerome had always acted differently than David. Maybe, at seven, when he was adopted, he was too scarred to let us be his family. He also came from a long line of foster homes, but was already a petty thief and a liar when he entered our household.

Our parents believed David needed a playmate—one of his own kind—so they brought Jerome home for David's sixth birthday. They should have known that David and I were fine just by ourselves. We were best friends, and Jerome didn't change that. He was a bully who stole toys and played too rough, and for the most part, we avoided him.

As we've gotten older, and Father's beatings have become more frequent, their blackness has finally united them. They are the outsiders, the basement-dwellers, Mother's failed mission to Africa. The black boys who get whipped by the white master. But while David still longs for a Hallmark card type of family— all frilly love and special occasions—Jerome has struck back, through me.

Over the years, I've noticed a pattern. After Dad beats him, Jerome comes to find me.

I've never told our parents our repulsive secret. While most children turn to their mothers for comfort, that's never been the case in our family. If I was sick in grade school and had to stay home from school, Mother would grumpily attend to me, making it clear that any extra claims I made on her time were a hassle. I'd frequently wake up vomiting in the middle of the night and would seek out my sister Laura, not my parents. Laura would help me wash the filth from my blanket in the bathtub, whispering comfort and quietly running the water, so as not to disturb them.

There's another reason I've never told. I don't want to be responsible for Jerome's yelps of pain, or fresh welts on his back. You don't do that to your brothers, you don't nark on them.

I just kept hoping and praying he'd leave me alone.

The fingernail scissors continue to jab at the tumblers. The alarm clock on my bedside table says it's 2:20. The house is quiet. My parents are asleep two doors down. I roll onto my back and fling the sheets from my body. Let it be quick.

The button lock finally pops and Jerome gently pushes the door inward, lifting the brass knob to ease the stress on the hinges. His massive form fills the doorway and I turn my head toward the wall so he can't kiss me. That's one thing he hasn't taken from me. A kiss should be special. I hear him lock the door and creep toward my bed. The mattress tilts under his weight. By the time he touches me, I'm far away.

I breathe deeply, pretending to be asleep, falling through layers of numbness, sensation draining from my body like dirty bath water. My mind flits through a collage of images and thoughts—a horse galloping across a field of clover, the conjugation of To Be in French, the marigolds on Deb's table. At some point, the collage fades, and time fades, but somehow I remember to keep breathing.

When I wake Sunday morning, the sheet is tucked around my shoulders and the door is closed. A choir sings "Abide With Me" on Rejoice Radio, and the welcoming scent of coffee wafts down the hallway from the kitchen.

Only when I pull my nightgown over my head do I notice the dried blood on my breast and remember Jerome. The tan circle around my left nipple is broken and raw; it's happened before. In my faraway place, I don't feel pain. I thrust myself into my Sunday dress, trying not to think about it.

We both bear our scars.

Lafayette Christian Reformed is forty minutes away by car—an epic journey by Lafayette standards—but it's the only Calvinist church in town and so we must go there.

We're always late, and today is no exception. In the van, Mother jerks the wheel right and left and stomps on the gas and brake pedals, as if she were pantomiming driving rather than actually doing it. Father is on call at Home Hospital, and David, Jerome and I each have a bench to ourselves in the back of the van.

We hurtle down thin country lanes while Amy Grant croons "Sing Your Praise to the Lord" over the tinny speakers.

Next to a cornfield is a Jesus advertisement:

> But unles you
> REPENT
>
> You will
> **PEARSH**

Farther down, someone has changed the wording of another message with spray paint:

> Get DOWN
> on yer KNEES *pads*
> and PRAY!

Jerome, sitting behind me, leans forward.

"Do you know what that means?" he breathes into my ear.

I scoot away from him, to the far side of my bench.

The line between town and country in West Lafayette is sliding as subdivisions creep onto farmland. "Quality Manufactured Home Living," announces a billboard at the side of the road. Behind it is a row of identical small houses, each with white vinyl siding, a gray shingled roof, two windows, and mud for a front yard. Instant houses—half a step above trailer parks.

Our church, in downtown Lafayette, is a severe brick structure surrounded by scruffy Victorians that have been divied up into apartments for poor people—the kind of people who don't go to our church.

Mother barrels into the parking lot and slides the van into the first empty slot. Her face is pinched as we hustle toward the three arched doorways of the church entrance, but the moment we enter the foyer she transforms, smiling and greeting people in her sweet telephone voice.

We kids sulk by the coatroom, watching her flit from person to person. She's in her element. She's well known in church circles for her charitable work with Vacation Bible School and the ministry to shut-ins. It's the next best thing to being a missionary for her: a chance to save souls, to receive gratitude, and to focus on something other than her unhappy family.

I dig around in the bottom of my purse for the Red Hots I swiped from the cupboard before church and dump several into my mouth, biting into their spicy cinnamon hearts. David holds out his hand and I pour a few into his palm. Next to him, Jerome leans his long body against the coatroom doorframe, crosses his arms and closes his eyes.

A woman with a blue poof of hair—Mrs. De Jong of De Jong Hogs fame—shuffles over to us. She's been old for as long as I can remember, wearing the same long black cardigan every Sunday, morning and evening, summer and winter, year after year. A yeasty odor spills off her as she comes to a wobbling halt in front of Jerome.

"Hello, Davey!" she shouts, patting the sleeve of Jerome's salmon-colored suit. "Don't fall asleep, now!"

Jerome slowly opens his eyes and looks down at her. She smiles, her face splintering into a spider's web of lines.

"He's Davey," Jerome says in a surly voice, nodding at David. "I'm Jerome."

"What's that?" Mrs. De Jong reaches up to fiddle with her hearing aid, and it buzzes loudly. Her eyes glaze over while she flutters her fingers behind her ear until the noise stops.

"What's that, Davey? I think I can hear you now."

Jerome thumps his chest with his fist.

"Me, Jerome," he says, before pointing to David. "He, Davey."

Mrs. De Jong waves her hand dismissively. "Oh, Jerry! It's so hard to keep you boys straight."

No one has called Jerome "Jerry" since seventh grade, when he surged over six feet and insisted on being called "Jerome." His face clouds over and he leans forward, dwarfing the old woman.

"The same thing happens to me with you whities," he says, grinning. Mrs. De Jong nods enthusiastically, her hearing aid obviously broken. "Y'all start looking the same to me after a while, too."

"Jerome!" I gasp.

Mrs. De Jong finally picks up on Jerome's menacing body language, and her smile fades. She looks confused.

"I just wanted to say hello," she says, doddering away. I give Jerome a dirty look, but he's back to leaning against the doorframe, his eyes closed.

At the front of the sanctuary, the choir launches into "Come Ye That Fear Jehovah." Mother returns from working the foyer and herds us to the usher stand, where Mr. Kylstra, a large grim man with a roll of skin bulging over the back of his suit collar, leads us down the aisle. I go first, followed by Mother, then the boys. We walk down the thread-worn red carpet toward our pew, spitting distance from the pulpit.

When there were eight of us, the parade went like this: oldest sister, middle sister, youngest sister, mother, father, youngest brother, middle brother, oldest brother. Everyone neat and ordered. Our entrance always caused a stir as people turned our way in nodding approval. I imagined their papery whispers: "Raising those black boys as if they were family. Talk about Christian sacrifice."

The sanctuary is a hot cave. The tiny openings at the foot of the towering stained glass windows aren't big enough to let air in, and the three giant fans that hang from the ceiling merely redistribute the heat. The smell of our church—of chalky plaster and dusty carpets and dark, moldy spaces—is as familiar to me as the smell of our home. We're here every Sunday morning and evening, and during grade school, we'd return for Wednesday night Catechism class and Saturday morning Calvinettes and Cadet meetings.

I rifle through the pew back and pull out a fan, a tongue depressor stapled to a cardboard square. The one I pick has a picture of a little girl in a pink dress clutching a Bible on it, and I put it back and choose another, this one of a quaint white chapel surrounded by autumn trees. New England somewhere, a fantasy church I'll never see.

At the front of the sanctuary, the choir director, Norm Seetsma, brings the choir to climax and then stillness with a series of epileptic movements. The singers sit in unison, and the men pat their foreheads with white hankies.

Reverend Dykstra steps through a side door to the left of the choir and climbs a small carpeted stairway to the pulpit. He's a small man in his forties, with a fat pink head and bulging gray eyes that make him look like he's about to cry. He raises the arms of his black robe in a silent benediction—a giant vulture stretching its wings—and heads bow around me. His robe billows as he blesses us, stirred by a small fan at his feet.

In the pew in front of us, the Van der Slew spinsters, Hansje and Uda, sit side by side in matching blue pillbox hats, their heads wobbling faintly. Spinsters and widows make up much of the congregation. They clump together in groups of two or three, sometimes accompanied by a crusty artifact of a man.

Our church is dying.

The young blood has drained to those modern churches where the preachers wear jeans and the choirs have been replaced by musicians wielding electric guitars. But we Calvinists ignore these changes, stubbornly clinging to our creeds and ceremony even as Reverend Dykstra urges his shrinking flock to "dig extra deep" during the offerings, which more and more frequently are taken twice during each service.

We rise to sing "Lead on, O King Eternal"—Mother's soprano soaring above the voices around us—before sitting for the first collection.

Elders in dark suits move down the aisles shepherding brass offering plates up and down the pews, and I place the fifty cents Mother gave me onto the red velvet circle on the bottom. The elders, deacons and ushers are all men. When I was in grade school, I wanted to be an usher like my brothers but was sent downstairs to the nursery instead. That's where the women work, in the basement—changing diapers, organizing potlucks and teaching Sunday school. In the basement, out of sight.

After another hymn the elders make a second sweep up the aisles, this time carrying silver trays containing cubes of Wonder Bread and glass thimbles of red wine, the Body and Blood of Christ. As I pass the wine tray to Mother I inhale the syrupy aroma and long to taste it.

David, Jerome and I are the only worshippers in sight with empty hands. None of us have stood before the congregation to make Public Profession of Faith and proclaim Jesus Christ as our Personal Lord and Savior, so we can't take Communion. Our classmates at Lafayette Christian all made Profession in seventh or eighth grade, but the three of us have held out. I don't know what the boys' reasons are, but I know my own: during the Profession ceremony, you must swear to forsake the secular world, and I'm not ready to do that yet. There are too many secular things that I like. Van Halen. MTV. Dancing. My friend Elaine, a Jew.

Behind the pulpit, Reverend Dykstra pinches a piece of Christ between his thumb and index finger and raises it over his head.

"Take, eat: this is my body, which is broken for you: do this in remembrance of me."

He sticks Christ in his mouth and chews, and the congregation follows suit. He then drains Christ's blood from his silver wine goblet in one long gulp, and the congregation mimics him with their glass thimbles.

Rick Hoolsema, my seventh-grade boyfriend, sits a few rows ahead of us in his family pew, and I watch him take Communion. Watching the back of Rick's head kept me awake during Reverend Dykstra's long-winded sermons when I was twelve, as I waited impatiently for the service to end so we could sneak off together. As soon as Reverend Dykstra pronounced the final "amen" and bustled down the aisle toward the narthex, Rick and I would rush up the back stairway to the windowless attic, where we'd feel our way through fusty stacks of Psalter Hymnals and the cool satin of hanging choir robes to a cushionless sofa. There, we'd sit facing each other in the darkness, taking turns running a fingertip over each other's palms, without speaking, as bats fluttered overhead and cars honked faintly in the parking lot. After Rick's glow-in-the-dark wristwatch marked five minutes, we'd slip back down the staircase to reunite with our families.

These fingertip caresses were exquisite, amplified by our inability to see the lust and embarrassment in each other's faces. There was only a tingling sensation and our open-mouthed breathing. But our caresses never progressed beyond our palms; years of Sunday school, Christian school, Calvinettes, Cadets,

Young Calvinists and Youth Group had taught us to keep ourselves pure for the marriage bed, and even the smallest token of physical affection was given with much hesitation and reluctance. "'Petting' encourages sinful thoughts," our youth group leader told us.

By the time Rick gave me my first kiss at the end of seventh grade—in a closet, during a party when the adult supervisor left the room and David pushed us inside, Rick skimmed my lips with his, then scrambled away—Jerome had already taken most everything else.

A second offering is taken—Mother gives me only a quarter this time—and Reverend Dykstra clears his throat and adjusts the microphone. I take a bulletin from the pew back; the sermon title is "God Is ALL You Need."

"Beloved in the Lord: All of us Calvinists are familiar with the first question and answer of the Heidelberg Catechism," he says, leaning forward and gripping the pulpit. "Our children memorize it in fifth grade, and I'm sure you adults can recite it by heart as well . . . that is, at least I hope you can. If not, there's still space available in Mr. Vanderkleed's Wednesday night class."

Laughter riffles through the pews, and Reverend Dykstra leans back and grins, taking it in, before putting on his stern preacher face again.

"It is a profound question, the cornerstone of our faith: What is your only comfort in life and death? The answer is equally profound: That I am not my own, but belong—body and soul, in life and death—to my faithful Savior, Jesus Christ, who preserves me in such a way that not a hair can fall from my head without the will of my heavenly Father.

"What does this mean, exactly? It means that God is the only comfort we need in a world where Communist missiles may fall at any moment and our families and friends may fail us. It means that nothing happens without God allowing it to happen. It means that He is in control."

My mind wanders, as it always does, lulled toward random thoughts by Reverend Dykstra's singsong voice. Sunlight streams in rainbow colors through the stained glass windows; green and orange stripes fall across my pale yellow skirt. Outside, a basketball thuds down the sidewalk next to the church. On the other side of Mother, David plays with a paper cut on his thumb, pressing the seam open and closed, and Mother elbows him sharply.

If God is in control, why does He allow so many bad things to happen? I lay my hands in the jeweled light on my lap and spread my fingers. If God is all we need, why does it so often seem that He is not enough? God may be enough for Mother, but I need other things, too. Immediate, solid things. I need Dad to stop beating the boys and Jerome to leave me alone and Mother to be kind.

". . . A passage from the Bible that helps put things in perspective is Proverbs 3 verses 5 and 6: Trust in the Lord with all your heart; do not lean on your own understanding; in all your ways acknowledge him and He will direct your paths."

Mother offers me a roll of butter rum Lifesavers and I take one before she passes the roll to David. He takes several, and Mother elbows him again as candy drops loudly to the floor and rolls under the pews. Mother shakes her head and closes her eyes, exasperated, and David peers over at me with a mischievous grin. I smile back at him. *Ding dong*.

"When we surrender ourselves to God and allow Him to take control of our lives, we can endure every battle and face every foe, confident of the outcome. We can say 'Thank you, Lord, for giving me all the comfort I need. You are mine and I am yours and I trust your authority.' What an amazing gift!"

Maybe God's punishing me for not praying regularly. I used to pray all the time, but cut back when I didn't see results. Jerome didn't stop bothering me, Mother didn't get any happier, and my chest is still flat.

Reverend Dykstra's voice softens and I look up to see his head bowed.

"Thank you, dear God, for all you have done for us. Apply your Word unto our every heart, and bring us into Thy courts again this evening. Forgive us our sins, oh Heavenly Father, and hear us in Jesus' name. Amen."

He raises his head and nods curtly at Mrs. Molestra, the hunchbacked organist, who launches into "Savior, Like a Shepherd Lead Us." The congregation rises. Mother thrusts a Psalter Hymnal into the space between us, and when I look at her she smiles; a warm, sweet smile, the one she reserves for church people and strangers. This throws me off-guard and I look away, unbelieving, before looking at her again and smiling feebly in return as I take a corner of the hymnal. *Mother smiled at me!*

They say that God works in mysterious ways that our finite human minds cannot comprehend. Maybe I should pray harder.

+   +   +

I grew jealous of him.

"What an adorable little black boy!" strangers gushed as Mother walked us down the sidewalk, me dangling from one hand, David from the other. "A miniature Bill Cosby!"

They'd pinch his cheeks, pat his spongy hair, ooh and ahh over him. And they'd ignore me. After all, Lafayette was swarming with tow-headed toddlers. David was unique.

After the strangers finished their poking and prodding, Mother would nudge David to say thank you. "Tank ew," he'd say in his high little voice, and they'd gush all over again. Sometimes I'd get so jealous, I'd reach behind Mother's legs and pinch him. Then I'd feel bad when he got in trouble for crying.

My competition for attention was fierce, and sometimes painful.

Once he rode his tricycle down the stairs at our house and crashed into a wall; everyone rushed over to console him. I took one look at all the commotion and rode my trike down the stairs right after him.

Another time we sang "King David: Kindhearted King" in Sunday school and I raised my hand to demand a song about "Queen Julia."

I was convinced that David got special treatment because he was black.

CHAPTER 5

BODY PARTS

The pool spreads out before me, purple-blue in the deep end and turquoise in the shallows. I stand on the high-dive platform, knees bent, toes curled over the sandpaper edge. Mary waits at the far end of the water.

"Ready?" I shout. She gives me two thumbs up.

I bounce twice and push off the board, soaring for a long moment before knifing through the cool surface, hands in prayer position over my head, elbows tight to my face. When I feel the counter-tug, I pull down my arms and frog kick, breaststroking underwater. I open my eyes in the scratchy chlorine and the world is pale blue. I glide past Mary's brown legs, reach the wall, and crouch down to kick off the hard tile, lungs burning, and manage several strokes back toward the deep end before rising to gulp in air. I turn to look at the marker at the edge of the pool.

"Five feet!" I yell, raising my arms in triumph. Mary made it to four. She freestyles over.

"Not by much," she says. "Do it again?"

"Sure." I shrug. "Just let me know when you get tired of losing, okay?"

She splashes me and as we swim to the side of the pool, a car horn blares one, two, three times.

"Gotta go," Mary says, hoisting herself from the water. She winds a towel around her thick body, grabs her gym bag from the bleachers, and bolts out the side door as the car horn sounds again.

"See you tomorrow," I call at the closing door.

Fluorescent lights buzz overhead. I pull off my rubber cap and lean back, letting the water cushion my head as my feet rise to the surface. As always, I'm the last girl in the pool after practice. This is my favorite part of the day, when I can float alone in the deep end and think.

My hair caresses my shoulders, and I close my eyes, pretending the white glare of the overhead lights is sunshine. David and I will have a pool at our Florida apartment. Not one of those dorky birdbaths that take three strokes to cross, either, but a decent plunger, ringed by palm trees and hot pink hibiscus, a stone's throw from the ocean. We'll float just like this under the brilliant blue Florida sky, listening to the waves and the seagulls as the gentle sun warms us.

Life will only get better when we're eighteen, and it's not unbearable now. I've got two friends and have won a few ribbons at swim meets. And now that I ride my bike to Harrison for the swim practice, I no longer have to endure the shame of the reserved bus seat or rush ahead of David on the sidewalk. Jerome rides the bus with him now, and nobody messes with Jerome.

David seems to be okay, too, consumed by Dungeons and Dragons. David calls Kenny Mudd the Grim Illusionist and Kenny calls him the Dark Cleric. Whatever. He seems to be happy. And no one's called me "nigger lover" since I stopped hanging out with him. Things will be different for us in Florida, but for now, it's best we keep to ourselves.

"Hey, little sister!"

Jerome. I drop my feet and scissor my arms and legs, backing farther into the deep end. He squats at the edge of the pool, twirling his hand in the water.

"What do you want?" I glance around; we're alone.

"Mom says to get home on the double."

I glance at the clock on the wall behind him.

"How come?" I ask him. "It's only 5:15."

He takes his hand out of the water and wipes it on his jeans.

"Fuck if I know. Maybe you're in trouble or something."

Maybe Mother found out that I borrowed her earrings without asking. When I returned them to her jewelry chest, I didn't remember which drawer I'd taken them from and dropped them in the top one.

"You coming?" Jerome asks.

"Yeah, I'm going," I say, glaring at him. "You don't need to wait for me."

I don't want him to see me climb dripping from the pool with my swimsuit plastered to my body. I don't want him to see me, period.

Jerome walks backward toward the side exit grinning smugly, turning at the last minute to slip through the door.

After he's gone, I rush to the locker room and throw my blue terrycloth sweat suit on over my Speedo, imagining Mother festering angrily at home. If she sent Jerome all the way down here

to get me, she must be pissed. I'll say I thought I'd asked to borrow her earrings, then apologize for forgetting.

The hallway is unlit. At the far end, Jerome stands on the
other side of the glass doors, straddling his bike and cupping his
hands to the glass. I halt and cross my arms, and he pedals out of
sight, the long shadow he threw over the floor refilled with orange sunlight.

As I'm pulling my wet hair into a ponytail, the boys' locker
room door opens and three figures emerge. They stand facing
me, but the hallway is too dim to see their faces; the fading light
is behind them.

"Hey there, Julia," one says; I recognize Scott's velvety voice.

They walk toward me in a row, arms curved slightly at their
sides, apelike. Squinting, I make out the two other boys, football
players I've never talked to before: Brad MacIntyre and Todd
Klondike.

"What's up?" I ask in a stiff voice, sensing something sinister
in their crouched walk.

One of them grunts something and there's a flurry of motion
and suddenly I'm on my back, swaying between them as if we
were on the beach and they were about to toss me into the ocean.
Scott's at my shoulders, Brad and Ted have me by the ankles.

"Easy, girl," Scott murmurs, as if he were calming a skittish
colt. "Everything's okay. We're just gonna have ourselves some
fun s'all."

I know what's happening. I've heard talk of this on Mondays
after a big party. A bunch of guys will single out a girl, drag her
away, and pull off her clothes. They'll do things to her, and if she
hollers, everyone ignores her.

It's called a gang bang, and it never happens to the popular
girls. The boys always pick a loner or a wannabe, a girl who

wants to be part of the in-crowd, but doesn't quite have the right attitude or clothes. She's flattered to be invited to the party, but on Monday she walks through school cringing, as the popular girls talk trash about her—*Who the hell did she think she was, anyway?*—while the jocks slap each other on the back.

It's happening to me. No, it *won't*.

"No!" I scream, and Scott stuffs a salty hand in my mouth.

"Come on, angel, relax," says Todd. He's wearing his varsity team letter jacket, orange sleeves and blue torso. He's got a zit on the side of his nose with a white tip, begging to be popped. His girlfriend is a varsity cheerleader named Brandi with big tits. He jerks on the bottom of my sweatpants and I kick my legs, seesawing back and forth between them. He drops my ankle, then snatches it back up, laughing.

Brad's curly brown hair falls over his face and he swings his head sideways to get it out of his eyes. I stare at his Big Boy T-shirt. *Big Boy Makes You Say Ohhh Boy!*

"I thought he said she was easy," Brad says, tugging on the cord at my waist.

A streak of hatred burns through me: Jerome set me up. He knew I'd be here alone. He lied about Mother wanting me home. She doesn't.

Brad keeps tugging at the cord; in my rush, I tied it in a knot and it won't budge. Thank you, Lord. Scott unclamps my mouth and snakes a hand down my top, groping my breasts through my bathing suit.

"Not quite ripe, but tasty all the same," he says. Scott, who stood in my driveway and shook my hand.

"Fuck you!" I scream up at him, craning my neck to look into his eyes. I've never said those words aloud before and am surprised at how easily they slip from my mouth.

Brad and Todd are now both yanking on the waistband of my sweatpants, trying to force it over my hips, and Scott is reaching under my swimsuit. I flail my arms and legs like a possessed rag doll, trying to twist from their grasp. Todd grabs my crotch and I spit at him, but the saliva falls on my chest. They whoop with laughter.

Brad steps forward, loosening his grip on my ankle, and feeling this, I yank back my leg and slam my tennis shoe into his balls. He crumples, shrieking, to the ground, his hands clamped between his legs. Half a second later, I'm sprinting down the hallway toward the exit.

"You wounded, MacIntyre?" I hear Scott yell as I crash through the glass doors.

I chained my ten-speed behind the school because the rack across from the gym entrance was full, and run to it and crouch by the front tire, fumbling with the combination lock, cursing the stupid tiny numbers on the dial and the setting sun. *Fuck, fuck, fuck.*

I hear the boys tumble outside into the cool October air.

"Where'd she go?"

"This way!"

The nightmare monster is chasing me, but I can't break out of slow motion. Any second now, a hand will grab my ponytail and jerk my head back, and it will all be over.

Miraculously, the footsteps run away from me, toward the front of the school. The lock finally clicks open and I fling the chain into the bushes and hop on, my muscles superhuman with fear as I pedal toward County Road 50. A single car is parked in the back lot, a navy Mustang sitting under a lamp pole. Light glances off its immaculate surface.

I'm about to reach the intersection with County Road 600 when I hear the Mustang vroom to life, tires squealing over the pavement. They're coming to get me. *Fuck, fuck, fuck.* There are bushes beside the road and I aim my bike for them, veering down a shallow ravine. My front wheel hits something and the bike pitches over, sending me skidding over sharp ground. I turn to see the Mustang's high beams swerving onto County Road 50 from the school driveway, and crawl toward the bushes, dragging my bike behind me. *Help me, God.*

As the Mustang bears down the road, AC/DC's "Hell's Bells" thuds from the speakers. The car skids to a halt at the intersection and I hear voices arguing under the music. The song clicks off and I hear someone say "Indian Meadow Lane"—my address—and then the music starts again. The car lurches forward and I lay under the bushes and watch the red eyes of the tail lights until they wink out and I'm alone in the dying light with the crickets and my heart pounding like a brick in my chest.

It's well after suppertime when I coast into the driveway. My bike chain derailed in the collision with the tree stump and I struggled with the greasy metal for an eternity before hooking it back over its ring.

When I open the front door, Mother rushes over, her bifocals flashing in the entranceway light. The boys peer over at me from the table, where they're eating bowls of pink ice cream.

"And just where have you been, Missy?"

Her voice is tight, as if someone were giving her a bear hug and crushing the air from her lungs. She hasn't smiled at me again since that Sunday two weeks ago, despite my renewed efforts at prayer.

She doesn't notice my dirt-streaked clothes or the scrapes on my arms from where I slid over sticks and stones. She keeps her eyes locked on mine. Sandi Patti's "Jesus, You're Everything" plays over the intercom.

"My bike . . . the road," I stammer.

"Your food's cold," she says, interrupting me. "I don't see why there should be a separate eating schedule for every person in this household. When I say supper at six, I mean it."

I nod, and her expression softens a hint.

"Make sure you get enough broccoli. We're entering cold season and I don't want you sick with your crazy swim hours."

She turns to walk back to her chair. In the kitchen sink, I scrub my hands with steel wool and dish soap, but the grease won't come off. I sit down at my plate of fish sticks, Tater Tots and broccoli with black fingertips. David notices shaking my hands and gives me a concerned look. Next to him, Jerome scoops pink ice cream into his mouth, a smirk itching the corner of his lips. I pick up my knife and fork and glare at him. *You are not my brother.*

Everything I know about being female I learned from a Kotex box.

At Lafayette Christian, there was no sex ed class. In Home Ec at Harrison, we learned how to care for babies, but not how to make them. Mrs. Lawton had each of us girls carry a raw egg around school for two weeks to teach us that babies are fragile and demanding and we shouldn't rush out and have one. Some of the girls drew faces on the shells and named them after their boyfriends: Jimmy Joe or Zeke or Bubba Johnson the Fifth. Most of the babies were dead by the end of the third day, their gut-yolks smeared across hallway and bathroom floors. Mine lasted until the fourth, when it rolled off my desk in Algebra and cracked between my shoes.

So I've had to self-educate regarding my female parts.

I don't have anyone to consult about these things. Even though my parents are both in the medical field, our family doesn't discuss bodily functions beyond Mother scolding us for wasting toilet paper. (*Two squares is plenty for a BM!*) After Adam and Eve ate of the Tree of Knowledge, they were ashamed of their nakedness, and so are we.

In sixth grade, when the other girls started getting breast buds and staining their pants, I'd lock myself in the bathroom with my sisters' Kotex box to read the pamphlet tucked between the stiff white tubes. From that piece of paper I learned my anatomy—urethra, vagina, rectum—in preparation for what the pamphlet called "my triumphant day of womanhood." I practiced sticking tampons in, but felt like I was ripping up my insides when I tugged them out.

Years passed, and I resigned myself to being a shapeless beanpole. So when I wake one morning with bloody underwear before swim practice, I actually do feel triumphant. I am normal after all.

But my triumph fades a moment later.

Now that I have my period, I can get pregnant. The unthinkable could happen. I get out of bed and open the bottom drawer of my desk. There, between the photographs of Lecka, polished seashells and my collection of plastic horses, I find the letter opener I got at a Christmas party gift swap a few years ago. The handle is engraved with Philippians 4:13: "I can do all things through Christ, who strengthens me." It's metal with a pointed, knifelike tip, and it's the closest thing I have to a weapon.

I slide it into my pillowcase, put on my robe and go to the bathroom to clean myself off.

There's another episode with David in early November.

I hear about it one afternoon while eavesdropping on him and Jerome. Our parents are at work, and I sit down at Mother's vanity and press the "rec room" button on the intercom panel, then slide the black button to "listen." They're playing ping-pong; I hear the hollow ball slap against the table and their paddles.

Things have gotten tense between David and me, and I've resorted to Mother's tactic of spying over the intercom. I know it's not right, but it's the only way I have to know what's happening in his life.

Things started going downhill a couple of weeks ago when he came to one of my swim meets with our brother Dan, who's studying business at Purdue. Afterward, in the crowded vestibule of McCutcheon High School, they walked over to congratulate me on winning third place in the fifty-yard breast event. Dan gave me a bear hug as David stood a few feet behind him.

"Ooh, Julia, introduce us to your brother!" said Tammy Withers, a varsity swimmer and cheerleader who'd never before acknowledged my existence. She hooked her arm in mine and stared at Dan. Women often find my big brother hot. Other girls crowded around, giggling, and as Dan shook their hands and flashed his dimpled smile, I felt proud.

"So, why didn't you introduce me to your friends?" David asked after Dan drove us home; we were walking across the driveway toward the front door.

His question panicked me.

"You could have been like Dan and come over," I shot back in an accusing voice. "It's not my fault you're such a loner. What were you waiting for, a special invitation?"

He didn't answer, and kept walking. I tried again. "Besides, everybody already knows you from school."

He turned to look me in the eye. "They don't know the first thing about me," he said, before slamming himself into the basement.

"Shit!" I hear Jerome yell over the intercom. "Stop spinning the ball!"

I pick up an amber necklace from Mother's jewelry cabinet and examine the bugs trapped in the hardened sap.

Did I ignore David on purpose? I was basking in the light of my handsome big brother and winning a race, and for a moment I wanted to be something other than the "black boys' sister." He could have interjected himself like Dan did; it's not my fault he's such a wallflower.

We haven't spoken much since that evening beyond "it's your turn to fetch in the trash bins" or "Lecka needs food." And now that Jerome's back, I avoid going into the basement, and the boys avoid coming upstairs. Allegiances have once again shifted into white/black, upstairs/downstairs.

"Sneed started it," I hear David say over the bouncing ball.

I put down the necklace and turn up the speaker volume.

"How so?" Jerome asks.

"He's the one who started chanting K.K.K. when I walked in the room," David says. "Then the whole class joined in, and Jones came at me with the welding iron."

I stare at the speaker, unbelieving.

"How's your arm?" Jerome asks.

"There's some pus . . . I think it might leave a scar."

"Those white fuckers touch you again, you let me know," Jerome says. "Next time, they'll get more than threats. I'll break some bones!"

The ping-pong ball slams hard against the table and they stop talking, as if they were concentrating all their anger on the game. I hear the garage door creak open—Mother—and rush to turn off the intercom and drop the necklace back into the cabinet before closing myself in my room.

At supper, I keep waiting for David to say something. I watch him intently as he picks at his Salisbury steak TV dinner. He's wearing a long flannel shirt, so I can't see his arm. How badly was he burned? Did those boys get expelled? What did the teacher do? After several minutes, he looks up.

"What are you staring at me for?" he asks testily, interrupting our parents' discussion of the church budget.

"I'm not staring," I say, my cheeks reddening.

"Yes, you are," David insists.

I turn to Mother.

"May I please be excused to get some more water?"

"Yes, you may," she says.

As I press my glass against the refrigerator water dispenser, I feel betrayed. Our whole lives, David has always confided in me, and now this horrible thing happens and he goes to Jerome instead. Jerome, who we've always regarded as a third wheel, an interloper. I long to ask him what happened in metals class, but if I do, he'd know I was spying on him and get angry. Then he'd go outside to talk privately with Jerome, just like he and I used to do to get away from Mother.

I look back at the table, at my parents on either end discussing churchy matters, at my brothers sitting side by side between them, their cropped hair identical, comrades in color. Where do I fit in this setup?

Jerome. Who else could David turn to when he's attacked by a classroom of racists? I certainly couldn't protect him, and our parents would just repeat their weary, useless advice: "Turn the other cheek." Jerome—with his size and his fury—is the great equalizer. Jerome's good for something after all.

When I return to the table, Dad clears his throat. He's still wearing his dark suit and his hair is greased over the bald spot, not a strand out of place. He looks like he's about to rush back to work.

"We have an announcement to make," he says, his fork poised over fluorescent orange cubes on his tinfoil tray.

"Your mother and I are going to California for a board meeting of the Wycliffe Bible Associates this weekend, and we trust you kids are mature enough not to require the services of a babysitter."

Mother chimes in. "Because if you do, we'll find one," she says.

They look sternly at us, and we look sternly back at them.

"Oh, please!" I say, acting insulted. "We'll be fine."

Oh, the possibilities! I'll stay up all night watching television, try on Mother's clothes and makeup, blast WAZY on the great room stereo and dance across the wood floor . . .

"We'll be fine," Jerome says.

David glances over at me and I can read the excitement in his eyes. This is a first. Whenever they've gone on trips before, they've left us in the care of some church person or a nurse from Dad's office.

"There's enough frozen potpies to last until we get back," Mother says. "And on Sunday, you may watch church TV instead of driving to town; we'll be back Sunday night."

Dad forks a carrot cube.

"We don't want you to have any visitors over while we're gone," he says.

"And," Mother says, "I want the house spotless when we return. Understood?"

"Understood," the three of us say in unison.

I'm allowed to drive the Corolla to swim practice now that the weather has turned, and when I pull into the driveway Friday afternoon, Jerome's waiting in the driveway.

"Give me the keys," he says as I get out of the car.

"What for?" I ask.

"I need to run some errands," he says.

He was forbidden from driving the car after he stole it, but he's in my face with his nearness and smell, so I drop the keys onto the gravel and walk away.

An hour later, I find him unloading cases of beer into the refrigerator. He's moved the eggs, orange juice, and milk onto the counter to make room for the silver cans.

"What are you doing?" I ask. "The food will go bad."

"Oh well," he says, dumping the vegetable drawer into the sink. His mail-order ID—"Tyrone Jefferson, DOB 1-19-62"—is on the counter right under Mother's "Missions to Africa" calendar. November features a group of ragged black children smiling as they hug Bibles to their bony chests.

I run downstairs and fling open the boys' bedroom.

David's hunched over his desk, peering at the top of his head in a hand mirror and holding a sewing scissors. He's got a row of small bald spots lining one side of his scalp.

"Ever heard of knocking?" he says, dropping the mirror and scissors into an open drawer. I step over to him and sink my fingers into the soft wool of his hair. They *are* bald spots.

"What'd you cut bald spots into your hair for?" I ask him. He jerks his head out of my hands.

"They're not bald spots, it's a part!"

"David, you don't *cut* a part into your hair, you *comb* a part into your hair."

He takes the mirror out of the drawer and strains to look at the top of his head, swiveling his eyes from side to side.

"But it looks okay, right?"

Something crashes onto the floor above us.

"It's fine," I say impatiently. "What's Jerome's doing with all that beer?"

"He invited some people over," David says, still peering at his head.

"What people?!"

"Some dudes from school. I told him it wasn't a good idea, but he doesn't listen to me."

Great, my evening is ruined. I had it all planned out—*The Facts of Life* at eight P.M., then *Star Wars*—at nine P.M., spumoni ice cream in the freezer.

"I invited Kenny since people are coming anyway," he says. "Why don't you invite Elaine . . . or Mary?"

He says this casually, but I know he's got a crush on Mary the size of Texas. He's tongue-tied whenever she comes over, and she treats him like an oversized puppy, patting him on the head and teasing him. David's always after my friends, but they don't take him seriously. He might as well belong to another species.

"My brother likes you," I once told a friend on his behalf in sixth grade. "Do you want to go with him?"

"David?" she replied, scrunching up her nose. "He's nice enough . . . but he's black!"

When David asked what her answer was, I lied and told him she already had a boyfriend.

"Elaine's out of town, and Mary's with her new boyfriend, some varsity wrestler from Central Catholic," I lie, again.

It's true that Elaine is gone, but Mary doesn't have a boyfriend; she's grounded for the weekend. David's face falls, and he stands.

"I'd best call Kenny and see what time he's coming over," he says, leaving the room.

Plan B: I'll barricade myself into my room and drink. It's Friday night, my parents are gone, and I want to party.

When I hear Jerome roar off in the Corolla again, I rush to the kitchen to extract the pantry key from Mother's hiding place, under the pen tray in the phone drawer.

I pour myself a Comfort and Coke (½ bourbon, ½ pop) and sip it while taking a twenty-minute shower, luxuriating in the heat and steam without Mother banging on the door *(That's long enough!)*. Afterward, I wrap a towel around myself and fetch another tall drink, then lock myself in my room.

WAZY is playing Van Halen's "Pretty Woman," and I prance naked in front of the dresser mirror, trying to grind my hips in circles and jiggle my boobs like those girls on MTV. Problem is, I have no hips to grind, no breasts to jiggle. But those boys must have found something about me attractive; why else would they want to pull off my clothes? Maybe I have that "special something that drives men wild" that *Glamour* talks about, I think, smiling slyly at the mirror.

I hear the Corolla race into the driveway and double-check the lock on the door, my head spinning pleasantly with alcohol, before pulling the December *Glamour* from under my mattress. David's been nice enough to hide my subscription from Mother for me when he gets the mail after school.

I lay belly-down on my bed and open it to the book-marked page:

Do's & Don'ts for the Man Hunt:

Don't put out too fast—he'll think you're a slut.
Don't make the first move—men want to be conquerors.
Do smile and be sweet—dazzle him with your femininity!
Do learn to converse intelligently—men don't like a chatterbox.

If Mother could only see me now: naked, drunk, listening to rock music and reading *Glamour* magazine. *For shame!* she'd say, and the thought of her pinched face makes me laugh.

I hear deep male laughter rumbling in the great room and stiffen, glancing at the door. *Yes, it's locked.* Who are Jerome's friends? The hoods he hangs out with at school? The laughter goes outside and a basketball slaps on concrete.

As I pull on the track suit, there's a knock on my door.

"Hey Ju-la-la, open up!" David calls.

He's smirking when I open the door, holding a glass of grape Kool-Aid in his hand. Kenny Mudd hangs limply beside him, dressed in funeral black, bug eyes staring at the carpet. *What a dork.*

"Kenny here wants to say hi," David says. I give him a dirty look; yesterday he told me that Kenny thought I was cute.

"Hi, Kenny," I say. "Nice you could make it."

"Hi!" Kenny shouts, thrusting a hand in the air, still staring at the carpet. I turn to David.

"So who are we tonight? The good guys or the bad guys?"

"The Dark Cleric knows not morality!" David says in a raspy voice. "He is the Master of the Mountain Minions, and he shall be feared."

He raises his left hand, Pope-like, to be kissed. A piece of metal winds around his middle finger, and I pull it to my face; it's a nail, hammered into a circle.

"Are you supposed to be some kind of religious figure?"

Kenny snaps to life.

"He's a barbarian from the Kingdom of Ork!" he barks, lifting his eyes to the knees of my sweat pants.

David makes a fist with the ring hand.

"It's the Band of Iron," David says in his queer voice. "No harm shall befall me as long as I wear it."

"He's aligned himself with the forces of Edgar!" Kenny blurts out. "Blood will spill, I tell you, and mightily!"

I raise my eyebrows at David and he smirks; Kenny entertains him.

"O-kay," I say. "David, who's out there?"

He shrugs.

"We've been downstairs," he says. "Why, are you expecting someone special?"

At this Kenny finally looks up. I glare at him, and his gaze falls again.

"They drinking yet?" I ask David.

"There's some hard stuff in the kitchen," he says. "But I don't think anyone's boozing it up yet but you."

David has developed a sixth sense for when I'm drinking, and he doesn't like it. He could smell it on my breath when we walked to the bus stop, even though I'd brush my teeth and chew gum. He says liquor makes me stupid and worries I'll become an alcoholic.

I put my hand on the doorknob; I don't need him to ruin my party.

"Well, you kids have fun playing make-believe."

"And you," David responds, as I close the door. "Party hardy—all by yourself."

Next to the spoiling food in the kitchen is a gleaming cluster of green and brown bottles. Four Roses. Night Train. Ever Clear. I grab a bottle of Bacardi Spice. This I know from the Home Hospital doctors' lounge at Christmas; David and I dumped it into our eggnog last year when no one was looking.

He took a couple of sips and gagged, so I downed both of our cups. As I'm filling my glass with Bacardi, the front door blasts open and smashes into a clay platter hanging on the wall behind it. The platter, which depicts the Aztec calendar—a gift to my mother from missionaries in Mexico—falls in pieces to the floor.

"God damn it," Jerome says.

I freeze, the bottle still pouring into my glass, and look over at the entranceway. Brad MacIntyre is beside Jerome, and they're both studying the broken shards. Through the open door, there are more male voices, and the sound of the basketball.

"That's gonna be fun to explain," Brad snorts, deliberately crunching a piece of clay under foot. He's wearing the same Big Boy T-shirt he wore the day he tried to stick his hands down my pants. He looks up and sees me.

"Well, look who's here," Brad says. I swallow, and Jerome pushes past him to snatch the bottle from my hands.

"You're wasting precious fluid, fool!" he shouts, exhaling sour beer breath. I back away from him and look down: the rum has spilled across the counter in an amber rush.

"I don't mind if she drinks my liquor," Brad says, winking at me.

We haven't spoken since the day I kicked him in the nuts, and the one time I saw him walking down a hallway toward me at Harrison, I ducked into a bathroom. I never told anyone what happened that day; how could I begin to explain why Jerome set me up?

Brad's eyes graze my body top to bottom, as if I were the centerfold in a dirty magazine.

"You up for some more fun tonight, angel?" he asks, grinning.

He can't do this to me in my own home. I walk to the sink and pour the rum into the silver basin, glaring at him. His smile disappears.

Jerome walks between us to the refrigerator.

"Dude, what's your poison?" Jerome asks, yanking open the door. "We got Bud, Michelob, that shitty malt stuff Whitman brought . . ."

"How about your little sister?"

Jerome straightens and looks at Brad.

"Afraid she's not on the menu tonight," Jerome says, holding out a beer can to him.

Brad ignores him and grabs the Bacardi Spice bottle from the counter. He tilts back his head and swigs rum into his mouth, gulping rhythmically for several seconds before slamming the bottle back on the counter. He wipes his wet mouth with the back of his hand and belches.

"How 'bout that, little sister?" he sneers.

"Leave me alone," I say, striding past him toward my room.

"Leave me alone!" he whines in a high-pitched voice, before growling: "You got it coming, you know."

The door's pounding. The alarm clock says it's almost eleven, and it takes me a second to realize why I'm lying on top of my bed fully clothed and Duran Duran's "Reflex" is thudding on the great room stereo. *Oh yeah, I'm partying.*

The door continues to pound.

"Who is it?" I call, my voice scratchy. The music is too loud to hear a response. I stand and my bedroom swirls like a merry-go-round. Close my eyes and sit back down.

The doorknob twists back and forth; the lock holds. It's probably David.

I stagger to the door and crack it open. Scott's leaning against the hallway wall across from me, two tumblers of honey-colored liquid in his hands.

"Truce!" he yells over the music, offering me a glass. He smiles, and his brown eyes are dreamy with alcohol. He's wearing his signature satin shorts, red this time, and a "Boilermakers" muscle shirt. Dressed for summer, despite the freeze outside. The arm offering me the drink is curved and tan and I stare at it. Despite what he tried to do to me that night in the school basement, I still find him hot. I know I've got some booze in me, but it's true. He *is* hot. The hottest boy who's ever shown interest in me.

"What do you want?" I yell back.

When we cross paths at school, he smiles and I scowl.

My hand is on the doorknob; I can slam it shut anytime. I have a sharp letter opener hidden in my pillowcase. David's right downstairs.

Whoops of laughter roll down the hallway from the great room; how many of them are there? I circle the doorknob with my fingers and eye the offered glass. I'm thirsty and could use a drink. I take it from him and sniff it—whiskey—and gulp a few swallows. It warms my throat. Scott takes a step toward me, and I start to close the door. He drops to his knees holding his glass.

"Please, please, please," he prays, and by the way he wobbles, I can tell he is drunk, harmless. "I want to talk to you."

The mighty Scott Cooper is kneeling at my feet. This is highly entertaining. Finally I'll have something interesting to tell Elaine and Mary on Monday as we sit on the floor next to the locked gymnasium, eating our junk food picnic.

I walk past him down the dark hallway, then turn and beckon to him like a femme fatale in an old movie. He's in my power now. He lurches to his feet.

The ghost of Mother's Enjoli perfume lingers in the air of the master bedroom. I turn on her bedside lamp and shiver with excitement as I sit on the spotless white bedspread of my parents' bed, sipping whiskey and waiting for Scott to walk through the door.

He sets his glass on the King James Bible on Mother's nightstand, and I move it to the carpet and put mine beside it. The Fixx's "One Thing Leads to Another" is now blaring from the stereo, and I giggle at this as I close the door and sit back down on the bed.

I turn to face Scott in the quieted room and his shorts shimmer red in the lamplight.

"Julia," he says, breathing out the three syllables of my name in a deep voice. "I've been wanting to talk to you."

He sits heavily beside me, his legs brushing mine, and suddenly I feel shyly stupid in his presence, my tongue big and sloppy inside my mouth. His breath is warm and yeasty on my cheek.

"You're so alone," he says, tucking a strand of my hair behind my ear, his fingers brushing my cheek. "You and me. We could be friends."

His hand slides down my neck to my shoulder, where it rests. He starts to fall back on the bed and steadies himself by tightening his grip on my shoulder.

"Your hair is beautiful. It's like . . . like . . . corn silk. Long and soft."

He pets the back of my head, a little too hard, but I yield to his hand and close my eyes. No one's ever talked to me this way before.

"Sorry 'bout the other day. Got out of hand. Jerome . . . "

"I hate Jerome!" I say, opening my eyes and leaning away from him.

"Shh, I know," he says, rubbing my back. No one's ever touched me this way before.

"Why do you hate him?" he asks softly. He pulls me sideways into his warmth, and I put my head on his shoulder, inhaling his brothy musk.

"He . . . he does things to me."

The words fall easily from my mouth, and I'm glad to have them gone. There. It's no longer a dirty little secret; someone else knows. Maybe Scott will know what to do.

"What kind of things?" he asks, still caressing my back.

"He picks the lock on my door at night and he . . . he . . ." I stop because these are things I cannot pronounce, and bury my face in his neck.

"Well, he's not your real brother."

True. But then neither is David. I start to sob.

Scott drapes his arms around me, rocks me back and forth like a monstrous baby.

"Shhh, it's okay," he says. His voice has thickened, deepened. "It doesn't matter. Everything's fine. I'm right here."

Hearing these words, a peace descends on me and I relax in his grip. Scott will protect me from Jerome and Brad and everything else. I wipe my nose and smile. Everything's fine.

Foreigner's "Waiting for a Girl Like You" floats down the hall. It's the song I practice kissing the mirror to, the most romantic song ever, and I'm listening to it with Scott.

Scott scoots back on the bed, lifts my head from his shoulder and guides it toward his lap. I close my eyes. Yes, I would like to lay my head down for a spell and rest. But my cheek doesn't fall against red satin, it falls against something warm and hard and flesh. I open my eyes, and in a boozy blur, see his penis jutting from his shorts. He grabs it by the root.

"Lick it," he says in his thick voice, pressing my head toward it.

I've heard girls giggle about blow jobs at school; it's something a boyfriend requires of you.

I stare at Scott's penis. There's a pearl balanced on the tan tip. It smells like liverwurst.

"Like a lollipop," he's begging now, breathing hard. He wags the penis with his hand to get my attention.

I close my eyes and stick out my tongue and it touches the side of it.

"Open your mouth," Scott says, and I do. He puts it between my lips and grabs my hair and pulls my head up and down on it. A moment later he groans and something slimy spurts into my mouth that tastes like pool water. Scott collapses onto his back on the mattress and I spit the slime onto my parents' white bedspread and roll onto my back beside him. We lay together in silence, not touching, and my head swirls with booze and what I've done. It was sinful, yes, but necessary. I need Scott to be my boyfriend.

Hours later, I wake alone and drag myself to my room. My stomach is in turmoil, but I'm elated. Now that I have a boyfriend, everything will change.

+   +   +

Mother got angry, and David got in trouble.

Seems he was always doing something to set her off: not paying attention, not eating all his food, not coming when she called.

I'd do the same things, but it was David she'd punish, digging her nails into his arm or whacking his butt with the handle of a toilet plunger.

One time we played hospital, washing our stuffed animals in the bathtub and wrapping them in gauze bandages. We were playing doctor and nurse, like our parents. Mother was not flattered. She tossed our patients into the trash, sent me to my room, and spanked David. It was a typical scenario.

In a photograph from the time, David is posed stiffly against a wall in a blue suit jacket, a white turtleneck, and plaid pants—Sunday clothes. There is no date on the back of the picture, but he looks about six or seven. He winces up at the camera, his eyes swollen with tears, his small hand clutching tissue, patently miserable. He wore that expression a lot in those days.

After Mother punished him, he'd stick his fingers in his mouth to stifle the sobs and gaze at me with those soulful brown eyes. At me, his twin sister. Wanting an explanation for life's cruel vagaries. I looked away, having convinced myself that Mother knew something about him I didn't, that he needed discipline to keep him from growing into a bad person.

It was years before I knew better.

CHAPTER 6

VIRGINITY

My heart's chugging like a runaway train when I walk into the cafeteria on Monday. There's Scott, sitting at the jock table, contorting in his chair as he says something that has everyone spasmatic with laughter. I stop walking and stare. Is he telling them what I did? I don't want to be one of those girls that guys make up nicknames for.

Mary and Elaine yell to me from the snack bar. I phoned them both on Saturday, impatient to share the news. I told them Scott kissed me, and it was beautiful and romantic and amazing. But it's a lie; he never did kiss me, not even after he dirtied my mouth.

"So, did he call you?" Elaine asks when I slip into line beside them. On the phone she called Scott a phony who flirts with all the girls, and said that no one takes him seriously because he's a half-breed.

"He's like one of those miniature horses you country folk keep chained in your yards," she'd said. "Amusing, but nothing you'd want to ride."

I almost hung up on her.

"Did he or didn't he?" she now insists, flipping her long red hair over her shoulders.

"I was gone most of the day," I lie. "He probably tried but . . ."

"Here he comes," Mary says, looking over my shoulder. I turn and see Scott strutting over in his varsity football jacket, a wide smile parting his face.

"Damn Sam! Got me all Charlie's Angels here at once," he yells, spreading his arms.

"What a dork," I hear Elaine mutter behind me.

He stops a few inches from my face. "So what's up?"

The corners of his almond-shaped eyes tilt upward when he grins, and his breath smells like the soy burger he ate for lunch.

"Not much," I shrug.

"Wanna go somewhere and talk?"

He cocks his head toward the dim hallway to the left of the snack bar, which ends in a glass doorway. Outside, gray sky hangs over dead fields.

I shrug again and follow him down the hall, wishing I had a piece of gum to freshen my breath. Halfway to the glass door, he stops and faces me.

"Didn't think I'd talk to you today, did you?" he asks.

I look at him, puzzled.

"Of course I did," I say. "I'm your girlfriend."

"My what?" He spits out the question, incredulous.

"I mean . . . after . . . the . . . bedroom," I stutter, as I sometimes do when I'm nervous. A boy sprints past us out the door, and a blast of arctic wind rips over us. I shiver and Scott starts to laugh, slapping his knees with his hands.

"You think that just because you . . . we're going out?"

I can feel my pulse throb in my temples, and stare at him in disbelief. I did that to him for nothing? Tears sting my eyes, and I start to walk away from him.

"Hold on!" he says, grabbing my arm and spinning me around.

"I wouldn't be here right now if I didn't want you, dummy," he says, pressing me against the cold metal of a locker. I stare at the collar of his pink Izod, which is starched straight up, preppy style. He leans into me, one hand resting on the locker behind me, the other lifting my chin. His lips are full and soft on mine, and his tongue swishes into my mouth, thick and wet and salty. I pull my head away; I don't know what to do with a tongue and don't much like it.

Scott frowns.

"You sure could use some practice kissing," he says, before smashing his mouth onto mine.

Mother's waiting for us after school. Swim practice was canceled today, so I rode the bus home with the boys.

"What in God's good name happened here?" she demands when we walk through the back door.

They got home late last night, after we'd gone to bed. I heard them tiptoe down the hallway and prayed they wouldn't notice their bedspread. I scrubbed it with soap and a nailbrush Saturday morning, but the faint yellow stain would not come out.

"What in God's name happened in this house?" she repeats, as we stand there in our winter coats and snow-crusted shoes, our backpacks still curved against us.

Mother ticks off a list of things she's discovered: spit tobacco on her rubber plant, beer cans under the sofa, her Aztec calendar in the trash!

On Saturday, Jerome vacuumed the great room and put the spoiled food back into the refrigerator before returning to bed, complaining of a headache. On Sunday, he slept right through church TV.

David and I now turn to glare at him, and he turns his blood-shot eyes to the ground.

"Someone's going to pay for this, or you all are," Mother says before pounding up the stairs and slamming the basement door.

"Well, what are you going to do?" David asks Jerome after she's gone. "Get us all in trouble?"

Jerome walks to the boys' room and slams the door, and David and I take off our coats and sit on the green cot next to the ping-pong table and listen to Mother bang pots and pans upstairs and Jerome bang drawers downstairs.

A few minutes later, Jerome emerges from the bedroom, still wearing his coat and carrying a duffel bag. He throws open the back door without a word and marches across the field as snow swirls around him. When he disappears behind the tree line, David stands and shuts the door.

"Guess that takes care of that," I say, turning to walk upstairs.

I pause at the bottom of the staircase and look back at David, who's still peering out the window into the frozen afternoon.

"He brought this on himself, you know," I say.

He doesn't respond. Mother's in the kitchen, busy at the stove.

"Keep that door closed," she says. "You're letting a draft in."

At supper, I blame everything on Jerome.

"David and I stayed in our rooms the whole time," I say. "We didn't want any part of it."

Dad listens grimly, his steel-blue eyes jostling from me to David, who looks at his tuna and potato chip casserole and says nothing.

"Jerome is officially persona non grata in this household," he says after I finish. "I'm changing the alarm code tonight, and I don't want either of you to let him inside. He's no longer welcome here. Understood?"

"Understood," I say, picking up my milk glass. Finally, I can sleep in peace.

David is silent.

"David?" Father says.

He nods, but doesn't look up.

"Heavenly Father," Dad prays after he's done reading the Bible, "protect this household from Jerome. Chastise him, dear God, and show him the error of his ways."

But Jerome doesn't stay away. On Thanksgiving Eve, I'm in my bedroom racking my brain over an algebra problem when there's a knock on my window. I look up to see a man crouched in a ski mask and am about to scream when I recognize Jerome's filthy orange anorak.

He motions for me to open the window, and I glance toward my closed door. David and Mother are in the great room watching television and Dad's at the hospital. I forgot to close the venetian blinds at dusk, something I started doing last summer after I caught Jerome peering through the glass one night while I changed into my pajamas. He climbed the rose trellis to the broad window ledge, same as tonight.

Snow sparkles in the floodlights attached to the roof and powders his dirty jacket. He hugs his arms to his chest and shivers; he's not wearing gloves.

We didn't see him at school this past week, but David found out where he was staying and called to tell him he wasn't allowed home. So why did he come back? Why doesn't he leave me alone?

No way I'm going to invite him into my bedroom after he forced his way in so many times before. I look back down at the squiggled rows of quadratic equations in my algebra book. I'm failing the class and the final's next week.

Jerome raps his knuckles on the window again, and I stand without looking at him and walk into the great room. They're watching *Little House on the Prairie,* the only show Mother lets us watch besides *The Waltons* and *National Geographic.* Wholesome TV, she calls it. Good family values. I pull up a chair beside David, but don't tell him what happened. He'd want to let Jerome in.

"Jerome's in the pole barn," David tells me the next morning, on our way to Thanksgiving service.

We're sitting in the back of the van as Mother drives herky-jerky past empty fields and gusts of wind shove us toward the rims of dirty snow lining the road. Hymns blare over the van speakers and David leans forward so I can hear him.

"He came to the window last night, but I told him I didn't want trouble with Dad," he says. "I gave him a blanket but couldn't get him food because the motion detectors were on."

The internal alarm's red lights zigzag the great room and rec room; normally we use it only when there's a breakout at the county jail. Now we use it to guard against a break-in by Jerome, a little late.

Mother stomps on the brakes at a yellow light, and the van's rear end skitters sideways into the next lane before she straightens it.

"Why didn't you tell him to leave?" I ask David. In the front of Hippensteel Funeral Home, a large mechanical Santa waves to passing cars, its arm yanking right for a beat, then left.

"He doesn't have anywhere else to go," David says. "Besides, he's our brother, our responsibility."

"Not mine," I say.

They put the same stupid Santa on that corner every year.

"Not your what?" David asks.

"Not my responsibility," I say. "He's a problem, and I wish he'd just stay away."

"I don't know why you hate him so much," David says loudly, falling back against his seat. "What'd he ever do to you?"

His outburst causes Mother to turn down the hymns.

"You kids bring your study Bibles?" she asks, looking into the rearview mirror.

We both hold up our Bibles.

"Good," she says, cranking up the hymns.

We have Young Calvinists before church, and Mother has Adult Bible Study.

Five of us Young Calvinists gather in a low-ceilinged room on the second floor of the church building, David, me, Rick Hoolsema and a couple of kids from Lafayette Christian. As we walk in, I nod at Rick, who broke things off with me after our closet kiss, saying "it just didn't feel right."

We meet here twice a month, shoving the warped ping-pong table against a wall and pushing the sagging, donated couches into a circle.

Reverend Dkystra bustles in, looking reduced without his billowing black robe, and writes the meeting's topic on a whiteboard as we take turns with a carafe, pouring hot water into Styrofoam cups, then stirring in packets of powdered chocolate.

THE IMPURITY OF ALL MEN, he writes in block letters, underlining IMPURITY three times. David and I exchange a glance as we stir our chocolate: sex is Reverend Dykstra's favorite topic. He thinks teenagers are obsessed with it, that our minds are filthy-full of it, and it's all he talks about when he's got us alone in this room.

"Adolescence is a difficult age," he says once we're all seated. "Your body is changing, your hormones are raging, and you become curious about sexual things."

In the parking lot below, a car engine turns, wheezing and straining, before falling silent again. Reverend Dykstra, standing before us in a blue suit, scans the room dramatically.

"But as Christian young people, you need to ask yourself the following question: Can you do the hanky-panky on Saturday night and shake it all around, and still call yourself a child of God come Sunday morning?"

His question booms off the walls, which we painted pea green last summer to symbolize our budding Christian identity. Everyone stops sipping their chocolate and is seized by an abrupt fascination with the frayed purple carpet.

As usual, Reverend Dyktsra is trying to be cool by using what he thinks of as teenage slang. I sneak a look across the circle at David, whose eyes are shining with mirth. Good. He's not sore at me over Jerome.

As Reverend Dykstra rails against the sins of the flesh, I think about the promise I made Scott last Friday during lunch. We were in a stall in the basement girls' bathroom, practicing kissing, and he kept trying to put his hand down my jeans, and I kept shoving it away. He was getting peeved.

"I won't be your boyfriend unless we do it," he said, his hard-on pressed against my leg. "I'll find someone else. There are lots of fish in the sea."

We'd spent the final fifteen minutes of every lunch hour last week locked in that stall, hoping no one would walk in as we wrestled in silence, Scott trying to stick his hands different places and me slapping them away. I wanted to take it slow, so our first time would be special, so it would be making love, not just sex.

Scott scoffed when I told him this.

"Sex is sex," he said. He narrowed his eyes. "Besides, I didn't think this would be such a big deal for you, considering . . ."

I grabbed his head and stuffed my tongue in his mouth to shut him up.

"Fine, I'll do it," I said after coming up for air.

Reverend Dkystra pauses to drink from his coffee mug and his sudden silence makes me lift my head. The other Young Calvinists are still staring at the ground with hot chocolate going cold in their hands, but David's staring at me.

"Stop spacing," he mouths when Reverend Dykstra turns to set his coffee mug on the ping-pong table. He clears his throat before continuing in his preacher voice.

"And you may think that playing with yourself is a fine substitute for carnal knowledge, but don't be fooled," he says, pounding the top of the bookcase beside him with the side of his fist. "You must have unholy thoughts to masturbate! You must sin!"

He pauses weightily. "I'm here to tell you today that you can't jack off with Jesus!" He pounds the bookcase to emphasize each word, unaware of the obscene gesture he's making. You. Can't. Jack. Off. With. Jesus.

Around me, there's weight-shifting and throat-clearing, and I slap a hand over my mouth and pretend to cough, my eyes burning with stifled laughter. David's also got a hand over his mouth, but I look away before my eyes meet his, lest we both burst.

During the church service, Dad joins us during the second hymn, sliding into the pew and sharing the Psalter Hymnal with Mother, but his pager bleats during the sermon—Unselfish Abundance—and he leaves as Mother sighs and shakes her head.

"Happy Thanksgiving," Reverend Dykstra tells me as I file past him after the service. He squeezes my hand in his, and I want to pull my hand away, remembering his obscene gesture during Young Calvinists.

"Where's Jerome?" he asks.

I glance after Mother, but she's halfway across the foyer, wading toward the coat room with David. She's got no time for greetings today; our relatives are due in from Chicago.

"Home sick," I lie. "Strep throat."

It's the first thing that crosses my mind. How could I begin to tell him the truth? I look down at the tips of his black loafers, which poke out under his robe, hoping he doesn't have a special preacher radar that detects lies.

"I'm sorry to hear that," he says, finally releasing my hand. "Tell Jerome I'll be praying for him to get better."

We walk into the house welcomed by the thick brown smell of the twenty-five-pound Butterball mother stuck into the oven before church. She rushes to tie an apron over her Sunday dress and peer through the oven window.

"We're going to feed Lecka before company gets here," I tell her, glancing at David. He nods.

"Take her the milk rinsings, and come right back to help," she says, pulling on oven mitts. She's a nervous wreck today, as she always is when her housewifey duties are on display. As she pokes the turkey with a long-handled fork, I swish water through the cereal bowls stacked in the sink and pour the cloudy white liquid into a glass. Mother says milk rinsings give Lecka needed calcium.

David holds the door open for me as we go outside into the blinding whiteness; the sun is a pinhole of light overhead, the sky blank of color. It's begun to snow again, and great curtains of it blow over our bodies as we crunch over the frozen grass to Lecka's doghouse. She strains joyfully at her chain, her shaggy winter coat snarled with knots and the hay that insulates her doghouse. We dodge her dirty paws as we look for her bowl.

"It's gone," David says. "Weird."

I follow him into the pole barn, closing the door quickly behind me. The air in the lofty metal space reeks of fertilizer and grease, and the small windows punched in the walls cast a dreary light over the concrete floor; it takes my eyes a few seconds to adjust. I shiver; for some reason, it feels colder here than it does outdoors.

We walk around the John Deere tractor and there's Jerome in a dark corner, crouched in a nest he's constructed from hay, and dirty rags and the blanket David gave him, still wearing his prison orange jacket and black face mask.

"Happy Thanksgiving," he says, his breath rising in gray puffs to the high roof. "I've been smelling that bird all morning; must be close to done by now."

He folds the face mask up and his eyes are bloodshot and his nose runny with yellow snot. He smiles at me and I look away. There, at the edge of his nest, is Lecka's bowl, the fake meat nuggets floating in red ice.

"You eating dog food?" I ask him.

"Nah, it ain't thawed," Jerome says. "But I was kinda getting hungry."

He blows his nose on an oil-streaked rag. My fingertips sting with the cold and I take a step backward, impatient to be gone.

"We'll bring you food right after we eat, Jerome, I promise," David says.

"Maybe I should just ring the doorbell and ask for table scraps, you know, in the spirit of Christian charity and all that," Jerome says, flinging the rag on the floor.

"Fat chance," I say, stuffing my hands into my coat pockets.

Jerome erupts in laughter, then starts coughing, snot rattling his lungs. He pounds his chest with his fist. Maybe he's sick after all. Maybe he'll die.

David throws him a concerned look.

"You need anything else?" he asks Jerome.

Outside, the brass bell clangs. Mother, calling us in. I start walking to the door.

"Wait!" David yells after me.

He shakes himself out of his coat and hands it to Jerome, then looks at me. I reluctantly unbutton my brand new green felt jacket—bought with four months of babysitting money at Sears —and toss it to Jerome, who drapes it over his head and shoulders like a shawl. I wince; the tag said I have to wash it by hand.

"Say hello to the relatives for me," Jerome says. "Tell them to come visit when they get a chance."

His snickering dissolves into hacking as we walk out the door.

There's enough food crammed onto the long oval table to feed an African village. Mother dons a fresh white apron to present the once-a-year china bowls—filled with canned cranberries and candied yams with marshmallow, and giblet gravy—to the guests and lights the cornucopia-shaped candleholders, one engraved with "Enter His gates with Thanksgiving" and the other with "Go into His courts with praise." Father appears at the last minute to carve the dead bird with his soft surgeon's hands as Aunt Cathy and Uncle Jake *ooh* and *ahh,* and David and I scowl across the table at each other because it's all so fucking Norman Rockwell.

And in the photographs we'll be the only ones not smiling for the camera and the guests because we are thinking about Jerome shivering in the pole barn about to eat dog food, and Mother will see these photographs and say that we are ungrateful. Not thanksgiving.

There's a recess before the pumpkin, apple, peach and banana cream pies; David's recruited to clear the table, so it falls to me to feed Jerome. I do so reluctantly, taking my time as I wad turkey and yams in tinfoil. David nudges me to hurry.

Mother sits with her sister on the sofa chatting about missionaries and the men sprawl in front of the television.

"Put a hat on," Mother calls from the sofa, when I tell her I'm going to make sure the dog has water. "You lose half your heat through your head, you know."

I rush to fetch a stocking cap from the mudroom closet before she notices I'm not wearing a coat.

It's stopped snowing, and powdery drifts ripple over the landscape like a frozen sea under the darkening sky.

"Jerome, I got your food," I say after I enter the hushed murkiness of the pole barn. I stand by the door, impatient for him to come get it so I can leave.

"Jerome?"

There's no answer. *What if he's lying in wait for me?* I lay the food on the floor and lift a pitchfork from the long line of tools hanging on the wall.

"Jerome?"

I walk around the John Deere holding the pitchfork in both hands, like a baseball bat. The nest looks empty, but I poke it with the tines to be sure. It is. I pick my coat off the ground and dust it off.

He must have feared I'd rat him out. Or that Dad would walk in to show Uncle Jake his farm toys. As I take apart his nest, returning the hay and rags to their rightful locations, I find Lecka's bowl upside down, icy chunks of dog food exploded over the concrete floor. Did he smash it in rage or hunger? Where did he go? They're predicting an ice storm tonight.

"The Cowboys are up by six!" Uncle Jake yells when I walk through the front door, wearing my coat and hiding David's and the blanket under it. I glance at the TV; miniature men swarm over a green field. The women are now in the kitchen, conversing in low voices as the coffee machine gurgles.

David's downstairs in the rocking chair next to the woodstove. The faint ghost of his reflection haunts the window, and he stares at it as he rocks back and forth. He does this a lot lately, rocking and staring at himself.

"Jerome's gone," I say, dumping his coat and the blanket in his lap.

"I'm not surprised," he says, laying his arm over them.

"Where do you suppose he went?" I ask.

He shrugs.

"Somewhere better, I hope."

"Well, do you want to go look for him?" I ask, surprised at his nonchalance after all his previous concern. "We could say we're walking the dog."

"If he left, it's because he doesn't want to be found."

The basement door opens and the noise of football and polite adult laughter drifts down to us.

"Time for dessert, kids," Mother calls. "Your Aunt Cathy made a spectacular Dutch apple pie!"

David gets up and walks to the boys' bedroom.

"Tell her I've got gastric distress," he says, before closing himself away.

It rained over the snow last night and then froze, creating a glass carpet in the field behind the house. We stumble over it, our feet punching holes into the snow, our ankles catching on the icy crust.

A car backfires on the lane and I turn in panic to see Mrs. Schneider's blue Mazda glide behind the cottonwoods. I don't think she saw us. Scott marches ahead of me, kicking free thick slabs of ice and sending them spinning over the glazed field like giant hockey pucks. He's trying to look cool with his bare hands stuffed in his letter jacket and his shoulders thrown back in a challenge to the bitter wind.

When I told him my plan at lunch, he picked me up and spun me around the empty hallway, muttering "thank you, thank you, thank you" into my neck.

I know that as a young Christian woman, my virginity is supposed to be my most prized possession, but Jerome stole it away from me a long time ago. Sometimes in my coma state, he does something that startles me to consciousness and an image—his hand groping my breast, his head descending my belly—burns itself into my mind before numbness again saves me. These images sicken me, and I want to replace them with others of my choosing. I can't become pure again, but I can decide who takes things from me, and when.

I pull my scarf over my face and trudge after Scott. Today's a good day for sex; David is at Kenny's and Mother's working a double shift. We parked Scott's Pinto behind an abandoned barn on 650, where it can't be spotted by nosy neighbors such as Mrs. Schneider, who lives at the end of the lane and whose three-year-old son I frequently babysit.

Lecka barks hopefully as we trample over the buried garden, but we don't have time to mess around. David's due back in an hour.

At the back door, I press the new code into the alarm panel and unlock the door. Scott struts into the rec room, and I close the door and lock it again.

The silent house presses down on us.

"Well, here we are," I say breezily, turning to Scott.

We haven't spoken since we ditched his car.

He sits on the bench by the back door to pull off his shoes and doesn't say anything, which surprises me since at school the teachers can't get him to shut up and are constantly sending him to the Time Out room for disrupting class.

"Would you like a snack?" I ask, wanting him to say something, anything. To act like he did before, like this was no big deal. "There's punch and Snickerdoodles."

He shakes his head and looks at me warily.

"You're sure no one's coming home?" he asks, unsnapping his letter jacket.

"Not for an hour."

Scott says he's already done this once before, last summer with a girl in Kentucky, a friend of a cousin or a cousin of a cousin, I don't remember which.

"We was fooling around and it just kinda happened," was the way he put it.

This does not make me jealous; I don't love Scott. He tried to gang bang me, and he writes me poems and makes copies for other girls. He serves one purpose: he blots out Jerome.

As he follows me up the narrow staircase, I feel his eyes roaming the back of my body and stiffen. Everything's about to change. Everything.

"Be back in a second," I tell him at my bedroom door. He perches on the edge of my bed and bounces up and down a few times.

In the bathroom, I reach into the towel cabinet for the Comfort I hid there this morning and empty it in my mouth, hoping it will dissolve the lump in my chest. Afterwards, I gargle and reapply my teal eyeliner and bubblegum lipgloss.

Although the alcohol leaps to my head—all I had for lunch was half a Payday, knowing the booze would take hold quicker on an empty stomach—it doesn't prepare me for the sight of Scott's nakedness beneath my pink comforter. I stop short in the doorway.

"Get yerself all purtied up for me?"

He grins and put his hands behind his head, back to his cocky old self. He's dumped my stuffed animals on the floor and stuck a tape into my cassette player; The Police's "King of Pain" drifts across the room.

"Can you change the song?" I ask.

He reaches over to the night stand and fast-forwards to "Wrapped Around Your Finger."

"You coming to bed or what?" he asks.

Through the window, the sun has burst through the clouds and the ice-dipped trees in the orchard glitter and sway in the wind. I walk to the venetian blinds and close them, then stand on the other side of the darkened room to strip to my bra and panties and rush to the bed before Scott has time to inventory my imperfections. He throws back the covers and I collide against his solid heat. I put my arm across his chest and press my face into his musk as Sting serenades us. If we could just do this, only this, I'd be happy.

Scott puts his arms around me and unhooks my bra.

"Roll over," he says. "I want to see you."

He pulls my hands from his neck and I cover myself with the sheet as I turn. He flings it off.

"But it's cold!" I protest.

He pulls off my underwear, then retrieves a silver square from the nightstand and kneels between my legs and rips it open. It contains a flesh-colored circle, which he rolls over his penis like pantyhose. *So that's a condom.*

"Ready?" he asks. I nod. He pushes my thighs apart with his knees and spits into his hand and wipes it between my legs before lowering himself onto me and prodding my inner thigh with his dick. I bite my bottom lip and look up into his eyes, but his face is turned to the alarm clock next to the bed.

When I was in grade school, I used the Sears Roebuck catalogue to plan my future. I'd rest it on its spine on the dining room table, and let it fall open at random. In the men's apparel section, I'd find the perfect husband. In the children's department, the perfect baby. In housewares, the perfect plaid sofa, Corningware set, chandelier lights. The smiling underwear model on page 107 would present me with a diamond ring on page 236 and we'd have a big church wedding, me in my white dress (page 340) and he in his white teeth. After the wedding we'd retire to our canopy bed (page 560) and whatever happened there would be soft and gentle and beyond imagining. If there was a color to describe it, it'd be pinkish yellow.

The only color I feel right now, as Scott pokes and prods at me, is gray. Cold, sterile, surgical, gray.

"Stop fighting me," he says as I scoot away from his fumbling. "You'll only make it worse."

I look at the clock—we've only got forty minutes—and inhale deeply, letting my legs fall flat on the bed. I know from the groaning noises he makes that he's inside me, and I try to feel something, to stay focused on the moment—this is Scott, my boyfriend—but it's numb there. I wonder if I'll ever be normal.

The Police are singing "O my God" on the tape player and I'm thinking "O God, let me feel something," and Scott's eyes are closed as he moves inside me. The light slanting through the venetian blinds is muffled, as if a cloud had slid across the sun.

It's over quickly.

"Did you like it?" Scott asks as he pulls off the condom. White liquid bulges at the tip of it. *Sperm.*

"It was fine," I say, wrapping the sheet around me.

"Want to do it again?" he asks.

I glance down at his penis, now deflated and pitiful, and he laughs.

"I mean later tonight," he says. "I'll come to your window."

I'd told him how Jerome climbed the trellis Thanksgiving Eve.

I shrug. I've sunk into my numbness as if it were a soft cocoon and don't care one way or another. He can do what he wants.

"What time do your parents go to bed?" he asks.

"Ten-thirty. Sometimes eleven."

"Okay, see you around eleven-thirty."

He takes his Police tape from the cassette player and pulls his clothes on, then goes to the bathroom, and when he comes back he kisses me, gently this time, without groping.

"You're a bitchin' girlfriend," he whispers in my ear.

I watch him from the window as he lurches over the glass field toward the gravel lane; as he cuts through the orchard, a flock of cardinals rises from the trees like droplets of blood.

Maybe if we practice enough, I'll learn to feel something.

"Guess what I just did?"

I'm in my parents' study, swiveling in my father's chair and twirling the phone cord with my hand. My fingernails are painted "Love's Blush," my face is zit-free, and Scott called me the moment he got home just to say "hey." I'm floating.

Across cornfields, Elaine squeals into the receiver.

"No way!"

"Way! He just left."

"And . . . did it hurt?"

"Gosh dang it, Elaine," I laugh. "Do you really think I'm going to tell you all the gory details? Jeez!"

I had to share the news with someone, and Mary, my first choice, was not home. I'm glad Elaine is excited for me despite her dislike of Scott.

There's a rustling behind me; I turn and Mother's in the doorway. I lower the phone and stare at her, stricken. How long has she been standing there? She taps her wristwatch and I look down at mine. It's almost six, suppertime, and it's my week to set the table.

Elaine's voice bubbles from the earpiece, indecipherable.

"Um, I have to go."

"Your mom?"

"Uh-huh."

I hang up and spin around. She's gone, the doorway a dark rectangle. I find her in the kitchen, her lips pinched into a small line, washing dirty tinfoil in the sink to reuse. I walk around her to the cupboard and open it, my heart pounding.

"I never want to hear that language from you again," she says in a tight voice.

I stop stacking plates and look at her.

"What language?"

"You know very well what I'm talking about."

"Actually . . . I don't."

"Gosh! Darn! Jeez!"

"What's wrong with those words?"

"You know exactly what they mean: God! Damn! Jesus!"

I stare at her mouth as profanity explodes from it, then swallow hard, as if I were the one caught using it and not her.

"But I use those words so I don't have to use the other ones," I say.

"Don't be flippant with me, missy," she says. "You're not too old to get your mouth washed out with soap."

How dare she threaten me? I storm into the dining room with the plates, muttering *I hate you, I hate you, I hate you* as I set down each plate on the plastic tablecloth.

"What did you say?"

I whip around to face her. She stands a few feet from me, her fists on her narrow hips, her blue eyes boring into mine. Despite her aggressive posture, she looks frail. The pouch of her abdomen bulges under her gray polyester slacks. Hard to believe I occupied that space once, that we were that close. She has never told me she loves me, or drawn me to her in an embrace. Never touched me with tenderness whatsoever. When I was a little, the closest she got was spitting in a tissue on the way to church and scrubbing my face with it, and I craved that attention.

Once in sixth grade, after spending a weekend at the Kuipers' house with my friend Sandra, I asked her why she couldn't be more like Mrs. Kuipers, who read us bedtime stories and took us to see a matinee and made us popcorn balls.

"What, Mommy too hard on you?" she asked in a whiny voice. I was horrified at her mockery and slammed myself in my room to write "I hate you" on every page of my diary, which I knew she read.

When did she start to despise me, and when did I learn to despise her back?

I should tell her what I feel for her, those three words, and pour salt on the infection of our relationship. Get it out in the open, clean and honest.

"I said . . . ," I start to say, but stop and shake my head. What if she says the same words back to me? What then? How could we live in the same house anymore? And I have nowhere to go.

"I didn't say anything," I say, setting a glaring white plate in front of David's chair.

The garage door creaks open, announcing Dad's arrival, and we quickly revert back to mother and daughter roles, she pulling a casserole from the oven, me setting utensils alongside the plates. This is what Father will see when he walks through the door.

At supper, we are four strangers, eating. We have nothing to say to each other.

The wind howls over the sharp corners of our house on the prairie and Rejoice Radio plays Christmas carols on the intercom.

"Your mother and I have something to tell you kids about Jerome," Dad says halfway through this silent meal of macaroni with cheese and hot dogs.

David and I look across the table at each other and then at him.

"Jerome's in juvenile hall. Apparently he got into a fight with another boy and put him in the hospital with a concussion. A judge will decide what to do with him."

So that's where Jerome is. "Juvi." Jail for kids. Kids who are hardcore screwups, beyond hope, total losers. Figures.

"Can I go visit him?" David asks, putting down his milk glass.

"Of course not," Mother says.

"Why not?" David asks.

"Well, for one thing, you have school," she responds.

"And what else?" David asks.

At this, Father jumps in, irritated at David's insistence.

"If your mother says no, it means 'no,'" he says loudly. "End of discussion, got it?"

Dad's got his fork in his hand, and David sees it and shrinks away from him. In eighth grade, Dad got angry at him during supper and pronged him in the head. He cried from the pain, but they wouldn't let him leave the table.

As soon as the "Amen" is pronounced, David mutely clears the table and slams himself into the basement. He doesn't even open up to me when I walk downstairs with two bowls of mint chocolate chip ice cream, his favorite flavor.

"I'm not hungry," he says through the door.

"Gastric distress?" I ask.

He doesn't respond.

"Okay, I'm going to leave it right here," I say, setting one of the bowls outside his door. I shut myself in my room to eat the other.

+   +   +

We were fascinated with the world outside our stern household and became chronic wanderers, given to poking around dank church basements, the secret back hallways of truck stops, the Lysol–scented wards of our father's hospital.

There were other places besides home, and we wanted to explore them all.

One summer morning when we were five, we struck out on our own. David pulled me down the sidewalk in our red Radio Flyer wagon, which I'd stocked with cookies, a blanket and my pet tick, Blinky, which I'd housed in an empty salt shaker.

We'd decided to join the outside world, the bright sun and sweet grass and playful dogs that beckoned behind fences. Outside was better than home.

But our adventure was cut short before we reached the end of the block, when a neighbor woman phoned our house.

"Your daughter's running off with the maid's son," she told Mother.

CHAPTER 7

SHARP OBJECTS

We're shoveling the driveway, scarves wound around our faces, heads and jackets soaked from the pelting sleet. It's Saturday morning, the sky is ash gray, and Christmas is two weeks away.

David jabs his shovel under the heavy snow, grating cement as he shoves it off the driveway. His glasses are fogged so I can't see his eyes, but I know he's still pissy at me.

On Tuesday, I was standing with Elaine at the snack bar when she remarked on the outfit she'd seen David wearing that day, a bright purple sweatshirt and green jeans.

"Good thing his sense of fashion doesn't run in the family," she sniffed, "because I wouldn't be able to associate with you."

"Good thing he's not my real brother," I'd shot back, "because he'd embarrass the hell out of me."

There was a commotion behind us, and I turned to see David racing away with Kenny trailing after him, the dictionary I'd lent him crashed to the floor.

I tried to apologize as he set the supper table that evening—"you know I was just kidding"—but he banged down the plates on the table, refusing to talk to me, and hasn't spoken a word to me since. Even yesterday, when we missed the bus and had to hike a mile and a half to Harrison as the below zero wind sliced our faces, he refused to open his mouth.

He's been acting strange lately, and my stupid comment didn't help matters. It's like something's been knocked out of him. Every evening he camps out in the downstairs rocker, swaying and staring at his reflection in the window.

Last weekend I tried to force him out of the chair, and the effort backfired on me. I went into the basement Saturday night with the Monopoly board and set it up on the carpet at his feet, spending ten minutes organizing the money and separating the Chance and Community Chest cards.

He refused to play. I grabbed his arms and tried to pry him out of the rocker and this devolved into a fierce battle of wills that ended with him kicking me in the stomach, knocking the wind from me. I fell onto the Monopoly board—sending money and cards flying—and lay there doubled over, gasping for air.

"I told you I didn't want to play," David said before locking himself in his room.

Although we'd had many brutal kick fights in grade school, his action on Saturday was unjustified and I was still angry at him when I made my comment to Elaine. But I know all too well that my comment hurt him more than his kick hurt me.

Mother's frustrated with him, too. Half the time he won't respond when she calls him on the intercom, and then she makes me go find him. She seems to think I have a sixth sense for locating my brother, as if some invisible leash tied us together. "Where's David?" she'll say. "Go find him." It's been this way since we were little.

The other day, I had to interrupt a manicure to find him. He was locked in his room.

"David, open up," I yelled, kicking the door with my shoe so I wouldn't ruin my nails.

"Hold on," he called.

When he opened the door, he had blue eyes.

"What do you think?" he asked, smiling for the first time in weeks.

His eyes were blue. Cataract, sickly, unseeing blue. He looked like a freak.

"They're contacts," he said, before I could gather words to respond. "I saved up my allowance.

First he cuts a part in his hair, then he gets blue eyes.

"When are you gonna stop trying to be white?" I asked.

His smile fell, and he stood there blinking his blue eyes for a moment before closing the door in my face. When he sat down at the supper table, his eyes were back to normal, but he didn't lift them from his dinner plate.

After the last patch of the driveway is cleared, we walk around the house to the basement door, stomping the snow from our boots before entering. The woodstove is burning, and Mother's set a pan of apple cider and cinnamon sticks on top of it; the aroma hits us as we walk through the door.

"Mmm, smells good," I say, looking at David hopefully. "You thirsty?"

He ignores me, sitting on the bench to peel off his snow pants.

"How long you planning to stay mad at me?" I ask him. "Forever?"

He doesn't say anything, but shrugs, which is something at least. A possible softening. As I'm arranging my wet socks and gloves on the rack next to the woodstove, Mother thumps downstairs.

"Don't hang those so close to the stove, you'll scorch them," she says.

I move the rack to the other side of the woodpile, and she starts to walk away, then stops.

"The judge sent Jerome to Cary Home for Boys, downtown," she says. "They're not going to charge him with assault because he's a minor, but they should have."

"Is he coming home for Christmas?" David asks, and I feel a twinge of jealousy at this concern for Jerome.

"Of course not," Mother says. "He's a juvenile delinquent!"

"He's not a juvenile delinquent, he's my brother!" David screams, jumping up. He whips his snow pants across the room and they flap against the ping-pong table like a giant tattered bird. His action startles both of us and we stare speechless as he stalks to his room and kicks the door shut.

"David, get out here and clean up your mess, right now!" Mother yells.

I hold my hands to the woodstove, thawing my blue fingertips. The cider is boiling in the pan, ready to drink.

Mother edges closer to David's door, hands on her hips, looking tired and old in her flesh-colored sweater.

"I'm warning you," she says.

The door stays shut.

"Just wait until your father gets home!"

I wince as she thunders back up the steps, slamming the basement door behind her, then walk over to pick up David's snow gear and put it away.

When his screams rise from the basement a few hours later, I wrap my head in my pillow and scream along with him. After twenty minutes tick by on my alarm clock, I unwrap my head and sit up. Pat Boone is crooning "O Little Town of Bethlehem" on the great room stereo.

I tiptoe to the mouth of the hallway. The ceiling-high Christmas tree flashes rainbow beads of lights on the walls and windows. David and I decorated it last weekend to the usual soundtrack of *A Christmas Sing with Bing,* but this year, it was just another Saturday chore. We used to sing along to the album as we decorated the tree, giddy with the idea of Christmas, with the idea that the presents our parents gave us would prove that they loved us.

Beyond the flashing tree, Mother and Dad sit on the sofa, reading the newspaper. I creep to the basement door in sock feet, the tree between us, and open it, lifting the doorknob to ease the stress on the hinges.

The lights are off downstairs, but the boys' door is open. I walk in and find David lying faceup on his bed, shaking. It's too dark to see his face.

"David?" I whisper.

He doesn't respond, so I turn on the lamp next to his bed and crouch beside him. Tears are drying on his cheeks, and his eyes are vacant as he stares at the ceiling.

"Are you okay?" I ask, although it's obvious that he's not. "Do you want some water or something?"

He begins to murmur.

"So sick of it, sick of all of it."

My heart contracts. He's giving up, and we're almost there.

"Don't do this now," I say. "A year and a half and we're eighteen. Remember Florida!"

He laughs bitterly—we haven't mentioned Florida in months, not since we started living our separate lives—and starts to sit up before gasping and putting a hand on his left arm. I notice, for the first time, the weird bend in the middle of his forearm.

"What's happened?" I ask him.

He turns his head to look at the carpet next to where I'm crouched and I follow his eyes. A 2x4 lays on the floor, one of the pieces from the pile beside the woodstove.

"Dad hit you with that?"

He nods.

"I think it's broken," he says.

My throat constricts and it's hard to breathe. What kind of father would do this to his own son? Unless it's true what Jerome said. That Dad doesn't consider the boys his sons.

"I'm so sick of it . . ." David murmurs again, and then he starts to cry in silence, tears dripping down his cheeks.

"Shh . . . I'll take care of you," I say, fighting tears myself.

I pull the bedspread off Jerome's bed and cover him, then go upstairs.

They're sipping coffee; Pat Boone's now singing "God Rest You Merry Gentlemen."

I walk over to them.

"I think something's wrong with David," I say, giving them each a knifing look. "I think somebody busted his arm."

I glare directly into Father's eyes after I say this, defying him to say something, then stride to my room and lock the door. Half an hour later, the garage door creaks open and I look out my window to see the Porsche disappear down the lane.

Jerome was the last person to break David's bones, in 1980. Jerome was being his typical bullying self, chucking pieces of asphalt at David in front of our old house as David sat on the curb with his legs stretched out in front of him, bouncing a basketball between them. I sat in the yard behind him, playing with my hamsters.

After a while, David got tired of dodging the rocks and lobbed a piece back at Jerome, hitting him in the head. Jerome yelped in pain, then ran over to him and jack-hammered his size-14 feet onto David's leg. I heard it snap from where I was sitting.

"That'll teach you to respect your elders," Jerome said as David screamed and twisted in the street.

The official story after church the next morning is that he fell off the bus and broke his arm. That's what David tells people when they crowd around him in the foyer. Mrs. De Jong clucks her tongue and asks me if I saw it happen. I look at David and he looks at the ground.

"No, I got off before he did," I say, my cheeks burning with the lie.

"I bet you heard him, though," Rick Hoolsema laughs. "I bet he yelled real good."

David manages a weak smile, and my eyes sting as I watch him.

Dad must have arranged to have David "taken care of" by one of his partners at the clinic or reset David's arm himself, so there was no need to fill out a police report on suspicious injuries.

"You kids are blessed with medical parents, they take good care of you," says Mr. Needam, an elder.

At this, I turn to David.

"Time to go," I say. "We're late."

David follows me mutely, his noninjured arm flung out for balance as he walks down the icy steps in front of church.

"Do you want to hold on to me?" I ask him.

He shakes his head no.

"I'm quitting the swim team," I tell Mother on Monday afternoon.

She's sitting on a stool at the kitchen counter, signing a large stack of Christmas cards. "Jesus is the Reason for the Season!" is printed in shiny green letters on the front of each card, and Luke 2:11 is printed inside: "For unto us a child is born, for unto us, a son is given."

"I thought you liked swimming," she says in an absent voice, signing "In HIS name, Dr. and Mrs. Jacob Scheeres" inside the card.

"I do, but I'm having problems with some classes and I can't do everything," I say, walking past her. I fill a mug with morning coffee, yawning loudly, and stick it in the microwave.

She looks over at me.

"Maybe you have that chronic fatigue syndrome," she says. "I'm calling Dr. Walters."

I shrug. The microwave dings and I stir milk into the stale coffee, clouding it gray, and yawn again.

She's threatened to drag me to the doctor for weeks because I'm always yawning and taking naps, but she never makes an appointment.

"That's high school for you," I say as I turn to go back to my room. "Exhausting."

What I don't tell her is that I already quit the team last week—I skipped so many practices that Coach Shultz was about to kick me off anyway, so I decided to beat him to the punch.

What I don't tell her is that I'm flunking half my classes.

What I don't tell her is that these things are happening because I'm up all night having sex while she and Dad sleep two doors down the hallway.

I wait for Scott each night dressed in a summer teddy, perfumed and painted and shivering under the blankets because Mother lowers the thermostat to 55 at night.

He walks forty minutes from his house to mine, down County Road 650 through unplowed snow. As I wait for him, I imagine myself his prize, one he must battle cold, dark and distance to claim.

When I hear the shuffle of his boots on the roof ledge, I open my window and he steps into my bedroom, tracking in cold as he peels off his layers, one by one, until he's standing there naked and brown and grinning and already hard.

We listen to The Police while we do it, and if the tape ends, Scott stops whatever we're doing to flip it over, and afterward he drums his fingers on my back to the music as we fade into sleep. And that's the moment I cherish most, when I'm stretched onto his warmth, my head on the soft pillow of his chest, his heart throbbing in my ear, his arms around me.

We don't talk much—partly because my parents are right down the hall, partly because we don't really know each other all that well—and when the alarm rings at 5:30, he dresses and slips back out the window into the rising dawn. I watch him cross the back field, a running shadow, then reset the alarm for 6:30.

At school, I'm so stupid with sleep that I cram myself full of No-Doz and Jolt Cola, but this only makes me jumpy *and* tired and I pinch myself to stay awake in class.

After a few weeks of practicing sex, I'm starting to feel something. Not the eyeballs-rolled-toward-heaven suck-in-your-breath immensity that Scott gets out of it, but a swelling pleasure that builds as he seesaws on top of me and ends all too quickly when he suddenly stops and says "fuck" in a small voice before rolling off me.

But it's enough of a something to make Scott clamp his hand over my mouth so I don't make noise and enough of a something to make me want to practice alone, rubbing the swelling place with a nail polish bottle and pretending it's Scott until my body

trembles and a brightness like heat lightning flashes through me
and I whisper "fuck" as well.

The first time it happened, I laid there marveling at the
beauty of it, wondering why God would forbid such bliss when
He makes us endure so much misery.

A slammed door wakes me and I slide guiltily into my desk
chair. It's dark outside, and I don't even remember lying down.

I hear Mother yell for David, her voice thin and agitated, and
then walk across the great room toward the hallway. I switch on
my clunky yellow desk lamp a moment before she opens my door.

"Where's David?" she asks, lifting a clear rain bonnet from
her head. "I told him to bring in the dumpsters after school and
they're still out there."

The stink of ammonia wafts over to me; she got her hair
permed in town, disciplined into tight brown coils. I frown
down at my hastily opened French dictionary, not wanting her to
notice my sleep-creased face. My final is tomorrow, and I'm
going to fail it.

"How should I know where David's at?" I raise the dictionary
to my face, blocking out her presence with neat rows of print.

"Come get the groceries in then." She lingers in the doorway.
"And if you can't find your brother, you'll have to get the dumpsters yourself."

I jerk my head up to protest, but she's already gone.

Ice scratches the window; the last thing I want to do right
now is drag the garbage bins a quarter mile over the slush-
covered lane in the dark. I push back my chair, and for the mil-
lionth time in my life set out to go find David.

He's downstairs in the rocking chair, as always. But he's got
the lights off for once, and is just sitting there, rocking, looking

out the window at the silhouettes of gray trees against the grayer sky.

"Didn't you hear Mother?" I ask angrily. "Go fetch in the dumpsters."

He doesn't answer, he just keeps rocking. I go to the wall panel and swipe on all the overhead lights. The room blooms into color.

"Are you deaf or dumb or both?" I shout.

I turn toward him and see the wall-mounted pencil sharpener in pieces at his feet. I take a step closer and see his right arm laying across his lap, slashed red. In his hand, he holds the razor from the pencil sharpener—he's sliced a bloody ladder into his brown flesh, and there's blood smeared on the cast of his broken arm. He continues rocking, now staring at his ghostly reflection. His eyes are wide open, unflinching.

I sprint back upstairs and Mother hushes me as I throw open the basement door. She's watching a news update about the Beirut embassy bombing on television.

"David cut himself," I say over the TV report, gripping the counter with both hands; the words are hard to say.

She walks around me to the stove, where corned beef hash fries in a skillet.

"Tell him to put a Band-Aid on it," she says. "Your father's going to be home any minute and . . ."

"He cut his wrist!" I yell, cupping my hands around my mouth as if she were half a mile away. She exhales, exasperated.

"Why can't I just have one day of peace?" she grumbles, handing me the spatula.

She walks downstairs braying his name.

"A White Christmas, just what everyone wanted!" the bleached blond TV reporter says. I push the pink and white paste around the skillet and wonder if I should call an ambulance or if Mother will take him to the hospital herself.

Next thing, she's beside me, snatching the spatula from my hand.

"It's burning!"

I wipe my hand on my jeans to erase her touch and watch her spoon four craters in the hash and crack an egg into each one. She says nothing.

"Well, are you taking him to the hospital?" I ask.

She snorts and jerks the salt shaker over the skillet.

"They're just surface cuts," she says. "If you want to kill your-self, you slice down, not sideways."

She illustrates with her index finger before bending to pull a metal lid from the tangle of pans in the cupboard below the counter.

"But doesn't he need . . ."

"He's just trying to get attention. Ignore him."

She drops the lid on the skillet and turns to open the refrigerator.

"Julia, the groceries!"

In the cold garage, three brown Marsh sacks poke from the Audi's open trunk. I jostle them onto my knee and then into my arms. As I walk back into the mudroom, the garage door opens and Dad's Porsche glides in. When I turn to nudge the door closed with my foot, I see him sitting in his silver car with the engine off, his head back, his eyes shut. Lacy flute music seeps from the closed windows. Mozart? Vivaldi? I didn't even know he liked classical music. I shut my eyes too and let the faint notes wash over me like a whispered prayer. If only we could live as peacefully as this.

"Julia, the milk!" Mother yells from the kitchen, and I jolt to consciousness and shut the door.

As we sit at the supper table—Mother in her apron, Father in his suit, David with his two damaged arms—I think about how I'll stretch myself into Scott's warmth in a few hours, and my cheeks flush with my secret.

I have a life apart from this.

They announce David's departure the day after Christmas. They're sending him to a Christian school, on an island in the Caribbean.

"He'll be better off there," Dad says, as if David were already gone, and not sitting on the sofa next to me. I recall how Elaine said David would be better off in Chicago, and now Dad's saying he'll be better off in the Caribbean, and wonder why he can't just be better off *here,* at home. His home.

Mother leans forward to take a Christmas cookie from a platter she's set on the coffee table. Dad unfolds a map and points to the island, the Dominican Republic, next to Cuba. They found the school in an advertisement at the back of *Christianity Today,* Mother explains. Mother hands one brochure to David, who reaches out awkwardly with his cast to take it, and one to me.

I look at David, but he's taking this news with the same dim eyes he's had ever since Dad fractured his arm. He twists his nail ring round and round on his finger, the one he made to protect himself from harm.

On the top of the brochure is a cross surrounded by a circle with the words "New Horizons Youth Ministries, Inc." inside it.

Do you have an adolescent who . . .
Rejects your family's Christian values?
Is out of control?
Has a low self-image?
Is irresponsible, showing lack of character?
Runs with a negative crowd or has no friends?

Is unmotivated and failing in school?
Is disrespectful, rejecting your love and others?
New Horizons Youth Ministries can help.

I look up at Dad.

"Is this some kind of punishment or something?"

He takes a drink of his coffee before responding.

"David needs help, and these people can help him," he says flatly.

He takes another sip of coffee.

"He'll leave after New Year's."

"How long will he be there?" I ask, looking at David, who is staring blankly at his brochure.

"He'll be there until the staff feel he's ready to come back," Dad says, rising from his chair. "Everything's explained right there in the informational packet."

Mother also stands.

"We have adult Bible study at the Vanderkoys at seven," she says. "There's leftovers for supper, and you may watch *The Waltons* at eight."

I wait until they walk into the garage before turning to David.

"What do you think about all this?" I ask him.

"Does it matter?" he asks.

He tosses his brochure on the coffee table with his good arm, and I continue to read mine, skimming down the page.

Concept
Why in the Dominican Republic? Three reasons: atmosphere, culture shock, and distance.

Atmosphere
Escuela Caribe is set far away from the pervasive influences of American society; the materialism, the social ills, the negative peers, and the struggles in one's family . . .

Culture Shock
A change in climate, racial differences, geographic surroundings,
friends, daily routine, and language all make adolescents remarkably
more dependent upon others for direction. This also renders them
more malleable . . .

Distance
Living in a structured environment, teens start to appreciate Mom
and Dad and begin to share their parents' dream of a united family
again . . .

"It's a reform school," David says quietly.

"But why?" I ask. "What'd you do?"

We both know there's no answer to this. We sit in a tight silence as Rejoice Radio plays stale Christmas carols over the intercom, not knowing what to say. Out the great room windows,
the sunset spills red across the snow-tossed landscape.

After a long while, David stands.

"I guess I'd best prepare myself," he says, turning toward the
basement.

The night before David leaves, I sit on his bed as he packs, next
to a pile of underwear with SCHEERES written in Marksalot
on the inside back of the waistbands. We've tuned his radio to
Rejoice and set it in front of the intercom so we can talk
privately.

"Don't leave me here alone with them!" I plead as he slowly
rolls a pair of jeans into a compact tube. They took his cast off
early, and he's being ginger with his arm.

"Come with me," he says, laughing darkly.

"Uh . . . maybe I'll come for a visit."

He and Mother trekked into town several times this past
week to revamp his wardrobe—*"no tight, torn, or revealing clothing,*

no T-shirts with logos"—and to get him a passport. In it, he glowers at the camera, dressed in a Sunday shirt.

I pick up a piece of paper lying next to his suitcase, a list the school sent, and skim down to the DO NOT BRING section:

No music
No secular reading material
No playing cards
No medications, without previous approval
Nothing that does not honor and glorify God

As he wedges the jeans into a corner of the suitcase, my eyes fall on his right forearm. The razor cuts have scabbed over into a row of dark tracks except for the places where he's picked them off, which are pink. He sees me staring at his arm and pulls it against his stomach.

I stand and walk to the window. Outside it's hailing, and there's already a foot of snow on the ground.

"Just think, you'll be lying on the beach down there, while I'm freezing my butt off back here," I say, watching his reflection in the glass. He straightens and looks at me, and I turn around.

The intercom crackles.

"Julia, David needs to finish packing and go to bed," Mother says over the sound of the radio. "We leave for Indy at 5:30 tomorrow."

I ignore her and walk over to David.

"Gonna be real lonely around here without you, Baby Boo Boo," I say, calling him by the nickname I never use anymore.

"You'd best write," he says, pausing for a moment before adding "Ju-la-la."

"I will," I say. "You too."

We stand there not looking at each other. We've never been separated for longer than a weekend since we were three. We take each other's presence—sometimes annoying, sometimes gratifying, always constant—for granted. The intercom speaker crackles again—Mother listening, waiting—and I punch him in the biceps, and he covers his arm with his hand and pretends it hurts. We've always expressed our affection through playful aggression—we don't come from a kissing and hugging family and it's the best we can do.

"I'll miss you," I say.

"I'll miss you, too," he says, smiling, "but not your abuse."

"Soon you'll be back for more," I say, backing toward the door.

"Julia," he calls when I have the doorknob in my hand.

I turn; he stands there with a serious face, eyebrows raised, eyes beseeching.

"Don't forget about me."

I shake my head.

"Nope. Never."

I leave his door open and walk up the stairwell. Mother and Dad are reading on the sofa. When I reach the hallway, there's the sharp crinkle of a newspaper hastily put down.

"Julia, the draft!" Mother calls. "How many times do I have to tell you to keep that door closed?"

I go back to it and gently nudge the door into its frame, so that it's shut, but not quite closed.

+   +   +

In preschool, color became a problem. There were kids who didn't like David because he was black and there were kids who didn't like me because I was his sister.

Others were just curious and asked stupid questions.

"How'd you get that color?" they'd ask. "If you scratch your skin, are you white underneath?"

I'd thrust myself between David and his interrogators.

"He was born that way, dummy!" I'd say. "If you scratch your skin are you black underneath?"

But their questions never ended.

"Is your blood green?"

"How do people see you at night? Are you invisible?"

"Is your hair plastic?"

They regarded him as a fascinating freak, and David dutifully answered their questions, letting them poke and prod at him.

But as we got older, this curiosity turned into rejection. Insults were hurled on the playground—"Jungle bunny," "Poo boy," "Velcro head." They called us the "Oreo Twins," and we were often left to play alone at recess.

That was fine by us, because we were best friends anyway.

CHAPTER 8

FREEDOM

A buzzer sounds and the cell door jerks open. I open my eyes, run them over the vomit-colored cement block walls, and close them again. The air con is still blasting down from the ceiling vent. I shiver and pull the stingy gray blanket around my shoulders, waiting for the next thing to happen.

"The time is six A.M.," a female voice announces. "Breakfast is served. You have fifteen minutes to eat breakfast, do your toilet, and return to your cell. Next meal, twelve noon."

Footsteps shuffle past my head on the other side of the bars. I swing my feet over the side of the metal shelf and stand, hiking up the waist of my XL orange jumpsuit before bending to put on my sneakers—the only "personal effect" they allowed me to keep.

In the common area, three girls in similar orange jumpsuits sit at a plastic yellow picnic table. There's a number on each girl's back and I wonder what mine is; I was too dazed last night to notice it.

Across from the picnic table is a long window and two female guards sit behind it, sipping coffee and watching *Donahue*
on a TV jutting from the wall.

I sit down next to LJ452, a fat girl with short brown hair. She
and the girl sitting opposite her are about my age, but the girl
sitting directly across from me still has baby fat in her cheeks and
looks to be about twelve or thirteen years old. What did *she* do?
She catches me staring and scowls, so I look down at the plate in
front of me, two chocolate-covered donuts and a cup of Tang. Juvenile food. Juvenile delinquent food.

The last month has been strange.

After David was sent to the Dominican Republic, things didn't
calm down at home.

Mother read my diary and found out I'd snuck into *Fast Times
at Ridgemont High*—"*They showed some teats is all*," I'd written—
and my parents started becoming suspicious of my whereabouts.

One evening Father confronted me in the kitchen, demanding to know where I'd gone after a baby sitting job the night before. I knew he suspected me of seeing Scott, whom my parents
officially disapproved of after learning his family weren't church
people and that a neighbor had spotted a porno magazine in
their living room.

That night I actually hadn't seen Scott, but Dad kept insisting I
tell him "the truth" and I kept insisting I had come straight home.
His face grew redder, his voice fiercer, until something inside him
popped and he threw me on the kitchen counter and came racing
at my throat with his hands. I instinctively knocked them away,
and then Mother—who was sitting on the sofa—stood up to say
she'd found an Arby's cup beside the driver's seat of her Audi,
which I'd borrowed because the Toyota was in the shop.

I'd forgotten about the Jamocha shake. I'd gone by the Arby's drive-through on my way home and had left the container in her car. Huge Mistake, apparently. Huger than I ever could have ever imagined.

That day I realized I wasn't immune to my father's violence. For years, while my brothers were whipped and I was spared, I thought I had some kind of biological privilege—that my father wouldn't harm his own genetic material. But in their absence, my father didn't have anywhere to train the spotlight of his rage on but me.

So when my parents left for another missionary meeting in California and the nurse from my dad's clinic who was staying with me caught Scott climbing out of my bedroom window one morning, I left home. If my father wanted to choke me over a forgotten milkshake, what would he do to me for losing my virginity?

I moved in with my brother Dan and his three roommates at Purdue and found a part-time job as a busgirl at the Howard Johnson's Hotel on Highway 52. I biked to work, and to Harrison—an hour's ride away—if I couldn't find someone to drive me. I didn't go to school if I wasn't in the mood for it, and a couple of teachers threatened to flunk me before passing me with D's.

Although I was dirt poor—I paid half Dan's rent, and frequently resorted to eating off the room service trays I was sent to collect from the hotel hallways—I was happy. I didn't have to go to church, spent hours watching MTV, and didn't need permission to do anything. I was free.

I listened to Van Halen's "Running with the Devil" on my Walkman as I rode through the streets of Lafayette on my bike, rewinding the cassette tape again and again.

It was the soundtrack of my rebellion. That was me, running with the devil. Doing bad things and liking it.

It was bliss for several weeks, until Mother called. She was crying on the phone, hiccuping with emotion. "You killed my baby," she kept repeating. It took me a while to figure out that her "baby" was our dog, Lecka. I had unchained her the previous night and taken her to Scott's house to play with her, but she ran away before I could take her back, and sometime during the night, she was run over in front of his driveway. His father had called Mother with the news.

"I loved that dog," my mother wailed on the phone. "And you killed her."

I hung up the phone on her—and—snapped. It wasn't just being responsible for Lecka's dying that set me off. It was my mother calling Lecka her "baby," and saying she loved her, and it was the emotion in her voice. It was my mother—who had never in my seventeen years told me that she loved me—getting all lathered up over the dog.

A few hours later, I was arrested.

I'd gone riding, racing down random streets on my bike, fleeing the conversation. I was shaking and sweating and not thinking. I just wanted to move, and move fast. I veered into a parking lot near campus and charged up the ramps until I could no longer pedal, then walked my bike past the rows of cars, peering into their windows.

There was a car with dozens of cassettes spilled onto the floor, and it was unlocked, so I sat in the driver's seat and looked at them. I was just doing things. Staying busy. My mind was blank.

Two police cars blocked the garage exit on my way out; someone had reported a break-in. When they asked me if I'd entered a car, I told the truth and let them search my backpack. I didn't take anything. But they arrested me anyway—cramming my ten-speed into the trunk of a patrol car—for breaking curfew. It was past midnight, and I was a minor.

At the police station, they stuck me in a small room with a metal table and chair chained to the cement floor. I howled at my reflection in the mirrored window until my eyes ached from crying, then slumped to the floor with my arms cradling my head. I was in jail, I was a criminal, I was following Jerome's footsteps. Things would never be the same.

An hour later, the door opened and a cop walked in with my father. They sat on the metal chairs and the cop motioned for me to join them. When I slid into a chair, my dad wouldn't look at me.

"Your father's here to take you home," the cop said.

I looked at my father, at the hostility churning beneath his surface, at his hair twisted out of place by sleep. I was afraid to be alone with him.

"I don't want to go home," I told the cop.

The cop said I had no choice. It was either go home or go to jail. I couldn't be out there on my own, he said, someone had to answer for me.

"I'll take jail," I told him.

He made me repeat myself three times, then he scratched his head and turned to my father, who hadn't opened his mouth, hadn't tried to convince me otherwise, wouldn't look at me, before sighing and writing something on a police document.

Dad left the room without a backward glance, and I was escorted to juvenile hall. What happened afterward I'd seen in movies—the stripping and being hosed down with soapy water by the large, mean-looking female guard (*"Turn around," "Bend over," "Spread your legs"*), the donning of the too-big orange jumpsuit. These things happened to the Julia who ran with the Devil, not to the Julia who attended Lafayette Christian.

Now I'm in Juvi, and a judge will decide my fate, Just like with Jerome.

The fat girl beside me sneezes and I look up.

"How long do they keep people in here before their hearing?" I ask the table.

No one responds. They keep shoving donuts into their mouth holes. I turn to the fat girl beside me.

"Do you know?"

She lifts her hand and points at a sign over the window. NO TALKING. A guard appears in the doorway.

"Toilet time!" she says, and I take a second bite of donut— as the other inmates form a line at the door.

"This ain't no vacation resort, LJ887," the guard growls, and it takes me a second to realize she's talking to me.

We follow her single file to a bathroom, where there's a row of toilets on one wall, and a row of sinks on the other. The kid marches to the farthest toilet, yanks down her jumpsuit—she doesn't even wear a bra yet—and starts to pee, her arms crossed over her skinny naked chest. I pick a spot in the middle of the toilet row and keep my eyes fastened on the gray tile floor in front of me, trying to ignore the farting and tinkling and odors around me. When we finish, we wash our hands and faces in the sinks and use paper towels to dry off.

"Cell time!"

Single file back to our cages. Lie down on the metal shelf, doze, snap awake, look for patterns in the dried paint dribbles on the vomit-colored wall, wonder how it will all end. Alarm at noon, peanut butter and jelly sandwiches, toilet. Alarm at six, eat-pee-shower.

Repeat for five days.

The Tippecanoe County Courthouse is the prettiest building in Lafayette and also one of the oldest, a hundred-year-old neoclassical wonder with a large central dome and a 3,000-pound bell that can be heard for twelve miles. The county's only execution took place on the southwest lawn in 1856, when three men were hanged for murder and riots broke out as hundreds of spectators fought for a view.

I learned these details during a seventh-grade field trip at Lafayette Christian, and remembered them every Sunday as we drove by the courthouse on our way to church.

And now here I am walking up the Indiana limestone steps in a flourescent orange jumper and wrist bracelets, wedged between two police officers. Passers-by crane their necks at me, and there's a group of school kids, fourth grade, fifth, and one points and then they all turn and stare, gawky-mouthed and googly-eyed at the scary criminal. The social reject. The bad person. I hang my head so my hair falls over my face—curtaining myself off—and stumble on a step. The cops tighten their grip.

They uncuff me in the middle of an airy chamber, where my parents stand against one wall and my big sister Debra stands against the other. She runs over and throws her arms around me, and although my hands are free, I am unable to return her embrace. Things are being done to me, and I can't do anything back. All I can do is wait for the outcome.

The four of us sit on a wooden bench outside a courtroom waiting for my name to be called. Across from us, there's a mural of white men on horseback shooting unarmed Indians on foot in the Battle of Tippecanoe, and I contemplate this while my family squabbles over my lost virtue.

Mother: "You gave her that *Glamour* subscription. You planted the seeds of wickedness in her."

Father: "You have no business being here, you're a poor influence."

Debra, in a trembling voice: "I'm here to support her, and I'm staying."

In the courtroom, I stand before the judge—dressed in a preacher robe, high up in her pulpit—and tell her the same thing I told the cop: I don't want to go home.

And like the cop, she gives me two choices: I can declare myself an emancipated minor or I can go to Escuela Caribe. I fix my eyes on the small circle of sunlight pouring through the window above the judge's head and think of David, as I've done often during the last five days.

"I want us to be family again," he wrote in his last letter, which Mother forwarded to me at Dan's. David had written me every week, always repeating the same things: "I want to come home." "I want us all to get along." "I want us to be happy."

I've heard him say these sorts of things his entire life. Maybe he holds the idea of family in such high esteem because he's always been the outsider, struggling to belong. The black boy in the basement.

He doesn't yet know that his Brady Bunch dream will never come true. A few days after he left, Mother cleared out the boys' room. I came home from school one afternoon and found her with rubber gloves and Lysol, scrubbing the walls.

"Who knows what went on in here," she'd said, pointing to a dark spot on the carpet. "Those boys were worse than monkeys."

"David's stuff!" I'd shouted when I opened his closet and found it empty. "Where is it?"

"He doesn't live here anymore," she'd said. "Neither of them do."

I grabbed the back of David's desk chair to keep from falling down.

"You can't do this to him!" I said.

She'd responded by plunging her scrub brush into the steaming pail and scouring away the remaining traces of his existence. And what power did I have to stop her, to prevent anything from happening? Bad things happen to you, and you can't do anything to stop them.

They didn't tell David that he was never coming home; the school staff thought such news would affect his progress in "The Program," of which he'd written very little, beyond calling it difficult.

And so to each of his letters asking if our parents had mentioned when he was coming home, I'd reply, "I don't know—ask them," to which he'd write back, "They won't tell me."

We're both homeless now.

". . . reached a decision in consideration of all this, young lady?" the judge asks, peering down from her pulpit.

"Yes."

"The Court did not hear the answer," the judge says. "Speak up, please."

"I said, I'll go. I'll go to the Dominican Republic."

I will go to David and be family to him. I can't live with my parents. I don't love Scott. I can't support myself.

I have nowhere to go but to David. We'll become close again, like we were when we were little, before everything got in the way.

PART TWO

+   +   +

TRUST NO ONE

CHAPTER 9

THE ISLAND

I follow the other passengers through a maze of roped-off lanes. We're headed toward a row of men in tan suits who sit at metal desks along the far wall. Aduana-Customs, says a sign over their heads.

A long cement barricade divides the low-ceilinged room in half; on the other side of it, brown faces yell staccato greetings in Spanish to the people around me, who shout back. Some passengers are already on the other side, folding themselves into welcoming arms, getting kissed and fussed over. This is their country. Their home.

I feel white, alone, exposed.

As the crowd jostles me forward, a large piece of cardboard is boosted into the air: JULIA SCHEERES, it says. Beneath it stand the only other white people in the terminal, a tall man with sandy hair and a fat woman wearing a lime green pantsuit. They frown in my direction. Bodies bump past me as I stop and look around. The room has two openings: the door to the runway that I just walked through, and a large glass entrance on the other side of the barricade; the red tail lights of idling cars glimmer beyond it. The runway door is wide open. I could sprint through it into the darkness and be free.

Free to do what?

When I turn back around, the white people are standing directly opposite me across the barricade. The man shakes my name violently and the woman shoots her hand into the air as if she wanted to answer a question. I give them a limp wave and catch up to the receding line of passengers as they follow my progress footstep by footstep on the other side of the barricade.

At the line of desks, an official smoking a cigar stamps my passport and jerks his thumb toward a narrow hallway behind him. The white people are waiting there for me, my name still thrust in the air. I saunter over and point at it.

"That's me."

The woman grabs my hand and squeezes it.

"I'm Debbie, the Assistant Director of Education at Escuela Caribe," she says with a lisp. The man leans the sign against his leg and cranks my hand up and down.

"I'm Ron, a teacher."

Debbie peels her lips back in a wide grin; she's got a gap between her front teeth that's big enough to jab a pencil through.

"Are you ready to begin your incredible journey?" she asks in a rah-rah voice.

I shrug and look at the cement floor.

"I s'pose."

"Alrighty then!" Debbie gushes. "Let's get your bags, and we're off!"

Ron strides to an overflowing trash can and throws my name on top of the heap, then punches it down repeatedly until it sinks from view; he walks back, slapping his hands together and grinning as if he'd accomplished some great feat.

We walk down the hallway into a large crowded room. Here, a man with a rifle guards a jumble of suitcases dumped in the middle of the room. He slings his rifle over his back and examines first my ticket stub, then my face. I smile at him nervously, and he steps aside. Ron helps me extract my bags from the pile.

"Now on to Customs," Debbie says. "Didn't bring any illegal contraband, did you?"

I look at her, preparing to smile, but she's not joking.

"No," I tell her. "I didn't."

We join a line snaking toward a row of conference tables where more uniformed men pick through the guts of splayed luggage. As Debbie and Ron stand a few feet away, the official frisking my belongings—a pimply-faced boy a few years older than me—scoops up a pair of my white cotton panties with SCHEERES scrawled on the waistband in Mother's handwriting and squeezes them, slowly winking at me. I look away, my cheeks burning.

When he's done fingering my underthings, the official dismisses me with a backward slash of his hand. Debbie rushes over. She picks up my toiletry bag and peers into it, shaking it around.

"Medications aren't allowed," she says, slipping a small bottle of aspirin into her purse. "Didn't you read the orientation packet?"

I hate her already.

She turns without waiting for my answer and leads the way down another hallway—Ron carrying one of my suitcases, me dragging the other—and we step through a door into an unlit parking lot. The hot air is sticky with moisture, and the full moon glances dully off parked cars.

Halfway across the parking lot, a gang of beggar kids appears, swarming around us and tugging at our clothes and the suitcases with tiny hands.

"Me help! Me help!"

Debbie barks at them in Spanish, and a girl in a tattered pink dress turns to her and sticks out her tongue before prancing off. I smirk; my sentiments exactly.

We stop beside a white van with "New Horizons Youth Ministries, Inc." on the sides and Ron digs in his pocket for the keys. A breeze churns through the yellow flowering bushes beside the van, filling the air with a dense perfume, and somewhere beyond the hedge, waves collapse on sand with a muted swoosh. My pulse quickens. I'm on Hispaniola, *Treasure Island*—the book I read three times in fifth grade. Maybe there are adventures to be had here, maybe this won't be so bad after all.

Debbie hoists herself into the front passenger seat and Ron slides open the van's side panel and heaves my suitcases inside before signaling me to get in. I bend my head to enter and stop short: There are no seats behind the front bench, just a metal floor. It's a cargo van. I turn to look at Ron.

"Should be a mat back there somewhere," he says. "Be about two hours, so try and make yourself comfortable."

I crawl in and the door clanks shut behind me. Ron walks around the van and climbs into the driver's seat, pausing to roll down his window before starting the ignition. There's enough space on the front bench for a third person, yet I am cargo. I can't find the mat, so I perch on a suitcase.

"Alrighty, here we go!" Debbie chirps, running chubby fingers through her cropped brown hair.

As we rattle down the dirt road leaving the airport, I clutch the window ledge with my fingertips and peer through the dusty glass at the Dominican Republic. Images blaze in the van's headlights then disappear. Clapboard shanties gussied up in jewel colors, pink, purple, green. Solitary figures with baskets and bundles of sticks on their heads who turn to regard our passage with blank faces. Ash-colored cows with enormous humps on their shoulders and turkey wattles under their necks. Everything strange and other-worldly. And everywhere the sweet stench of smoke and rot and vegetation.

We speed up when the road turns concrete and curves along the ocean. The van's rattling is replaced by the low thrum of the tires gripping asphalt, and the air thickens with the briny smell of the ocean. I gaze at a giant moonbeam rippling over the water, and for the first time since my arrival, think of David.

"So, when can I see my brother?" I ask.

My question hangs in the sweaty air like a large object. An object that is ignored and grows dim and shrinks and is finally sucked out the window into the rushing night. I clear my throat to repeat the question, louder this time, when Debbie speaks.

"He asked to wait up for you, but I told him no," she says, her rah-rah voice gone.

"How come?" I ask. "I haven't seen him in months!"

"Because it's the rules," she says flatly.

I start to protest, but she lifts a hand to the dashboard and shoves a tape into the cassette player, and Sandi Patti's "Lord Oh

Lord, How Majestic Is Thy Name" bursts from the speakers and ricochets off the van's metal walls. It's the same tape Mother used to play to block us out in her van.

I shove my suitcase perch into a back corner, away from the synthesized organ music and these strangers who now control my life. Plugging my ears, I scowl out the rear window.

After jail, the judge sent me to a children's home until my parents completed the paperwork for Escuela Caribe.

I got my first square meals in weeks at the home, but also had to do chores and participate in activities with the other kids, all of whom were much younger than me. I avoided them as much as possible until the social workers came around and forced us to participate in humiliating activities like finger painting or charades.

Then, I went home to pack. My parents were chilly to me, but Rejoice Radio played so loudly during supper that we didn't have to talk. Afterward, I listened to WAZY for hours and hours in my room, trying to memorize the words to the songs, knowing that it would be a long time before I could listen to secular music again.

Scott showed up at the airport with a promise ring. He'd become protective of me after I left home; just as my feelings for him iced over, his flared up. As I walked down the tube to the airplane, he lurched after me, begging me to run away with him.

"Run away to what?" I asked.

He couldn't come up with an answer before a security guard came and escorted him away.

I wake when the van bangs over a pothole and I'm chucked against the metal siding. Sandi Patti is still wailing for Jesus on the tape player, but the air pouring through the windows is cooler now, fresher. I climb back onto the suitcase and look outside. We drive down a dirt road flanked by pine trees, and then the pine trees end and the road winds through pastures dotted with the deformed ash-colored cows.

A sign spelling out JARABACOA in white reflectors appears in the headlights and I tilt my watch to the moonlight; it's a little after two. A dim streetlamp appears at the side of the road, and then another, and then comes a row of shanties. As we drive through the tight streets of the dark village, a pack of dogs lopes silently behind us, herding us toward our destination. They stop when we forge a shallow stream crossing the road. The van tilts up a hill and bushes rake the side paneling as vegetation closes in on us.

"We're here," Ron calls over the music when a metal gate looms abruptly before us. He taps the horn twice, and it swings open. A Dominican with a long knife hanging from his belt and a German shepherd at his side salutes us as we drive through the gate, then closes it behind us.

Just inside, two buildings—long and low like cement chicken coops—face each other across a courtyard, and Ron pulls up to them and cuts the engine. Sandi Patti finally shuts up.

"You'll stay here tonight," Debbie says, switching on a flashlight and dancing it over the buildings. "Tomorrow you'll move into your home."

Home. Group home, she means. Ron opens the side panel, grabs a suitcase, and carries it toward the buildings, and I stumble out on cramped legs.

The school is built on a steep hillside surrounded by a barbed wire fence. Far below lays a dark valley, and above us are four small buildings, the residences. Three for boys, one for girls, David wrote.

"Let's go, it's late," Debbie says, wagging the flashlight at me. I jerk my suitcase from the van and tug it over the gravel, following her across the brick courtyard to a small room at the far end of the first building. I set my suitcase next to the one Ron brought in. There's a cot shoved against the far wall, but no other furniture. Debbie unhooks a flashlight from the wall and hands it to me.

"No lights?" I ask.

"Nope," Debbie says. "No electricity. We're pretty much isolated out here. Pretty much alone."

No electricity. That means no TV. No radio. No VCR. No ColecoVision. No hair dryer or curling iron. Why didn't David mention any of this? These things are important! I shine my flashlight on a large green bug crawling up the wall over the cot.

"Ron't worry, those ones don't bite," Debbie says.

I turn to her.

"When do I get to see David?" I ask again, because I really need him to explain some things to me.

"We'll discuss that in the morning, along with everything else," she says curtly, turning to leave. "The bathroom's two doors down. I'll be by to wake you at seven o'clock sharp."

I wait until her footsteps fade before stepping outside; the moon has set and the sky glitters with billions of stars. A breeze shuffles through the palm trees at the edge of the courtyard—*shh shh shh*—and foreign noises come from the jungle on the other side of the barbed wire. *Birds? Animals? People?* I contemplate the residences on the hill and wonder which one holds my brother.

A sick squalling prods me toward consciousness at dawn, and it takes me a second to recognize the crow of roosters. In the next second, I remember where I am. *Reform school*. I squint at my watch in the gray light that leaks through a small window above the cot. 5:20. Before the roosters started croaking, I was dreaming about swimming in the Harrison pool. I was naked and alone in the warm turquoise water, my hair streaming over my shoulders, happy. Then Jerome walked naked out of the boys' locker room and dove into the water and the pool turned into a murky ocean. I thrashed through the cold waves in a panic, searching for the shoreline, waiting for his hand to tug me under.

My heart is still pounding as I grab my jean jacket off the cement floor and wad it under my head as a pillow. Sometime in the dark, the deadbolt slid shut on the door, locking me in. Where could I have run?

I drift in and out of sleep until the deadbolt slides back and the door swings open. "Time to begin," Debbie says, her wide form filling the doorframe. "Meet me in the courtyard in five minutes sharp."

After she pulls the door shut, I jump from the bed and salute her, *Heil Hitler!* before tugging on my clothes. I take the safari hat I bought at Tippecanoe Mall last week from my suitcase. The jungle look was in, and I was going to the jungle, so I bought it. I jam it on my head and walk out the door. Let the adventure begin.

Outside, the sky shimmers like blue cellophane. Underneath, everything's green. The valley below is combed into orderly rows of plants and water, which I recognize from *National Geographic* as rice paddies.

I walk past picnic tables that I didn't notice last night to the bathroom. These picnic tables are made of real wood, they're not the plastic jail kind. Maybe that's a good sign. Debbie sits at one of them with her back to me, shuffling through sheets of paper.

The bathroom reeked last night and reeks again this morning and now I find out why. Next to the toilet is a wastebasket brimming with wadded-up toilet paper, some of it smeared brown. A sign is taped to the side of the stall: Do NOT put ANYTHING but human waste in the toilet, it will CLOG!

I hold my nose as I pee, then add my dirty paper to the pile. At the sink, I twist the hot water handle all the way open, but the water stays cold. No electricity, no hot water, broken toilets. With our parents shelling out $4,000 a month to keep us both down here, I'd expect the baby-sitting service to be a little better.

I lean into the mirror over the sink and cake foundation onto a ripening cluster of zits on my forehead, then sweep electric blue mascara over my eyelashes. There, my mask is on, and I'm ready to make my debut at this new school: *Party Impression, Take Two*. Maybe I'll have better luck here than at Harrison. I think fondly of the Comfort still hidden in my closet. I wish I had some now.

"Go wash that stuff off your face," Debbie says when I sit across from her. "Makeup is a privilege you have not earned."

My mouth flops open at the thought of my blistering forehead. Privilege? No, makeup is a necessity. But something tells me not to press the issue and I bite my lip and shuffle back to the bathroom.

I'll play the reform school game, just like I played the jail game and the children's home game and the family game. And when I'm eighteen, I'll stop playing games and start living for real.

Debbie slides a fat binder printed with the school's logo toward me when I return to the table. "Escuela Caribe Rules & Regulations" it says on the front.

"Read this carefully," she says. I open it.

General Rules updated 3/85

The student will not abuse alcohol, tobacco or any other drug at Escuela Caribe, nor will they engage in unfitting corporal contact.

The student will not discuss negative (check) subjects such as rock music, alcohol sex, drugs, etc. Exceptions may be made for staff-led therapeutic discussions.

The student will comply, immediately and willingly, with all rules and staff orders.

The Authority Problem will be addressed. "The rod and reproof give wisdom but a child who gets his own way brings shame to his mother." (Proverbs 29:15) The student must be willing to accept this form of discipline.

Rod and reproof?! What, are they going spank me if I say "Duran Duran"? Why didn't David mention any of this? I glare at Debbie, who's leafing through a pile of papers. On closer inspection, I recognize my last report card from Harrison (C–/D+ average) and a letter in my mother's loopy handwriting. I squint at the up-side-down sentences and make out the words "boyfriend," "rebel-lion" and "condoms." They must have found the stash of condoms under my bed; in my rush to leave after Scott got caught descend-ing the trellis, I'd forgotten to take them with me.

In her hands, Debbie holds the results of my last Pap smear. She looks up and I lower my eyes to the binder.

A Dominican woman in an apron emerges from a doorway on the side of the courtyard carrying a tray with coffee cups, or-ange wedges and toast. She sets the tray on the table without looking at either of us, turns, and walks away.

As we eat, I pretend to read the rules and steal glances up the hill, looking back down whenever Debbie lifts her head to sip at her coffee. A small figure with a ponytail walks onto the patio of the middle building with a mop and pail. That must be the girls' home. Which one is David's? Debbie burps, and I continue read-ing, my alarm growing.

Rank System:
The Student will begin The Program on Level 0 and work his way up to Level 5.
Level 0
Must be watched at all times

Must ask to move
Must ask to sit
Must ask to stand
Must ask to eat
Must not communicate with members of the opposite sex or other
zero-rankers
Level 0 carries no privileges—no makeup, jewelry or house pops.

I grunt in disbelief. Ask to sit down? To begin eating? This has
got to be a joke.

Requirements for Level 1.
memorize Matt. 5:1–1
memorize Isaiah 53:1–6
memorize Titus 2:11–14
memorize names of New Testament Books
3 minutes of leg lifts
15 sit-ups
15 push-ups
15 suicides (squat thrusts)

Titus? Suicides?

Ron walks over to the picnic table holding a crossword puzzle book.

"Hey Debbie, how do you spell independence? Does 'dence'
have an 'e' in it like in 'fence' or an 'a' like in . . . like in . . ."

I look up at him and he gulps and looks stricken.

"Like in 'dance?'" I suggest.

Debbie shoots me a cool look.

"It's spelled with an 'a,' like in . . . in . . . 'pants,'" she says.

"Thanks," Ron mutters before rushing away.

Debbie turns to me.

"Finished?"

I haven't reached the third page, but nod anyway. She reaches
over to shut the binder and drag it back to her side of the table,
then she smiles her gap-toothed smile and leans forward.

"Basically, this is what happens: everything you think, do and say will be scrutinized to measure your progress in The Program. We keep Escuela small, about the same number of staff and students, so we can keep a good eye on everyone."

She picks up her coffee mug without taking her eyes off mine and raises it to her mouth, slurping at it as I hold her gaze and struggle to make my face blank and unimpressed. *You can't scare me.*

"You earn points for attitude, academics and good old hard work."

She glances down at my mother's letter.

"And in your case, it sounds like you need some major improvement in your personal relationship with Jesus Christ as well. Any questions?"

I shake my head numbly and look up the hill.

"David will be down shortly," Debbie says. "You'll have ten minutes to catch up, and then you're not allowed to communicate with him again until you reach Second Level. And I mean no communication—no smiling, no gesturing, nothing. You'll have to pretend he doesn't exist."

My mouth drops open.

"Are you serious?"

"Very."

"How come?!" I spit the words out, grabbing my coffee mug with both hands and squeezing.

"Because it's the rules. You read them. No communication with boys until Level Two—that's about a month if you perform well."

"But David's not a boy, he's my brother!"

She inhales deeply, as if mustering up a great patience.

"To succeed in The Program, you must trust our authority," she says slowly. "Just as Jesus requires blind faith from His

believers, we require blind faith from our students. We are here
to help you. To save you."

This woman is out of her mind. This place is out of its mind. I
thought it would be like *Facts of Life,* only set on a Caribbean island. I expected a pleasantly cranky Mrs. Garrett, not a mean,
cranky Debbie. I scowl down at the unfinished surface of the picnic table. The boards are pocked with termite holes, and someone has carved HEL into one of the boards. *Help? Hell?*

We sit in silence, Debbie scanning my face, me glaring at the
table. No doubt she's trying to scrutinize my thoughts at this
very moment. *Scrutinize this, barf bag: Screw you.*

A bird squawks overhead, and I lift my head to watch it soar
blue and red up the hill before noticing the line of people wind-
ing single file down the cement drive connecting the school to
the residences. Boys. All dressed in jeans and short sleeves, all
white except for a figure slouching at the back. David. My pulse
quickens; I've never been happier to see anyone in my life.

While Debbie scribbles into a notepad with one hand shielding
her words, I impatiently watch the boys snake downhill. When
they finally reach the courtyard, I stand and wave my arms.

"David! Over here!"

A grin spreads over his face, and he jogs toward me in a
purple T-shirt emblazoned with "God Rules!" on the front.

"Hey you!" He tenses his biceps and I punch his arm, and he
grimaces as if it hurt, and I punch him again.

"So what took you so long to get here?" he asks.

I shrug.

"Been busy."

He has white tape wrapped around the nosepiece of his athletic glasses like a nerd. Even so, he's a welcome sight. Debbie
gathers her papers and walks over to the boys, who are standing
outside a door at the far end of the courtyard, staring at us.

"I can't believe you're actually here," he says, still grinning.

"Me neither."

We sit across the table from each other for several moments, grinning and shaking our heads. Here we are, me and David, in the *Dominican Republic! A* warm piney breeze puffs over us, and at the top of the hill, a flock of lime green birds flutters onto the jungle canopy. This would be prime exploration territory if we weren't caged in by barbed wire.

The boys file into the room as a group of girls arrives. My housemates. I stiffen as they all turn to look at us.

"I'm missing the morning prayer meeting because of you," David laughs. He looks thinner than I remember, and he's got dark circles under his eyes. I guess he didn't sleep too well, either. The deadbolt, Titus, and "rod and reproof" come to mind.

"What is this place?" I ask, squinting across the table at him in the high tropical light.

He pushes his glasses up his nose.

"What do you mean?"

"How come you never told me what it was really like?" As I talk, my anger swells. "Do you know I had to get special permission to talk to you just now? And that after this, that fat lady says we can't communicate?"

"Shh!" He presses a finger to his lips and glances around, a deep crease etched into his forehead.

"Well?" I ask, glancing at my watch. "We've only got, like, eight minutes left."

He leans forward.

"I *couldn't* tell you—they read the mail," he says in a low rush. "If you write anything negative about The Program, they dock your points and throw away the letter."

I look around at the now empty patio, the residences on the hill, the barbed wire circling everything.

"What is this place?" I repeat.

Footsteps slap across the courtyard and I turn to see a tall man in a blue windbreaker walking over to us. He halts at the end of the table and regards me.

"I'm Ted Schlund, the Dean of Students," he says.

He doesn't offer his hand.

"I'm Julia, David's sister."

"I know who you are," he says, lifting his eyebrows. "I know *all* about you."

He cuffs me playfully on the shoulder with a large hand before wheeling around and marching toward the prayer hall. David watches him go with flared nostrils.

"Okay, this place is really starting to creep me out," I say, adopting David's quiet voice.

"Ted's bad news," he says. "Stay away from him."

"Great. Got any other helpful hints?"

A muffled piano strikes up a hymn, accompanied a moment later by the mutter of singing.

> *Blessed assurance, Jesus is mine*
> *O what a foretaste of glory divine!*

David looks behind him, then leans forward again.

"First off, don't trust *anyone* down here . . . except your lovable little brother, of course." A smile flits over his face and I narrow my eyes at him.

"Seriously," he says. "Everyone wants to get out of here as bad as you do. The place is full of narks and cheats and backstabbers. Best thing you can do is keep your head down and don't make a fuss."

His flippancy—to use one of Mother's favorite words—is unbelievable.

"But it's your fault I'm down here!" I say loudly, not caring who hears me. "You got me into this! That whole bit about 'keeping the family together'? I think you just wanted company. I could be an emancipated minor right now! Do you know what that means? Free!"

"Free to do what? Flunk out of high school and be a busgirl for the rest of your life?"

We glower at each other and the hymn swells between us.

> *Perfect submission, all is at rest*
> *I in my Savior am happy and blest . . .*

He's right, of course. That is where I was heading. An image of me as a shriveled-up old woman in a busgirl uniform flashes into my mind. The music ends and a man's deep voice holds forth, his words not quite loud enough to be clear. I glance at my watch—three minutes left. If we can't talk for a month, I don't want our last conversation to end so harshly.

"So, what happened to you?" I ask him, sweeping my eyes over his "God Rules!" T-shirt and taped glasses.

"Broke them playing dodgeball."

"And this?" I reach across the table to grab his sleeve. "They turn you into some kind of Jesus freak on me or something?"

He looks down at his chest and shrugs.

"I got it for Third Level. This and a Study Bible."

"How nice. Did they give you a sucker, too?"

David rolls his eyes and laughs. The Dominican guard walks through the courtyard with his sword and German shepherd, whistling. He nods curtly at us and David nods back. The dog sniffs at something under a picnic table and the guard yanks on the leash, knocking its head against a bench.

"So, does he use that sword to chop kids up if they try and escape?"

"It's called a machete, dufus," he snorts. "And he's here to keep the Dominicans out."

". . . and the Americans in."

He shakes his head and grabs my wrist, twisting it around to look at my watch. The old-man worry line crimps his forehead again, and I start to wonder whether this is a permanent blemish on his seventeen-year-old face. He looks up at me.

"So, did they say when I'm coming home?"

"I don't know, ask them," I tell him, as I did in all my letters.

"But they won't tell me."

His brown eyes beg for good news, for hope, and I think back to the boys' dark basement room, emptied and reeking of Lysol.

"I dunno . . . they might have said something about the end of the year," I lie, pressing my thumbnail into H of the HEL knifed into the table.

He breathes in sharply, as if he'd been holding his breath underwater for a long time and just broke the surface for air. His smile is one of pure, unfiltered joy.

"Maybe we'll both be home for Christmas!" he says.

Christmas. That's more than six months away. I plan to be out of here long before that.

"Maybe, but now that I'm down here, you have to stay with me, you hear?" I say. "No leaving me here alone."

He smirks and is about to say something when the prayer room door bursts open and kids pour out; he lifts his head to watch them disappear into rooms on either side of the courtroom. I ignore the commotion, my eyes still trained on David's face. *Say it. You won't abandon me.*

"You two have a nice chat?"

Debbie looms over us with a Bible tucked in her armpit, her loose dimpled flesh spreading over the cover under her short sleeve.

"David, time for class. Julia, let's get you moved into Starr."

"Yes," David says, as I look down at the HEL in the table. *Go away. Leave us alone.*

David stands and walks to my side of the table. I grab his thin wrist in my hand.

"Guess I'll be talking at you later, then, bro," I say. The crease reappears on his forehead, and I don't want to let him go.

"Take care," he says. "And remember not to . . . don't . . ." He looks at Debbie, then at the ground, shaking his head.

"I know," I say, squeezing his wrist.

I watch him cross the courtyard with stooped shoulders and walk into a dark room, before turning to follow Debbie.

The van Debbie drives to take me to the girls' home is a passenger van, also marked with the school's New Horizons logo. When I open the side panel, prepared to crawl in after my luggage, it's got four benches.

Debbie offers no explanation, and I realize, as I sit behind her and fume, that making new students ride for two hours in the back of a cargo van over potholed roads must be part of the "psychological disorientation" tactics mentioned in the school brochure.

STARR is painted on the side of the girls' residence, a yellow box with a corrugated lid that crouches between the two boys' homes on the hillside. All three buildings are simply more elaborate versions of the shanties we passed last night.

When we pull into Starr's driveway, I drag my luggage over a flagstone patio and through a sliding glass door into a room crowded with furniture. Half the room contains a long dining room table surrounded by wooden chairs; the other half contains iron patio furniture with no cushions. The walls, painted a flamingo pink, clash nauseatingly with the orange-and-green tile floor.

Despite the crammed space, the room gleams with order and sterility. The sliding windows that open onto a small deck overlooking the valley are invisible but for a blaze of sunlight on the glass. The dining room chairs are precisely spaced along the table, and there is not a plant, book or personal effect in sight. There is no sign of life whatsoever.

It reminds me of the time our parents took David and me to the Model Home Show in Indianapolis. The "homes" were double-wide trailers parked in a stadium parking lot: The Kitchen trailer, The Bedroom trailer, The Bathroom trailer. Each space was reduced to its basic function: Here you cook, here you sleep, here you shit.

I survey Starr's sterile Dining room-Living room. Here you do time.

"The house parents are Bruce and RuthAnn McMillan and they come to us from Canada," Debbie says. "You'll meet them later; they're in staff Bible study now."

She gives me a quick tour of the building. An archway at the far end of the dining/living room leads to the kitchen, which is also eerily immaculate—no crumbs on the counters, no plates in the sink, no grease on the stove. Each jar in the spice rack precisely spaced, dust-free, with the label facing forward.

"Looks real clean," I say.

"Cleanliness is next to godliness," Debbie says.

"So they say," I mutter.

She points to a closed door off the kitchen. "That's the house parents' quarters. You're not allowed in there."

Out back, there's a small patio strung with clotheslines. On one wall, a row of brooms hangs over dustpans. On another, mops over buckets, and the strands of the mop heads are spike-straight, as if they'd been hot-picked.

"A Dominican washes the clothes, but you must wash your own underwear if you soil it with menstrual blood," Debbie says.

She leads me up a short staircase to a dark room. Light seeps weakly through a tiny widow at the back and from the crack be-tween the slanted wave of the metal roof and the cement wall. Debbie turns to a tall tank beside the doorway and fiddles with a knob at the top; the tank begins to hiss and a faint whiff of rotten eggs fills the air. She strikes a match, and *whoomph,* a fist of or-ange fire explodes atop the tank then shrinks to a stubby flame.

The bobbing light reveals a room crammed with bunk beds. Clothes hang from a pole suspended horizontally down the mid-dle of the room. Here again, order reigns supreme: Sheets are snapped tightly over thin mattresses, blouses are buttoned and centered on their hangers, shoes aligned beneath the pole, laces tucked in.

My bunk is in a corner. Debbie points at the top mattress, a three-inch-thick piece of foam resting on wood slats. Space has been cleared for me along the pole and in the bottom half of one of the rickety dressers that separating the bunk beds.

She excuses herself to use the toilet and I start to unpack, stuffing my clothes into the drawers.

"Not like that," she says when she returns. She grabs a pair of my panties and kneels beside the bottom bunk, motioning for me to join her on the floor. I do.

"Watch carefully," she says. She folds the panty crotch to the waistband, left side to center, then right side to center, reducing it to a small white envelope, then holds it up for me to admire.

"There's a right way and a wrong way to do everything in The Program," she says. "Even folding panties."

I look at her with raised eyebrows and you've-got-to-be-kidding smirk, but she's not. Her face is dead serious.

The lesson continues. Socks must be rolled into tight balls, bra cups fitted together with the straps tucked underneath, jeans doubled butt cheek to butt cheek, then folded in thirds, every crease perfectly aligned. Every button must be buttoned, every zipper zipped. These things are important, she tells me. My success in The Program depends on them.

I bend over the polished floor, folding and refolding a pair of panties, and each time Debbie tells me I'm doing it wrong. After several minutes, she shakes her head and stands.

"You can finish that later. They're waiting for you at school."

+   +   +

We vowed to marry so we could live together forever. In the tree-strained sunlight of the basement playroom, we mapped out our lives. We'd live on the beach, eat nothing but ice cream sandwiches and own dogs. Lots of dogs.

They called our plans ridiculous, of course. We couldn't marry, they said, despite the fact that we weren't really brother and sister.

So we decided to become real family, blood brother and sister.

We held the ceremony in the early spring of 1976, in the woods behind our house, under a canopy flecked with dogwood blossoms. Snow still lingered at the bases of the trees, and the shooting star flowers had just begun to push their pointed lavender heads through the rotting leaves.

We sat side by side on a fallen sugar maple tree and David unfolded his hand to show me the blue thimble-headed tack he'd taken from Mother's missionary bulletin board. Blue, his favorite color.

"Are you ready?" he asked.

I nodded and squeezed my eyes shut, holding out my hand. The tack bit sharp and quick, and I opened my eyes to see a red bead welling on the tip of my thumb.

A bell clanged in the distance; Mother calling us to supper.

"Hurry," he said.

But I couldn't bring myself to prick David; I didn't want to hurt him. Finally he had me hold the tack skyward and he pushed his thumb onto it.

Afterward, we pressed our thumbs together, black and white, until our blood ran out the side.

"Now we have the same blood," David said, beaming.

"Now they can't say we're not real," I said, smiling back.

The evening wind stirred, and dogwood petals drifted down on us like blessings.

Uphill, the bell pealed impatiently.

CHAPTER 10

THE PROGRAM

Debbie points at a door in the middle of the courtyard. Economics, she says.

"Your parents signed you up for college prep. They have high hopes for you, and I'm sure you won't disappoint them again."

I approach the door with my backpack clamped against my chest and my heart booming. This is it. *Party Impression, Take Two.* Debbie stands behind me and watches as I knock.

"Hello!" a male voice calls from inside the room. I remove my safari hat, fluff my hair, and paste on my Farrah smile before turning the doorknob.

Seven students sit in a single row at the front of the room as the teacher—a short, thick man—bangs out a list of words on the chalkboard.

I slip into an empty chair desk next to a girl with a blond bob. She's cute in an upturned-nose, cheerleader type of way, and I wonder what got her sent down here. I train my Farrah smile on her, but she rolls her eyes and looks away.

Maybe she has a personality disorder, I think, pulling a notebook and pencil from my backpack. The teacher straightens and slaps chalk dust from his hands. He peers at me through large glasses.

"Excuse me, aren't you forgetting something?" he asks.

"Sorry, I didn't want to interrupt you," I say with a carefree laugh. "I'm Julia Scheeres."

Someone snickers.

"Did you ask for permission to enter this room?" he asks.

I stare at him in disbelief as he rubs his jaw with his hand and looks at me with mock confusion.

Must ask to move
Must ask to sit
Must ask to stand
Must ask to eat

This is really happening. Fine. Play the game.

I stand and start toward the door, but the sound of tongue-clucking stops me short.

"Did you ask permission to stand?"

I walk back to the chair and sit down, but the tongue-clucking continues.

"Did you ask permission to sit?"

The cheerleader smirks and my cheeks burn. I dig my fingernails into the palms of my hands.

"Can I get up, please?"

"Can you speak proper English?" the teacher asks, prompting more snickers.

"May I get up, please?"

"Yes, you may."

"May I walk to the door, please?"

"Yes, you may."

"May I go out the door, please?"

"Yes, you may."

"May I come in the room, please?"

"Yes, you may."

"May I walk to the desk, please?"

"Yes, you may."

"May I sit down, please?"

It's a nightmarish game of "Mother May I?" By the time I'm again seated, I've cut four bloody crescents into the palm of each hand.

The teacher picks up a notepad from his desk and jots something into it, then noisily crosses out what he's written and walks over to me, bending until his face is level with mine.

"I'll give you a break today because it's your first day," he says. "But from now on, you give me attitude, and you'll pay for it. Do you understand?"

I nod, unable to speak.

He cups a hand behind his ear.

"Yes, sir," I say in a weak voice.

My pencil shakes violently as I copy the vocabulary list off the chalkboard into my notebook: *Unlimited wants, limited means, correcting for externalities, adaptive expectations, absolute advantage.*

When the noon whistle sounds, the other students bolt from Remedial Math and the game of "Mother May I?" starts in earnest. The math teacher gives me permission to stand and walk to the door, but disappears into the mass of bodies crowding the picnic tables before I can ask her to enter the courtyard.

There's another zero ranker across the courtyard from me, a boy. He's as scrawny as a plucked chicken and looks to be about thirteen—a mere kid. He hangs from a doorway in a yellow T-shirt, braying at the staff table.

"May I enter the courtyard, please?"

They ignore him. Apparently he isn't demonstrating proper Courtesy and Respect Towards Authority Figures, one of the categories on the daily scorecard Debbie showed me, along with Attitude, Cooperation, and Being Totally Truthful and Honest, Facing Reality. We get points for all of them.

After braying his request four more times, Boy 0 hammers the doorframe with his child's fist, muttering cuss words only I can hear. He catches me staring and squinches his face at me; I look away.

Unlike him, I refuse to call out. I won't ask permission to sit, stand, walk, to *exist,* one more time. I simply won't. I'll stand in this doorway like a statue until the world ends around me.

"I said! Please, may I please enter the courtyard, please!" Boy 0 bellows again, his voice growing thinner and higher with each word.

At the picnic tables, there is no pause in the eating activity; no one even glances in his direction. I regard the chewing faces, the glaring sky, a three-inch, half-smashed cockroach that drags itself over the bricks to my sneakers. I kick it away and it lands on its back next to a cement bench, where it mechanically probes the air with its good legs. After several minutes, it bumps against up the bench and manages to flip itself over.

The next time it lugs itself to my feet, I press the toe of my tennis shoe onto the working half of its body. It pops, and a yellow pus squirts out.

A hot wind races through the courtyard and I take off my safari hat and fan my face with it. In the valley below, the sun glints off the rice paddies. Some of the kids cast their eyes in my direction as I fan myself, but mostly they just stare at their plates and chew. None of them talks much.

A large parrot lands in a palm tree next to the picnic tables, where it screeches down as if it found the presence of humans on this hillside offensive. At my feet, a line of ants streams toward the cockroach's glistening innards.

I contemplate the hazy green horizon and wonder which way is home. Not that I have one anymore. At this very moment, Mother is probably in my bedroom, erasing the stain of my existence with rubber gloves and hot bleach, just like she did after David and Jerome left. "Our children are gone," I imagine her writing to her missionaries. "Now it's just Jake and me and our dedication to God."

Across from me, Boy 0 has sunk to the bottom of the doorframe, where he hunches over, chewing the side of his hand and glaring at the picnic tables.

The Dominican woman from this morning shuffles into the courtyard carrying a glass pitcher of red liquid. Strawberry pop? Cherry juice? Raspberry? She refills glasses at the staff table and ice cubes tumble from the pitcher along with the sparkling red cascade. I swallow dryly. The staff are the only ones demonstrating proper behavior at this picnic, chatting and laughing as if this were a church social and not some hell devised for teenagers.

At my feet, the ants have swarmed over the cockroach. I'm about to crush them as well when a body rises from a far table and turns in my direction. David. We stare at each other for a sour second before he walks to the staff table and bends to talk to someone I can't see. A moment later, Debbie is marching toward me, a napkin tucked into the collar of her blouse like a bib. Boy 0 jumps to his feet.

"Debbie! Over here, Debbie, over here!" he yells. She pays him no mind, and comes to a halt before me, her left sandal

falling squarely on the insect sacrifice. She swallows before
speaking.

"Yes, Julia?"

I clear my throat, look down at her sandal, and croak out the
words. "May I enter the patio, please?"

"Yes, you may."

She follows me to the girls' table, where I stand behind the
sole empty place setting.

"May I sit down, please?"

"Yes."

"May I begin eating, please?"

"Yes."

There are five girls at the table, all about my age. No one says
hello or looks at me, but I'm not much for pleasantries at the
moment anyway. The cheerleader sits across from me; she gazes
at a space just over my hat, nibbling the sandwich she holds in
both hands.

There's orange liquid in a cup by my paper plate and a basket
with bread in it at the far end of the table.

"Will someone pass me the food, please?" I ask.

When the basket reaches me, it contains the smashed remains of half a sandwich—egg spilling from white bread. It
looks like someone punched it; I can see the knuckle marks
clearly. I glance around.

"Are there any more of these?"

"Nope," says the cheerleader, still gazing over my head. She
looks like the girl in the Sea Breeze commercial, all clear skin
and white teeth perfection, and this makes me hate her all the
more.

I shove the basket away and take a drink of Tang.

"They'll dock your points if you don't eat it," says the girl sitting next to the cheerleader. She's wearing a pink T-shirt with

"Praise Jesus!" on the front, and is shredding a napkin and watching the pieces fall like snowflakes onto her plate.

"But it's been smashed!"

She shrugs and a small smile flashes over her face and I realize that my food was ruined on purpose, for their entertainment.

The girl sitting next to me pushes an orange wedge toward my plate.

"You can eat this if you so desire," she says in a soft Southern twang. She lifts her sorrowful brown eyes to mine. "Being as I'm not all that hungry anyway."

"Susan, you know you're not supposed to . . ." the cheerleader says before lifting her head and breaking into a smile-for-the-camera grin. Hands clamp down on my shoulders, and I jump and turn around. A bearded man with a protruding belly stands behind me.

"Howdy, I'm Bruce, the Starr housefather," the man says, his hands still on my shoulders. "How are you liking Escuela so far, eh?"

Oh yeah, he's Canadian.

"Everything's great," I respond, knowing this is the only acceptable answer.

"That's what we like to hear!"

He digs his fingers into my shoulders in a painful massage, and I arch my back away from his belly.

"Everyone been properly introduced?" "Been" he pronounces like "bean."

"We were just getting acquainted," says a girl with bad acne at the end of the table. She waves at me, and a rainbow of jelly bracelets ripples down her arm. "Hi, I'm Carrie, Starr high ranker."

The girls go round the table stating their name and rank and how long they've been in The Program. The cheerleader's name is Tiffany (of course), and the sorrowful girl sitting next to me is Susan; she was the lowest-ranking girl before my arrival. They've all been here under eight months, except for Carrie, who's been here two years. (*Two years!*)

"If you need anything, please don't hesitate to ask," Tiffany gushes with her fake smile. I glare at her.

Bruce bounces on his toes and his belly jostles my spine.

"Okay, we'll see you up at the house," he says. His footsteps recede, then return, and my hat is lifted from my head.

"Nice topper!"

I turn to see him yanking my new safari hat over his thick curls; he bends the brim over one eye and juts out his hip like a fashion model. All the girls laugh politely except for Susan, who looks at me with her sorrowful eyes. Bruce struts back to the staff table swaying his hips like a faggot, my hat crunched on his head.

I glance at my watch—it's 12:26, four minutes to the next class—and stuff the sandwich into my mouth, trying not to gag on the snotty texture.

A teacher blows a whistle, and kids stream across the courtyard into the classrooms. Alone at the picnic table, I search for an adult who will notice me and grant me permission to move, but none of them pay attention to me. My eyes fall on Boy 0, who's slumped at the bottom of his doorway, rocking and raking his fingernails over the bare flesh of his forearm, over and over.

There's a soft tap on my back, and I turn. It's Susan. She brushes back my hair with her hand and bends to whisper in my ear: "This place is Hell."

I see David several times in the courtyard between classes, and because we're not allowed to communicate, we just stare at each other. All I can do is drink in the concern stamped on his face, which makes me feel a little bit better and a little bit worse.

When I need to use the toilet, the English teacher follows me to the bathroom and stands on the other side of the stall, tapping her sandal on the cement floor as I piss. They must fear that given half a chance, newcomers will either make a break for it or bash their heads against a wall. Both options have crossed my mind.

During the last class of the day, P.E., we play soccer on a flattish part of the hillside next to the entrance gate. As we run over the curved field, the Dominican guard sits in the shade of an enormous banyan tree near the gate, mopping his face with a rag as the German shepherd pants at his feet.

My jeans are pasted to my legs with sweat and it's hard to move. There are far too many players on the field and no way to get near the ball. After a while, I stop running and let the game swarm past me. I look around for Boy 0 but don't see him.

David throws me stern glances as he sprints by me, trying to get me moving, but the whole setup is too retarded. Everyone claps whenever a goal is made, no matter which team makes it, and when the ball lands in a thicket, everyone jogs in place or does jumping jacks while it's fished out. What's *wrong* with these kids? The object of the game doesn't appear to be winning, but to "be a good sport" and to stay in perpetual motion. The P.E. teacher—a tall man in shorts—frowns at me and scribbles in one of those notepads all the staffers carry around with them, along with the referee whistles that dangle from their necks. No doubt he's scrutinizing my performance. What bull crap. David pleads at me with his eyes, but I shake my head at him. Am I the only one who realizes how asinine this all is?

At the end of the hour, the P.E. teacher blows his whistle one last time and we sort ourselves by house and rank and trudge up the steep cement drive to our residences. I lag behind my house-mates, stopping several times to catch my breath.

"You'd best not be poky," Susan tells me, but I can't help it, I'm out of shape. Six months of junk food and little exercise have taken their toll.

At Starr, the after-school hours are chopped into Housework Time, Supper Time, Homework Time, Free Time, Bed Time. Too much Time.

My housework consists of "mowing" the grass around Starr with a machete, Becky, the Starr Group Leader, tells me.

Becky's from Rhode Island, pencil thin, and a recent gradu-ate of some junior college in the East. She talks even queerer than the Canadian housefather, and she's an American. She tells me that she lives in a locked room next to the upstairs dormi-tory, and that it's her job to watch me in the bathroom.

She gives me a quick lesson on how to use the machete, squatting on the ground with the handle of the machete in one hand and the tops of the weeds in the other.

"Pretend you're scalping the earth, Juliar," she says, swiping the sharp blade against the base of the grass.

But I have nothing against the earth, only against certain people treading its surface. When Becky hands me the machete, I try to think of someone I'd like to scalp, but there are too many of them—my mind skips from Jerome, to my parents, to the cop who arrested me, to the social workers, to the Eco-nomics teacher, to the cheerleader, to the housefather—before settling on a generic anger at the world in general. I chop the grass-hair with such vehemence that Becky compliments me on my skill.

As I weed whack, she stands behind me and tells me how she came to Escuela Caribe.

"Juliar, I was driving my *cah* home from a church *potty,* when I had the idea*r* that Gawd was *cahlling* me," she says, fanning herself with a straw hat. "On that *dawk* road, Gawd *tawked* to me, just as He did to Paul on the road to Damascus. He told me to come *heah* to *minista* to the girls and precious unborn babies."

I want to ask her if she drank booze at this potty and if Gawd's voice sounded like it does in movies, as if it were booming down from a megaphone in the sky. And what do unborn babies have to do with reform school?

But I know it's better to keep my thoughts to myself, so I bite my lip and hack grass. After a while, Becky goes to lean against the shady wall of the house and watches me from afar. By the time the five o'clock whistle blows, my palms are blistered but I've cut only a tiny patch in the huge swath of field grass surrounding the house.

"You will improve," Becky says, and I don't know if I'm meant to take her words as encouragement or a threat.

After Housework Time ends at five, we're summoned to a "special function." We walk down the cement driveway ordered by rank and join the crowd of boys gathered by the banyan tree. A makeshift pen, constructed from metal stakes and twine, has been erected in the dust.

"What's it for?" Tiffany asks Bruce, and he raises his eyebrows and presses his lips together in a "you'll just have to wait and see" gesture. I spot David across the pen and we stare at each other.

Suddenly, the Dean of Students comes barreling through the throng, bare-chested in shorts and hiking boots and wearing orange gardening gloves. He trots to the pen, jumps over the twine, and beats his naked chest with the gloves.

There's a commotion, and again the crowd parts. Boy 0— also bare-chested and wearing shorts and gloves—is thrust forward by a male staffer. His face is red and his mouth raging and all manner of profanity spills from his lips, this time loud enough for everyone to hear.

"Fucking assholes! Fuck you! Fuck you all to Hell!"

The staffer shoves him over the twine and he stands opposite Ted cussing and hugging his bony little boy chest, both defiant teen and cowering child.

Ted walks to the middle of the ring and shouts over Boy 0's profanity.

"Proverbs 23 tells us: 'Refrain not from chastening a child; for if thou beat him with the rod, he shall not die. For thou shalt beat him with the rod, and shalt deliver his soul from Hell.'"

He turns to face Boy 0, who stops cursing to scowl at him.

"Andrew has refused to accept the staff's authority, but he has accepted my invitation to a boxing match. May the best man win."

Boy 0 spits in the dust.

This can't be real. I glance at Susan, but her sorrowful eyes are pinched shut. Across the pen, David lowers his eyes to the dirt at his feet. I look around the crowd. Some students watch the spectacle unfold with expressionless faces, and other focus their attention elsewhere—on the stalactite roots of the banyan tree, on the dirt under their nails, on the unknown country beyond the barbed wire fence.

Ted steps into the center of the ring and raises his garden gloves and Boy 0 raises his, but does not budge from his corner. Ted walks to him and towers over him, like an adult over a child, and Boy 0 sneers up him.

"Go on and hit me," Ted says, taking a step back.

Boy 0 thrusts out a small fist that glances off Ted's broad chest. Ted jogs half a step back, then swings his glove, hitting Boy 0 squarely in the jaw. The thud jerks his head sideways and I wince.

"Please, God," Susan whimpers beside me, her eyes still pinched shut.

Boy 0 totters unsteadily on his feet, a smirk on his face. He refuses to give in, but I wish he would. He charges Ted and pummels his chest with the sides of his fists and Ted shakes his head and grins down at him in a "Can't you do better than that?" way before stepping backward and swinging at his face again. Boy 0 crumples sideways to the ground and sits there.

Ted extends his orange glove to help him up, then punches him again, and this time Boy 0 collapses into the dust and stays there.

He lays on his back staring up at the vacant sky, his bony chest heaving up and down, a trickle of blood running from the corner of his mouth.

Ted pulls off his gloves and kneels beside him.

"Dear Lord," he prays in a loud voice. "Please help Andrew accept this discipline. Help him become a true child of Christ."

I don't bend my head or close my eyes while Ted prays. I stare at him in shock.

Afterward, he dismisses us, and as we march back uphill, David's house is ahead of mine and I keep focused on his narrow shoulders. Halfway to Starr, I look back at the boxing pen. Boy 0 is still stretched out on the ground, and Ted crouches over him, dabbing his face with a white cloth.

At Supper Time, Bruce sits at one end of the long wood table and RuthAnn at the other, in the father and mother places. Becky sits at Bruce's right hand, and we girls are arranged according to rank, with me at RuthAnn's side, and Carrie across from me.

RuthAnn has prepared meatloaf with catsup squirted on top, instant mashed potatoes and pan-fried carrots. After Bruce says Grace, he serves himself from the platters of food, which are then passed down the table to RuthAnn, then back up the table to Becky, then back down the table to Carrie, who passes it to Tiffany, and so on, in descending order of rank. As I watch the food move back and forth across the table, my stomach growls audibly; the half sandwich I ate for lunch was reduced to acid hours ago.

By the time I'm handed the meatloaf, it's been carved down to the burnt rump, but I dump it on my plate and chomp into it, savoring the salty rubber as if it were filet mignon.

"Excuse me!" Bruce yells down the table. "Aren't you forgetting something?"

I stop chewing and look up to find everyone staring at me. Bruce shakes his head with great disgust, as if he found my eating a repulsive activity. Must ask to eat. I consider spitting the meatloaf back onto my plate, but decide to swallow it instead. It gets stuck in my throat; I try to dislodge it by gulping cherry Kool-Aid.

"Excuse me!" Bruce yells.

"I'm sorry!" I gasp, once I'm able to speak.

"Pay attention, really think about what you're doing!" he says.

"I said I'm sorry! May I please eat?"

He raises a forkful of carrots to his hairy mouth.

"Sorry's not good enough," he says, before eating the carrots.

He says no more. The food on my plate blurs into a brown mass. I curl my hands into fists under the table, pressing my nails into the half-moons I cut into my palms earlier. Water pools along my lower eyelids, and I tilt my head back so it won't spill down my face.

For a long time, no one speaks and the only sound is the clink of metal against porcelain and the hiss of the gas lamps on either side of the room. I lower my head and stare out the patio window until the crimson puddle of sun oozes beneath the horizon, and then I stare at the reflection of the family of rejects eating in their cement house. I wonder how Boy 0 is doing, and if he can eat with his wounded mouth.

After a while, RuthAnn brings a bowl of orange slices to the table and these are passed around. When the bowl is empty, Bruce clears his throat.

"Julia, you may now eat."

I pick up my fork to swallow my food, but I can no longer taste it.

After Bed Time, I lay awake for hours doing calculations on my foam pad. With the right combination of superior housework, grades, and attitude, I figure I can get through all the levels and leave of here in six months.

I just have to playact, same as David and I did as little kids in the basement with our dress-up clothes. He'd pretend to be a Texas cowboy, and I'd pretend to be an evil witch. Now we just have to playact the part of repentant teenagers.

When I get out, I'll go live with Deb and find another job as a busgirl. I'll save up money to buy a junker and drive down to Florida, where I'll rent an apartment on the sand and wait for David to join me. Unless, of course, he gets out first, in which case I'd join him. I'll work my way up to a waitressing position and go to college at night.

I imagine the two of us living in our beach apartment, dunking each other in the warm waves and going for long bike rides on the boardwalk. *We'll be fine after all, David, we will.* My thoughts start to wink out like a stuttering television screen when I'm brought back to consciousness by a hiccuping sound.

I squint at the gray lumps in the bunk beds around me, but none move. The noise continues, rising and becoming more ragged, until it reaches a full-blown howl of rage and misery. I stuff my fingers in my ears, but it's too loud to block out.

"Shut up!" someone screams.

"Let the rest of us sleep!" someone else yells.

The howling weakens, then stops, and the bunk shakes beneath me. I peer over the side, and in the dirty moonlight shining through the tiny window, make out Susan lying on her back with both hands clamped over her mouth.

"You okay?" I whisper.

She unclamps one of her hands to give me the thumbs-up sign, then clamps it over her mouth again.

I roll on my back and try to conjure up the beach and the waves and the cozy apartment, but they are gone to me. *Someday, David.* I listen to the sighs and moans and rustlings around me and close my eyes.

"Dear Lord," I pray. "Please help us get there."

+   +   +

There came a day when David denied his skin color.

We were in trouble for kicking a basketball into the television set and shattering the screen, and as usual, David got the brunt of the punishment: He was spanked while I was scolded.

Afterward, we commiserated over a pile of marbles under the ping-pong table. David squatted on his heels, his butt too sore to sit on, and I felt guilt at our unequal punishments.

I was still trying to understand the reason for it. I thought maybe Mother was harder on him because she didn't want him to grow up to be one of those black people on the six o'clock news, the ones who wore orange jumpsuits and handcuffs. The ones who stole and killed and sold drugs. They were the only other black people we knew of.

"I know why you always get spanked," I told David that day under the ping-pong table. "It's because you're black."

He picked up a big marble and dropped it on the pile, knocking the gleaming circles across the carpet.

"No, I'm not," he said quietly.

I looked at him.

"What?"

"I'm not black," he said, louder.

Upstairs, Mother was banging pans, making supper.

"Of course you are!" I said.

He shook his head.

"No, I'm not."

"You're blacker than the place the sun don't shine," I said, parroting a phrase I'd heard flung at David on the schoolyard. I had no idea what it meant, but I knew it was bad and instantly regretted saying it.

"Shut up!" he screamed.

Mother opened the basement door.

"What's going on down there?" she yelled down the stairs.

David glared at me before crawling out from beneath the ping-pong table and running to his room.

"I'm sorry," I whispered a moment later at his unyielding room door.

CHAPTER 11

DEAD BABIES

In the milky predawn, the Third World roosters start croaking as if someone were choking the new day from them and I wake with a shudder. A heaviness presses down on my chest like a boot. This place isn't some conjured-up nightmare that fades with the morning light, but it is real, and it is an island, and it is inescapable.

I wonder if David is awake, and whether he's thinking of me right now as I think of him. If we concentrated hard enough, I wonder if we could learn to communicate by brainwaves alone.

David, someday we'll laugh about all this in Florida.

A distant alarm clock sounds and a moment later Becky unlocks her door and shuffles into the dormitory. She ignites the gas lamp—*whoomph*—and the room is washed in dreary light.

"Six o'clock," she calls. "Everybody up."

There's a collective groan as bodies tumble from bunks and thrust themselves into clothing. The two highest rankers enter the bathroom to do their toiletry while everyone else starts their Room Job. I watch Susan crease her sheets into precise forty-five-degree angles at the corners of her foam pad and try to imitate her. This is my first day on points, and I must score high.

After five minutes, Becky yells "Time!" and the next two highest rankers enter the bathroom. As Susan stands at the dresser straightening her bottles of perfumes and potions, I'm still struggling to fit the sheets over the floppy foam pad.

When it's our turn to wash up, Becky gives me permission to enter the bathroom and stands in the doorway as Susan and I sit on the two exposed toilets and urinate with our eyes fixed on the floor in front of us. The small room has twin sinks, twin toilets and twin shower spigots, everything out in the open like in jail. I need to relieve my bowels, but refuse to do so with an audience.

"Remember to put your t.p. in the wastebasket," Becky tells me as I wipe myself.

After we scrub our faces with cold water and comb our hair, we drape our towels on the rungs at the end of our bunk, making sure they're perfectly centered with aligned edges, before proceeding to wipe down every surface in our space with bleach-soaked rags.

At 6:30, there's a whistle blast and a stampede down the stairway. Becky shadows me as I get permission to go downstairs, to cross the imaginary line dividing the living room into the dining room and to sit down at the long wood table.

A large bowl containing a fluorescent pink substance steams in the middle of the table; the girls regard it with suspicion as they drape napkins over their laps.

Susan leans toward me.

"It's oatmeal," she whispers. "RuthAnn puts Kool-Aid in it."

Bruce emerges from the house parents' quarters buttoning his shirt over his soft hairy middle and pads to the head of the table.

"Good morning, Bruce!" the girls sing out, their sour faces suddenly sweet.

"Mornin'," he responds, reaching for his coffee mug. RuthAnn rushes from the kitchen with a metal carafe to fill it, then takes her place at the mother end of the table.

We bow our heads as Bruce blesses the pink oatmeal. By the time everyone has slopped the required spoonful into their bowl, there's only half a serving left for me, but I experience a small thrill at this when I discover that the only thing more revolting than regular oatmeal is Kool-Aid–flavored oatmeal.

As we eat, we discuss how Bruce slept and what he dreamt about and what he'd like for supper, and when the large black-rimmed clock over the kitchen doorway marks 6:55, we bow our heads in prayer again, before everyone rushes off to do their House Job.

Since I'm the lowest ranker, I get the bathroom. It's my job to make it look tidy, despite the large swaths of blue paint peeling off the walls that expose the concrete blocks underneath and the rusted metal ceiling, which looks like someone attacked it with a can of orange spray paint.

"Bruce will scrutinize your housekeeping skills when you finish," Becky tells me. Scrutinize. People love that word down here. *Scrutinize, scrooge, screw, scrotum.* I smirk as I shake smeared toilet paper into a plastic bag.

As I scrub the porcelain throats of the toilet bowls, Becky talks about abortion. She asks me how many teenagers get abortions in Indiana and I tell her I don't know. She asks me if I know that abortion is a deadly sin against Gahd Our Maker and I tell her yes. She tells me Gahd sent her down here to convince us troubled girls not to abort His precious unborn babies and I nod and she repeats the story about the church potty and the dawk road.

When I can no longer stand the pressure in my bowels, I tell Becky I need to use the toilet for private business. She considers my request for a long moment, then agrees to stand outside the bathroom with her head pressed to the door. There's no lock on the knob.

When the whistle blows at 7:30, she tells me to drop my cleaning utensils or my points will be docked and I protest that I haven't finished the mirror.

"Timeliness is next to Godliness," she says.

I give her a sideways look, and she adds: "And cleanliness is next to Godliness, too."

Bruce scrutinizes my work, running his hands over the floor and walls, sniffing crevices, peering into corners. He holds up his index finger; there is a gray smudge on the tip.

"This is not acceptable, eh?

"Nor this, nor this, nor this," he says, pointing out more mistakes. There's goop beneath the shampoo caps, a dead cockroach stuck to the bottom of a wastebasket, pubic hairs in the shower drain.

We proceed to the dormitory, where he flings open my panty drawer and traces a finger over the bottom of it.

"There's grit."

He pulls out the drawer and dumps it upside down on the floor. Does the same with the sock drawer. Stands and squints at my bunk.

"Look at those corners!" he says, shaking his head.

I stand beside him, my heart sinking. The angles are more seventy-five degrees than forty-five, but it's still the neatest bed I've made in my life. Bruce rips the sheets off the mattress, and it slumps off its metal brace and falls onto the socks and panties on the floor. I bite my bottom lip and follow him to the closet, where he flings shirts and shoes on top of the mattress. By the time he's done, it looks like a tornado touched down on my belongings. I survey the damage, blinking away tears.

"You need to try *harder,* really *think* about what you're doing," Bruce says. He writes a 2 on my point chart next to Room, Done Well and On Time and another 2 next to House Job, Done Well and On Time.

"You've got five minutes to do your corrections before school," he says, turning to walk away.

"As if," I mutter.

He whips around, his face a bearded tomato.

"What did you say?"

I press my fingernails into my palms.

"I said, 'Yes, sir.'"

He eyes me a second longer, then leaves.

I bend to furiously rewipe, refold, redo and am still bent when the whistle blows and footsteps pound out the front door to the patio.

Bruce stamps upstairs as I'm struggling to reinsert the dresser drawer onto its runner; clothes and shoes still litter the floor at my feet.

"Come on!" he yells. "Everyone's waiting for you!"

Panicking, I sprint past him, down the stairs, and onto the patio to join the other girls. Only when Susan turns to me, wide-eyed, do I realize what I've done. I dash back into the house, and there's Bruce, standing in the living room.

I start to babble an apology, but his face is as unyielding as a concrete wall and I stop. RuthAnn rises from the dining room table holding a magazine and a coffee mug and disappears into the house parents' quarters, closing the door behind her.

"Get down and give me fifty push-ups," Bruce says.

"What?"

"Fifty push-ups. Now!"

I glance down at the gleaming tile floor and at the girls on the patio, and Bruce starts counting "One . . . two . . ." and I don't know what happens when he reaches three, so I stretch out before him like a crucifix and lower myself to the ground. I'm dipping into my fourth shaky push-up when Bruce squats beside me.

"Get lower! Count out loud!"

"I can't!" I gasp.

"You can and you will!" he orders.

My arms fail, and I collapse on the gleaming floor, hot snot and tears burbling from me. I feel no shame at this messy outburst, but rather relief, a lightness that balloons in my chest and replaces the suffocating weight that woke me. I could weep happily for hours on this gleaming floor if only he'd let me.

"Get up," Bruce says. "We'll finish this tonight."

Bruce leads the way downhill in my safari hat, his brown hair fluttering beneath the brim, and I swear that if I ever get my hands on that hat again, I will bite it, and I will piss on it, and I will cut it to pieces, and I will burn it.

Becky catches up to me and lays a hand on my shoulder.

"I know The Program must seem very difficult to you right now," she says. "But all these experiences will help you build character."

I don't respond because I know that whatever noise comes out of my mouth will not be human. I shrug off her arm and she falls behind me.

The boys are singing "Amazing Grace" when we walk into the chapel. Mrs. Madsen, the P.E. teacher's wife and school therapist, plunks out the hymn on a small piano under a floor-to-ceiling wooden cross at the front of the room.

We file into the pew in front of David's house, and when I lift my bloodshot eyes to his, he stops singing. I hold my songbook to my face and try to focus on the words, but singing about grace and mercy just makes me feel more wretched and I begin to sob anew.

There's a surge behind me and I turn to see David seething at Bruce as the boys on either side of him grip his arms, holding him back. I slash at my tears with the back of my hand and smile at him. *Everything's fine.*

On Tuesdays and Thursdays, the last class of the day is "Group" instead of P.E.

"It's where Becky teaches us to be proper Christian young ladies," Susan tells me as we stand outside the History classroom with the other girls, waiting to be let in.

Becky's inside, slamming drawers and doors and otherwise preparing a "surprise" lesson for us. She's put me in the custody of Tiffany, who leans against the wall with her arms crossed, scowling at me.

When the door swings open, the other girls push past me as Becky gives me permission to enter, walk, sit. At the front of the room, under photocopies of the American and Confederate flags taped to the wall, seven large pieces of cardboard are propped on chairs.

Becky stands before them.

"Today's lesson may disturb some of you," she says in her high bird voice. "But I've given it much prayer, and I believe the Lahd has guided my decision.

"The topic of today's lesson is the legalized murder of precious unborn babies," she says as she walks to the first piece of cardboard in the lineup.

Susan tilts her head toward me and rolls her eyes—Becky's talking abortion again.

"In Ephesians 5:11, Gahd tells us to 'Take no part in the fruit-less deeds of darkness, but instead expose them' and that's my intention here today. I special-ordered these posters from the States to do just that, to expose this great evil."

She flips over the first poster. It's a close-up of a doll's hand resting on a quarter, fingers spread across George Washington's face, adorable in its miniature perfection. No, it's not. It's not a doll's hand, it's a real hand, a transparent, guppy-like hand. An amputated baby hand. You can see the webbing of nerves, the shadows of bones beneath the skin. A red jelly oozes from the wrist.

"Ewww!"

"Yuck!"

"Nasty!"

Several girls clap their hands over their mouths.

Becky flips over the second poster. A tiny baby curled on a pink sheet next to a small gold cross, napping. Its skin is streaked black, its lips are gray. It looks like a marble paperweight.

"It looks real," Rhonda says in a choked voice.

"Yeah, real *dead*," I whisper to Susan. She hushes me.

Becky crouches next to the poster of the baby paperweight and studies it.

"This is Sara," she says. "All these babies have names. They are all Gahd's children, our brothers and sisters in Christ."

The hand she calls Hannah.

She stands and flips over the third poster. A butchered baby in a bedpan, yellow and quartered like a stewing hen. A tab of flesh pokes out of the crotch—it's a boy. His head leans uncom-fortably against the bedpan, and his eyes are shut, but his mouth gapes open in an eternal scream.

Someone shrieks. Someone else mewls. There are gasps and moans.

"Meet Samuel," Becky says, patting the screaming head. "Little Sammy."

She turns the remaining posters, and each one is more gruesome than the last. By the time Becky reaches a red blob of slime she calls Rachel, many girls are crying. Beside me, Susan peeks through her fingers at the gore.

Becky kneels before the dead babies and contemplates them silently for a long moment. Suddenly she yelps and plunges her face into her hands, and the crying becomes wailing.

Susan's lips contort into an upside-down U as she bawls and she wipes her snot on the sleeve of her blouse.

I look at the posters and the warped faces around me and feel nothing. I have exhausted my emotions and have no more to give. I press my forehead against the cool surface of my chair desk and review the vocabulary from Spanish class. Chair, *silla*. Window, *ventana*. Door, *puerta*.

After the crying subsides, Becky has us pray for the dead babies and the people who killed them. We slide to our knees on the cement floor and take turns, each girl trying to out-pious the next, and some even addressing their prayers to "Dear Babies."

"Heavenly Father," I say, when it's my turn, "deliver us all from evil, the living, the dead, and everyone in between."

As punishment for getting 1s and 2s in Courtesy and Respect Toward Authority Figures and Attitude and Jobs and a bunch of other boxes, Bruce has me haul rocks during Work Time while the other girls polish silverware or practice folding napkins into fans and bishops' hats.

The work consists of carrying a pile of rocks from the field below the house and making a new heap beside the driveway.

Becky watches me from the deck with her legs dangling over the side as I cradle the rocks in my arms and lug them uphill. When I stop to rest in the shade of the house, she quietly urges me to keep moving, glancing back into the living room where Bruce sits reading *The Thornbirds* with his feet up and a pillow tucked under his butt. We watched the miniseries based on the book a few years back, and to see Bruce caught up in a torrid affair between a priest and a ranch girl grosses me out. It's not the kind of book men are supposed to read.

After an hour, Bruce blows his whistle, but I've barely made a dent in the rock pile.

"Now I'm giving you two casitas," he says, walking over with the romance novel in his hand.

He explains that casita is Spanish for little house, and English for running up the hill, a quarter mile from the entrance gate to the top boys' house, TKB. Normally, he says, he'd assign me one casita for every point under a 3—and so far today, I've earned seven such points.

"But I'm a nice guy and making an exception for you," he says.

I stare at my sneakers and wait for him to stop talking before turning to start down the driveway.

Three boys are pounding up the cement track as I jog downhill, including Boy 0, who staggers behind the others. The TKB group leader swoops past me on a moped and nips at his heels, trying to herd him up the hill, but he won't speed up. His eyes, when he passes me, are dull, unseeing.

Bruce moves to the deck to continue his love story, looking up now and again to roar "faster!" but I can barely walk up the hill, much less run it. I pump my arms to make myself look faster, and it seems to work because he stops yelling.

At supper, I stare into my Velveeta casserole and wonder where I'd be right now if I'd run away with Scott. Staying with his cousin in Kentucky? Living out of his car in Happy Hollow Park? In his backyard tent? We couldn't hide forever.

After supper, Becky is teaching me to fold clothes when a whistle blows downstairs.

"Time for the meeting," she says brightly.

I look at her warily.

"This isn't a 'special function,' is it?" I ask, thinking about the "special function" boxing match.

"No, it's Starr Family Unity," she says. "It's a good opportunity for you to get to know the other girls."

She gives me permission to walk downstairs, enter the living room and sit on a metal chair. Everyone's already there, arranged in a circle. Bruce sits across from me with his butt pillow. Beside him, RuthAnn embroiders a dish towel.

After I sit down, Bruce lifts his chin and peers around the circle.

"I'd like some water," he announces.

Hands shoot into the air. "I'll get it, Bruce!" "Oh, pick me!" "Please, Bruce, let me!" high voices plead.

I look around in disgust; even Susan's hand is raised, although she waves it with a little less vigor than the others. Bruce considers each girl in turn, tapping an index finger against his mouth.

"Umm . . . Tiffany!"

The other girls fall back against their chairs in disappointment as Tiffany sprints to the kitchen. She returns carrying a tray with a single glass of water, smiling triumphantly. Bruce takes it from her without a word.

"Carrie, you start," he says. "Tell Julia your story."

Carrie inhales sharply and frowns down at her nails, but when she speaks, her words are loud and slow and clear:

"I smoked pot pretty much every day. I couldn't stop. Got so bad I was getting high before church and flunking school."

A drug addict?! I look around the circle in astonishment, but no other face mirrors my alarm. I've never met a druggie before.

Janet's next: "I snorted cocaine and hit my mother when she tried to take away my stash."

Again, no one's face registers alarm. One by one, the girls gaze into their laps and tell their stories. From their steady voices and polished lines, it's clear they are called upon to do this often.

Tiffany: "I stole money from my parents to buy clothes. And sometimes I shoplifted."

Rhonda: "I ran away from home and sold my body for money."

A prostitute?! She's not even sixteen.

When Susan's turn comes, she glances at me, and her eyes now contain both shame and sorrow. She pulls at the hem of her T-shirt and mumbles something.

"What?" Bruce says loudly, cupping a hand behind his ear. "We can't hear you!"

Susan pinches her lips together before speaking.

"I was a member of the Church of Satan," she says mechanically. "I renounced Jesus Christ as my Lord and Savior and bowed down to Beelzebub."

I gasp. *A devil worshipper?!* I'd heard rumors of such activity back in Indiana, of animal sacrifice and orgies and possession by demon spirits. *But Susan seems so normal, so nice! How could she possibly choose Satan over Jesus Christ?*

I lean away from her and look around the circle; blank faces gaze back at me. I sweep my eyes back and forth across the orange and green tiled floor. *What am I doing here, among these criminals?* Something large screeches in the darkness beyond the patio door. *I am surrounded by danger. Tonight I'm to sleep in a roomful of druggies and whores and Satanists!* At least in jail, everyone had their own cage.

Bruce clears his throat, and I look up. All eyes are on me.

"So, what's your story, Juliar?" asks Becky, sitting beside me. She smiles warmly. "What brought you to Escuelar Caribe?"

I study the floor, the traces of "Love's First Blush" still stuck beneath my cuticles, the red high-tops Mother bought me at Kmart a few days ago, when I was still free. Bruce taps his foot impatiently.

"I . . ." I fall silent, wondering which "behavioral problems" my parents listed on the school application.

"I left home."

"Correction!" Bruce says loudly. "You ran away."

I stare at the tiny green seeds clinging to my shoelaces. Dominican seeds. I hate that term, "run away." Dogs run away, people don't. I walked away, slowly, deliberately, with a suitcase in each hand.

"Say it!" Bruce orders.

"I ran away."

"What else?" he prods.

I shrug; those seeds are going to be a real pain in the ass to pick off.

"You drank alcohol," Bruce volunteers.

"I drank alcohol," I repeat, still staring at my shoes.

"You were an alcoholic."

I jolt up my head. A drink now and then before school is not alcoholism.

"I was not!"

Bruce goes rigid on his butt pillow.

"Will you defy my authority?!" His voice booms off the flamingo pink walls. RuthAnn pulls a purple thread through her embroidery hoop, and in the abrupt silence you can hear the *sssss* of the silk slicing cotton.

Becky turns to face me.

"Juliar, admitting our faults is the first step toward recovery," she says. "And confessing our sins is the first step toward forgiveness."

"But I didn't . . ." I start to protest, but stop short when I notice Bruce leaning forward with his hands planted on either side of his butt pillow, as if he were preparing to spring from the chair. *Don't make a fuss, David said. Keep your head down.* I ball my hands into fists.

"I was an alcoholic."

"What else?" Bruce demands, still on the edge of his seat.

I remember the word "condom" in the letter from my mother that Debbie had at the picnic table.

"I made love with my boyfriend."

"You fornicated. You had unholy sex."

I clench my fists tighter.

"I fornicated . . . I had unholy sex."

"You were an alcoholic and a fornicator."

"I was an alcoholic and a fornicator."

I see Becky pat my arms with her hand, but I don't feel her touch. My pulse pounds in my temples. *Boom boom boom.*

Bruce nods at me before saying "Let us pray."

I bow my head and stare at my fists.

"Heavenly Father," Bruce prays. "Thank you for bringing Julia to The Program. Please open her heart and her soul to receive Your rich blessings, and forgive her rebellion. Let her know how much You love her, and how much we do. In His name, Amen."

When he finishes, Bruce stands, his palms lifted heavenward.

"Let us make a joyful noise unto the Lord!" he shouts.

Becky gives me permission to stand, then reaches behind her chair to pick up a guitar leaning against the wall. She strums it

ESCUELA CARIBE
WEEKLY RECORD OF POINTS

Level: 0   Week: 1

Student: Julia Scheeres

Dates: 7/8—7/15

5-Excellent 4-Good 3-Average 2-Poor 1-Attempted Rebellion 0-Rebellion

	S	M	T	W	T	F	S
Responding promptly and up on time			3				
Room Job, done well and on time			2 slow				
House Job, done well and on time			2				
Pleasant and mannerly at meals			2 spacing				
Neat and clean in personal appearance			4				
Being totally truthful and honest, facing reality			3				
Courtesy and respect toward authority figures			1 jobs				
Courtesy and respect toward other people, places and things			1				
Being a helpful and positive influence			2				
School—attitude			2				
School—cooperation			2				
Physical education or Group participation			3				
Work time participation			3				
Target goal—abiding by rules and procedures			2				
TOTAL possible 70pts/day 560 pts/week			32				

with twiglike fingers as we sing all five stanzas of "Kum Ba Ya," each girl hugging herself tight and wailing at the floor.

Life becomes a loop of school, chores and punishment.

All the things I took for granted just last week—listening to the radio, talking on the phone or simply walking into a bathroom and closing the door behind me—seem like a wonderful dream. I never knew how good I had it, even when I was eating off room service trays at Howard Johnson's.

Bruce stops explaining my housework deficiencies, and simply goes about destroying my work.

"Wrong," he says, as he upends a drawer of clothes onto the floor.

"Wrong," as he rips the foam pad off its frame.

"Wrong," as he tears clothes from hangers.

Afterwards, he studies my face for signs of disrespect, but I've learned to hide them well; my brain curses him out even as my mouth apologizes for my inadequacy.

When he tells me to get down and do push-ups, I dip low and count loud.

When I finish hauling the rock pile to the driveway and he orders me to move it back downhill, I say, "Yes, sir, right away."

When he's thirsty or he sneezes, I join the "me, me, me" chorus for the privilege of fetching him water or Kleenex.

I have gotten with The Program.

As I haul rocks, run casitas and scrub toilets, I've got a big "fuck you" smile on my face. It scores me high points in the Courtesy and Respect Toward Authority Figures box. Academics are another area where I shine. School is easy when you have a compelling reason to pay attention.

David and I develop a code language to check in on each other when no one's watching:

An upward jut of the chin means "How are you doing?"

A shrug: "As good as can be expected."

A nod: "Okay . . . for the moment."

A head shake: "Bad."

Raised eyebrows: "You don't look too hot" or, when something weird happens, "Can you believe this?!"

A combination of crossed arms and a loud sigh: "I hear ya. Hang in there."

Once when I was having a particularly rotten day and arrived at school snot-faced and raw, he left me a yellow hibiscus on Starr's picnic table. I watched him from where I stood in a doorway, waiting for permission to cross the courtyard to my next class. There were a lot of people milling about, and nobody noticed when he laid the flower at my place at the table. Hibiscus, a Florida flower.

I wore it in my watchband until Debbie said it looked like I was wearing jewelry—a priviledge I haven't earned—and told me to take it out. By then, half the petals had fallen off, but I pressed it inside my Geography book anyway.

At Starr, Tiffany narks and brown-noses her way to the top of the trash heap and becomes high-ranker. She ratted out Janet for sneaking a piece of bread between meals because she was hungry, Susan for using a kitchen rag to clean the dormitory, and Carrie for yelling "shit!" when she jammed her thumb during dodgeball—that's what got Carrie demoted from the top spot.

That's how The Program works. Snitch on people, and you score big in the Being a Helpful and Positive Influence box. Susan is the only girl I trust; I avoid the others as much as possible. You never know who will betray you.

After she busted Susan, Tiffany walked into the bathroom as I was scrubbing the toilets, and I glared at her in the mirror.

"Live and let die," she said, bending back the tip of her cheer-leader nose to check for buggers. She now spends all her time primping—rubbing sugar into her face and lemon into her hair and filing her toenails—in preparation for her release.

"I'll be playing tennis at the Hartford Country Club next month while the rest of you rot down here," she said, picking up a bar of soap and streaking it over my clean mirror.

By the time I realized what she'd done and scrambled to my feet, she was already out the door, flashing a fake smile.

On Saturday, Starr takes a field trip to a waterfall on the out-skirts of Jarabacoa. We drive through the center of the village—past plywood shacks and trash fires and open sewers and malnourished children with swollen bellies and blond-streaked hair and women carrying baskets on their heads and men who yell "Americanas!" at us—and bump up a narrow dirt road until we reach a dead end. "Salto de Jimenoa" says a hand-painted sign at the edge of the jungle.

We line up by rank outside the van and Bruce leads the way up a muddy path as the dense vegetation whirs with hidden birds and insects. Above us, the sapphire sky glitters through the high lattice canopy and the smell is green and living. The steamy air clings to us as we brush past giant ferns, and for a few moments I forget where I am and feel excited about being in a foreign country.

I roll up my jeans to keep them from dragging in the orange mud and watch a blue parrot swoop up the trail ahead of us. When we reach a wide shallow stream, we ford it by hopping over moss-covered rocks, tic-tac-toe, racing to see who reaches the other side first.

"Wait for me!" a man's voice shouts when we're halfway across. I turn to see Bruce teetering between two rocks at the lip of the water, his arms spread out to steady himself. Janet rushes back to guide him across, and Susan and I exchange a sneer because he's such a Canadian pansy. All the girls secretly despise him; they giggle at his jokes and fall all over themselves to fetch his water, but roll their eyes as soon as he leaves the room.

After Janet leads him safely across, Bruce strides to the front of the group.

"Let's go!" he commands with a forward wave of his arm, The Man once again. Susan and I exchange another look, and I lean over to hawk my disgust into the weeds.

Becky turns to scowl at me as I wipe my mouth with the back of my hand.

"Pardon me, I swallowed some crud," I tell her as Susan smirks.

As the roar of the waterfall gets louder, Susan and I lag behind the others. RuthAnn stayed at Starr and Becky is ahead of us talking abortion with Rhonda, and finally, we can finally talk privately.

We swap information about the events that got us here. Susan tells me she's not really a Devil Worshipper, but joined a clique called the Squires of Death after the preppies and the New Wavers turned her down. The Squires held meetings in the town graveyard, where they recited the Satanic Verses dressed in black choir robes that they found at a secondhand store. Afterward, they'd drive through town in their pickups, blaring Black Sabbath and chugging Apple Slice and Everclear and stopping to spray-paint 666 on churches.

"Wasn't like we was fixin' to sacrifice babies or nothin'," she says as the trail steepens. "Although we did catch this stray cat this one time, but we were too scared to kill it."

She inquires after my alcoholism, and I tell her about the Comfort in my closet.

"Guess they found it after I left home," I shrug. "That, and my stash of condoms."

She asks if I love Scott and I tell her no, but that he was fine to pass time with. She tells me she had her share of boyfriends back in Texas too, but none more special than the others.

We climb a ramp of slippery rocks, then wind through car-sized boulders before the waterfall roars into view ahead of us, catapulting through a crack in the mountain and smashing into a pile of foam on the river below. A cool mist billows from the thundering ejaculation, which drowns out all other noise.

The group stops to take pictures at an overlook, and Becky and several girls lean over the guide rope, craning their necks to watch the water disappear below. Bruce stands behind them, clinging to a tree branch and shouting something no one can hear, and we laugh openly at him.

Neither of us is in a hurry to catch up to the others. As we watch them from a distance, she grabs my elbow. I turn to her.

"I ain't no virgin neither!" she yells. "But that's one thing they never learnt. That's one thing that's all mine."

When she says this, her eyes are shining, and she is not sorrowful.

+   +   +

When the word "nigger" crept into the vocabulary of exclusion—yelled by public school kids at the bus stop and roller rink—I had to look it up in the dictionary. It wasn't in the Webster's, *so I asked Mother what it meant. She said it was a bad word for a black person, and that if we heard it, we should ignore it and turn the other cheek.*

But it was hard to ignore a word that was suddenly everywhere.

"Nigger cooties!" they'd screech when we jumped into Kingston pool, fleeing before us as if we were Jaws.

"*Nigger alert!*" *they'd yell as we climbed onto the Witch's Hat at Happy Hollow Park.*

We'd pretend not to hear them, but of course we did, loud and clear. I'd look over at David and see a cloud wash over his luminous brown eyes and his little boy smile.

Those kids didn't even know his name. They didn't know that he was a champion ping-pong player, or that he knew the best places to hunt salamanders or that he could pop a wheelie for an entire block.

When he got braces in sixth grade, a boy in a grocery store hollered at him: "*Black people don't wear braces, only whites!*"

The more they cut us off, the more we clung together.

CHAPTER 12

NEW GIRL

A new girl arrives from eastern Kentucky. This means I'm no longer the lowest ranker in Starr. This means that I no longer scrub toilets. This means I have a better shot at a second helping of dessert. I welcome her arrival.

Her name is Jolene and she's fifteen. She's got bleached, permed hair that cascades to her skinny butt in straw-colored coils and at night, she sits in her bunk and combs it out with a special rubber-tipped pick, one coil at a time. It is her pride and joy.

Jolene's taken hard to the loss of freedom and often plunges her face into her hands with a small moan, as if all this were a thing too ghastly to behold.

When Bruce gives her push-ups, she chews on her bottom lip a few seconds before lowering herself to the ground, and all his tomato-faced shrieking won't speed her along. Sometimes I catch her staring at me with confused eyes, as if she were waiting for an explanation. I look away; she'll soon find out there's none to be had.

On a Sunday before Vespers we learn why Jolene is here. Bruce picks me to fetch his water, and then we sit in the metal circle to tell our stories.

I now know my line by heart, as I am called upon to repeat it often.

"I was a fornicator and an alcoholic," I say whenever a staffer asks me what brought me to The Program. As I say my line, I gaze at my shoes, striving to appear humbled. I do this well, and get consistent high points for Being Totally Truthful and Honest, Facing Reality.

When it's Jolene's turn to confess, she looks around the circle blankly.

"Ah honestly don't know why I'm here," she says in a hillbilly drawl so backwoods it makes Indiana rednecks seem positively citified.

Bruce narrows his eyes at her response, and the girls around me shift uneasily on their patio chairs.

"You do so know," Bruce says in a tight voice. His voice rises several octaves when he's upset, into the soprano range, and it's a scary thing to behold. "You know perfectly well why you were sent here."

"Well, Ah do know that Momma married herself a borned-agin man, and that's when my troubles began," Jolene says, flipping a long corkscrew over her shoulder. "Ah shoulda known they was storyin' about this place. That rich old Briggity Britches was up to no good, no how."

When she says this, I stuff my fist in my mouth to keep from laughing and Susan coughs into her hand to do the same.

Becky turns to Jolene.

"Jesus forgives his children, Jolene," she says in her earnest bird voice. "He loves you. But to receive His forgiveness, we must first admit our mistakes."

Jolene sucks in her cheeks as if she were preparing to spit.

"Ah don't need no forgivin', cuz Ah ain't done nothing wrong," she says, her black eyes flashing. "And Ah cain't say Ah much care for this Jesus character anyhows."

Bruce bolts to his feet.

"Would you like *me* to tell everyone why your parents sent you here?"

"That would be my momma, cuz my daddy died when I was . . ."

"Jolene here had a game she played with the boys in her town, called 'Health Clinic'. . ."

"Nah, it was 'House Call' and it . . . "

"This ritualistic sexual abuse took place at her home, while her poor mother was slaving away as a maid in order to . . ."

"Wasn't no maid, she worked in a hospital . . ."

"Quiet!" Bruce roars.

Jolene crosses her arms and hunkers down in her chair, glaring at him.

"These boys would take turns having carnal knowledge of Jolene, right there under her poor mother's roof."

Becky puts a hand on Jolene's shoulder and Jolene jerks out from under it. I study her baggy Kentucky Wildcats T-shirt and wonder what's so special about the stick figure underneath that all these boys would crave it. She lifts her chin and stares back at me defiantly.

"Well, what do you have to say for yourself?" Bruce asks her.

"All that happened 'fore Momma found herself that rich old Bapdist and decided to become a fancy lady. 'Fore that, she paid no mind at all."

Bruce raises his index finger with an ah-ha expression on his face.

"So you confess to being a fornicator."

"A forni-what?"

"You had sex before marriage."

She shrugs. "So?"

"Fornication is an abomination in the eyes of our Lord!"

"An abomini-what?"

"Sin! Evil! Wrong!"

"Wasn't like we was hurting no one," Jolene giggles, looking over at me. "Actually, it was kinda fun."

Bruce orders the rest of us out of the house, so he can converse alone with Jolene. We all know what this means: calisthenics, threats, tears. Big 0s in the Facing Reality and the Courtesy and Respect boxes.

Becky leads us into the darkening field beside Starr, where we sit on the machete-hewn grass and sing "Seek Ye First" and "Sandy Land" and "Humble Thyself."

But no matter how high we raise our voices, we can still hear Bruce bellowing inside the cement house. We slap no-see-ums from our bare arms and scream the lyrics at the fading horizon. We sing until our mouths go dry and the night wraps itself around each one of us like a shroud, and the raging finally stops.

At Vespers, Jolene bends her head to pray and doesn't raise it up again.

The pastor, a preacher-in-training from Kansas named Stephen ("Call me Stevie") Erickson, asks us if Jesus will find our hearts 100% pure and hate-free when He returns to earth, and I wonder how such a thing is possible.

David is also in a mood tonight. He scowls at the cross nailed to the front wall during the sermon—"Our God is a Tubular God"—with the old-man worry line creasing his forehead, and he doesn't once look in my direction.

After the benediction, we congregate in the courtyard for Social Time. Debbie sets a platter of chocolate chip cookies on a picnic table, and this provokes squeals of delight. The cookies were held up in Customs for two months and are hard and stale, but they are Chocolate Chip Cookies just the same, the first some kids have tasted in over a year.

Susan and I sit on a cement step with our Bibles cushioning our butts and dig out the dark beads with our fingernails. We melt them on our tongues, one by one to make them last, each morsel a piece of Home.

"Been five months since I had chocolate," Susan says dreamily, lifting a morsel to study it in the gaslight before dropping it into her mouth.

It's the little things that keep you sane at Escuela Caribe, an extra hour of sleep on Sunday, chocolate pudding cake on Thursday nights, a lukewarm shower instead of a cold one, stale chocolate chips.

Ted Schlund holds forth at the center of the courtyard, surrounded by staff. He twists and gesticulates as he recounts some story, and his audience hoots with laughter. As usual, his wife lists quietly at his side, her face upturned like a waiting child.

Across from us, Janet and Tiffany huddle with their boyfriends at separate picnic tables while Becky hovers nearby to guard against any "unfitting corporal contact." The definition of said contact—as well as the Program boys we'd like to have it with—is a frequent topic of conversation for Susan and me. She believes that anything beyond a quick peck on the lips is considered inappropriate, but I think the definition could even include hand-holding, if it's done in a perverted manner. Like when a boy tongues the space between your fingers and you can feel it down between your legs.

Janet's boyfriend rises stiffly from the picnic table, a bulge tenting the front of his Sunday slacks.

"My Lord, look at that woodie!" Susan whispers as he walks to the boys' bathroom. "Do you think he's going in there to abuse himself?"

We laugh, and I remember Reverend Dykstra telling our Young Calvinist group that "you can't jack off with Jesus" and laugh even harder. I look across the courtyard at David, but he's standing alone, scowling at the ground and he won't look up at me, so I can't use our secret code to ask him how he's doing.

A group of boys find a tennis ball under a bush and chuck it against the school building and it echoes loudly *poing poing poing*. One of them is Tommy Atherton, a seventeen-year-old Californian whom Susan and I secretly call "The Clydesdale."

We'd both like to have unfitting corporal contact with Tommy; he's got a basketball player's physique and talks like Sean Penn in *Fast Times at Ridgemont High*. We suck the chocolate from our tongues and watch his tan biceps curl beneath the sleeve of his lavender polo shirt as he chucks the ball against the wall.

When a housefather roars at the boys to stop, they arrange themselves in a glum circle and toss the ball to each other underhanded. Tommy sees us staring at him and grins, and Susan perk ups, sticking out her boobs and grinning back. When he sees this, Tommy smiles wider, and Susan sticks her boobs out further.

"You look real stupid doing that," I tell her, sore because I have no boobs to stick out. She ignores me.

A whistle blows to signal the end of Social Time, and Susan and I reluctantly stand to join the other girls.

No one notices that Jolene's gone until we've lined up to march back up the hill and there's an empty space behind me.

Bruce and Becky run back through the courtyard shouting Jolene's name. They're joined by other staffers who poke flashlights into the classrooms and toilets calling "Jolene! Time to go, Jolene!" as if she'd simply misplaced herself. Susan and I exchange a wide-eyed look; we know better.

Ted struts around with his hands on his hips, barking orders. The Dominican guard trots up with his German shepherd and machete to consult with Ted and lopes off into the darkness, shouting in Spanish.

She's gone. Vanished onto the Dominican side of the barbed wire.

Bruce and the other men pile into the school's two vans, and the vehicles careen through the front gate, tires spitting gravel, and shoot down the narrow road toward Jarabacoa. We listen to them fade into the distance, and then Becky turns to us, her face as pale as a mushroom.

"Let's go," she says, her voice barely a whisper.

We walk up to Starr under the moon's unblinking gaze in deep silence, no one daring give voice to the thought swirling through her head:

She's free.

The vans growl back up the hill a few hours later. I'm awake and thinking about Jolene and listening to the girls in the bunks around me as they sigh and moan and cry out at the demons who pursue them even in their sleep. Tires crunch over Starr's driveway, a metal door slams, then footsteps clack across the tiles into the houseparents' quarters. Bruce, returning without Jolene.

At the breakfast table, Bruce says Jolene made it all the way to the village by hiding in the shrubs alongside the road; the men passed her several times before one of them looked through the back van window and saw her metallic silver purse sparkling in the moonlight. I stare into my grape oatmeal as he speaks and imagine her tottering down the dirt road in her gray satin pumps, her white eyelet dress glowing in the moonlight. *Did she have a plan, or was she blinded by panic? Was she happy? For a small while at least?*

They hauled her back to the property and locked her in the room at the end of the courtyard where I spent my first night. Kids call it "The Hole."

After lunch, Ted Schlund tells us to remain seated for a special function and I prepare myself for the worst. David and I exchange a grim look across the picnic tables before Bruce leads Jolene into the courtyard, where she is seated on a stool before us. She's dressed in jeans and a T-shirt, and she perches on the stool with her back curved in defeat, her platinum hair snarled with knots and draped over her face like a corn tassel.

Ted quotes some scripture and makes some pronouncements, but my attention's fastened on the scissors in his hand. When he's done talking, he grabs a fistful of Jolene's hair at her neck and nips in with the long blades. A thick swath drifts to the ground, where it is dragged over the brick courtyard by a gust of wind.

By the time Ted has finished with her, Jolene's pride and joy winds around the bushes, the table legs, and our shoes in a vast golden spider web. Jolene slouches on the stool with her arms crossed tightly over her chest, her pale face naked to the sun, her eyes closed. Her hair has been reduced to a jagged butch cut that's blond at the tips and black underneath, her natural color. She looks like a punk rock star; all she needs is a safety pin in her ear.

Ted prays aloud for God to help her accept this punishment, and we echo his "Amen" in a mumbled chorus before he dismisses us for the class.

On Sunday afternoon, I stand before Bruce to recite Bible verses, then prostrate myself before him to do leg lifts and push-ups and suicides. The house votes to approve my promotion to First Level, and suddenly I can move without asking and use the bathroom without an audience. And these simple freedoms— which just two weeks ago were as natural to me as breathing air—fill me with awe, and I circle the house several times, marveling at the ease of it all.

Bruce pins a silver-colored medal on my T-shirt that says "Achievement" and tells me I'm now entitled to use one make-up item and one accessory. He returns my safari hat, and I thank him before walking into the kitchen to spit on it and stuff it deep into the garbage can.

Two more weeks of this playacting, and they'll let me talk to David.

First Level also means I can read a letter Scott sent a week ago. I carry it around unopened for days, savoring the anticipation of opening it, prolonging the suspense.

The staff have already scrutinized the letter and taped it back into its envelope, but I don't care. A letter is proof that I once lived in the real world beyond the barbed-wire fence, and that the real world has not forgotten me.

Between classes, I take Scott's letter out of my backpack and trace his cramped handwriting with a fingertip, imagining his fingers gripping the blue pen that scrawled my name. His tongue licking the back flap. His callused palm smoothing it shut, the same callused palm that skimmed my back as we laid in bed after sex. At night, I sniff the letter for traces of his musk and sleep with it under my pillow.

On a Friday evening, I sit on the patio during Free Time to open it while everyone else plays Scrabble at the long wood table and Sandi Patti wails on the house cassette player. The small speakers make her voice all the more annoying. Thank God that batteries are hard to come by in the Third World, so we're restricted to only one hour of Jesus music a night.

I peel the tape off the envelope and pull out the letter. Black marker blots out half the words. *Jerks.* I wonder how much of my letters to David were crossed out as well. Now I believe that he couldn't warn me about this place—Bruce and Becky check our letters home for "negativity" and "lies" about The Program, and if they find a hint of nonconformity, they dock our points and make us rewrite them. I quickly learned not to refer to Escuela Caribe as a concentration camp after scoring a 1 in the School—Attitude box. Our parents must continue paying our tuition, and The Program must go on.

I read Scott's letter in the gaslight as the evening breeze tugs at the corners of the page.

> *Dear Julia,*
> My love, it's only been a few days since you've left but it feels like an eternity.
> After you got on the plane, I had some "words" with the bitch and bastard. I told your dad he was a ▮▮▮▮▮▮▮ and a ▮▮▮▮▮▮▮ and that if he wanted to ▮▮▮▮, then ▮▮▮▮▮▮▮.
> 'Course your mom pulled him away, and that was that. Reckon they didn't want a scandal to ruin the good doctor's name.

Since you've gone, I've scarcely moved from my room. I don't have energy to do anything. When the boys came round the other day to see if I was up for shooting squirrels I told them no, I'd rather ███████████████████.

I can't stop thinking about you, about how they seperated us like this. Even as I write this, my hands are shaking. I want to be with you and in you so bad it hurts. I miss your ██████ and the way your you ████████████ when we ██████ But it's not just ██████, it's you, the way you are good to me in ways no one understands.

I've never felt this way before, this pain is the first I've suffered purely from emotional problems. You are my first, last, and only love. When this is all over I want you to come back to me and be mine. And if you want, I will marry you.

Yours 4 Ever,

Scott

I reread the last sentence and snicker. Scott's always good at saying what he thinks people want to hear; he likes to be liked. But in this case, he's wrong. I don't want to get married. I like boys well enough, but the last thing I need is a husband bossing me around after being bossed around by everyone else my entire life. I just want to be left alone.

The Sandi Patti tape ends, and the player clicks off. The jungle explodes to life on the other side of the barbed wire, buzzing and shrieking. Wild things out hunting at dusk.

In the valley below, the moon lies shattered in the rice paddies.

I tuck the letter back into its envelope and reseal the tape, thinking about the words Scott used to get inside me—*beautiful, love, special*—and wonder if he meant any of them. I miss his touch and playfulness, the way he'd put an ice cube inside me on hot afternoons and drink the water out of me, the way he'd cover my mouth so my parents wouldn't hear us having sex. But, then again, he also copied my poems for other girls and visited them when I was busy.

Susan comes out to the patio to sit beside me and we talk about the trip we're taking to Santo Domingo next month, and what we'll see there. If there will be McDonald's and Pizza Huts and places to buy tampons and M&Ms. I long to talk to her about boys and the urgencies they create, but I know that everything we say will be overheard and scrutinized and assigned points.

We veer left on County Road 50, our bike tires skidding across the crumbled pavement. The sky is quilted with low clouds, the air hot and wet.

"Race you!" David yells.

We rise in unison to stomp on our pedals, blasting past Hanke's Dairy, the Workmans' cornfield, the abandoned trailer home with the windows smashed out.

David zooms ahead of me and looks back over his shoulder grinning because he thinks I won't catch up. He's scrawny, but strong. And a bit too cocksure of himself. I blink sweat from my eyes, lean over the handlebars and click my bike into tenth gear. *Watch out, here I come.*

A shriek rips through the dormitory, one, two, three times. I jolt upright in my bunk, my heart jackhammering, my dream racing away. Bruce is in the middle of the room with his silver referee whistle plugging his mouth. He blows it again, and I clamp my hands over my ears.

"Everybody downstairs, now!" he roars.

Night-gowned bodies rise from bunks like ghosts, and Susan gets out of the bottom bunk and looks at me.

"You'd best scurry," she says, her eyes sparking with fear. "We're fixing for a session."

I have no idea what that means, but her tone prods me into action. I flip onto my belly and slide over the bunk's metal frame backwards, conscious that my nightie is creeping up the back of my thighs as Bruce watches.

"Get moving!" he yells. I stumble down the narrow stairway and behind me, Jolene, fresh from a week in The Hole, gurgles something and Bruce screams, "Yes, you have permission! Go!"

I join the other girls clumped in the middle of the living room, my eyes still foggy with sleep. Becky sits in a patio chair in the corner regarding us with a grim face. I give her a questioning look, but she turns away. I tilt my watch to the lamplight; it's two A.M. Tomorrow, already. Bruce pads downstairs in slippers.

"Everyone get down and give me twenty-five push-ups!" he shouts.

I drop to the ground with the others and start humping air. We count in unison as the satin and lace of our nighties kiss the floor and Bruce paces between us, exhorting us to get lower, move faster, count louder.

What have we done to deserve this? I rack my brains for reasons. Bruce didn't seem grumpier than usual today. No one even got chewed out for an exposed bra strap or spacing at supper.

"Fifty jumping jacks!" Bruce yells, when we finish the push-ups.

Janet's boobs flop obscenely under her nightgown and Tiffany's is so short you can see her teddy bear underwear.

As we pant, Bruce rages.

"I am sick and tired of the negativity in this household! I should send the lot of you back to Level 0, eh? All I get from you girls is ingratitude! But things are going to change around here, eh? I want to see PRO-gress and I want to see it now!"

Who does this Canuck think he is, anyway? He's not even an American, and here he is, he's in charge of us American girls!

His hands are balled at his sides, and his face looks ready to explode.

"You have lost enthusiasm for The Program!" he shrieks. "You have no respect for authority! You are not right with God!

"Thirty-five leg lifts!"

It's true that some girls have gotten more depressed since Jolene's botched escape. Her ravished head is a constant reminder of how hopeless our situation is, and there's been a lot more snuffling under pillows at night, a lot more sour faces at the dinner table. But then again, we're in reform school. How can we *not* be depressed?

"I can't do it no more!" Jolene wails after three minutes of running in place. She falls to the floor and curls onto her side, rocking herself like a baby. The rest of us continue to jog, our bare feet slapping the tiles.

Becky crouches over Jolene and rubs her back.

"Jolene, do you want to go back into The Hole?!" Bruce shouts.

Becky looks up at him with hard eyes.

"I think Jolene should rest," she says. They regard each other for a long moment before Becky turns back to Jolene, who's still rocking and moaning.

"It's not fair!" Susan gasps as she jogs. "How come she gets a break?"

She starts to cry.

"Mind your own business, eh?" Bruce shouts. "Twenty suicides!"

Soon we're reduced to a blubbering mass of snot, sweat and tears. Bruce make us promise we'll show him PRO-gress and that we'll try harder, really *think* about what we're doing.

Afterward, we kneel on the floor in a circle, sweat pasting our nighties to our bodies, and hold hands. Bruce leads us in prayer, asking God to forgive us our trespasses against Him, but what exactly those are, I'm not quite sure.

We wake the next morning transformed into godly women, adorned with meek and mild spirits from sleep deprivation. We brim with enthusiasm for The Program. We are happy to be here. We are *grateful* for this opportunity. We sing hymns during House Jobs, as we walk to school, during Work Time. We bring Bruce tea during Free Time, massage his doughy shoulders and clean his shoes without being asked. We are models of Christian femininity.

As we wash up that night, Susan informs me that a session can occur at any time, for any reason. Past reasons have included low points on House Inspection, general mopiness and a per-ceived lack of respect for Bruce.

"You never know when one's coming," she whispers into the mirror at me. "That's how they keep us on our toes."

For the next week, if a girl so much as stops smiling, all we have to do is hiss the word "Session" at her and she gets right back with The Program. One person's bad attitude can drag the entire house down, and no one wants to be responsible for a loss of dream time. Sleep is everyone's favorite Time, for it is Divine Nothingness.

On Saturday, there's an all-school outing to Salto de Jimenoa, but I'm not grateful for it. I'm angry. I failed my Room Job because my panties weren't folded right, and when Bruce told me my score, I rolled my eyes, prompting him to give me a 1 in the Courtesy and Respect box, as well as a 2 in the House Job box. So I have two casitas to look forward to after the daylong hike.

I lag behind the other kids on the trail while Becky tries to distract me with small talk about the flora and fauna. I grunt responses to her observations, and after a while she moves on to someone else.

I want to focus on my misery. I want to roll around in it like a dog in a pile of shit. I want to claim it as my own. Right now, it's all I have. I still can't believe that a place like Escuela Caribe exists, and that I find myself enrolled in it. All I did was try to wring some happiness from life, a little fun and a little affection, and as a result I was banished to an island colony ruled by sadistic Jesus freaks. Mother says the greatest thing you can do in life is die for Jesus Christ, but all this suffering for Him had best score me some major brownie points, too.

My mood gets darker as the waterfall gets louder. Why does God always have to make everything so difficult? I know we are put on earth to test our faith, but why can't He make our time here a little more enjoyable? Why does everything have to be such a cross?

We hike farther than the last time, and the boys rush forward, jostling each other to be the first to reach whatever lies ahead.

The trail ends and the guide rope ends, and we climb onto a crown of bald rock. A few of the boys throw themselves to the ground and belly crawl to the lip of the gorge, and soon everyone's laying down and peering over the side, staff and students alike.

Everyone but David and me. He's leaning against a solitary pine tree, eyeing me warily, aware of my foul mood. Everyone's so preoccupied with the view that I could easily flash him a forbidden smile to let him know I'm okay, but I don't because I'm not. I'm forced to playact with everyone else here, but I refuse to playact with my brother.

I turn away from his concern and walk toward the cliff, treading carefully on the mist-slick rock. I crouch on the curved edge and hug my knees. On either side of me, prostrate boys shout into the canyon, but the waterfall drowns their voices, reducing them to red faces and ranting mouths. They might as well be shouting profanities into the cold mist and thunder. They probably are.

I decide to try it myself.

"Fuck this place!" I scream. "Fuck you all! Fuck you, assholes!"

I scream so hard that my throat gets scratchy, but I still can't hear myself over the catapulting water.

"Fuck!"

"Fuck!"

"Fuck!"

It feels good to be profane. I smirk and gaze down at the river, which lies at a dizzying distance below. I close my eyes against the wet wind churned up by the fall, and cold dew collects on my face. I can feel the hugeness of the void before me; it would be so easy to slip into it and disappear. One slip and it'd all be over: casitas, sessions, Escuela Caribe.

I'm moving.

I open my eyes, and I'm moving, slipping over the wet rock into the abyss. I arch my back away from it and flail my arms, every atom in me roaring *stop! Not yet!*

Two brown hands slap down on my shoulders, forcing me to sit down. I turn and scramble up the rock on my hands and knees to level ground, and when I stand, there's David, sauntering back to the pine tree. No one has seen what happened; they're all still peering over the ledge.

David goes back to leaning against the tree, and we face each other with astonishment. My brother was watching over me. Gratitude floods my eyes and I sit at his feet, craving his presence like solid ground. We stay like this for a long time, watching wispy clouds move across the sky over the canyon. My skin is covered in goose bumps, but I'm sweating, and as I sit there, shivering and sweating, I feel a connection to my brother that is physical, as if his hands were still on my shoulders, protecting me.

When Ted blows his whistle to round people up to hike back down the mountain, I reluctantly move away from him, lest anyone think we were communicating.

Two days later, I walk up to David after the morning prayer meeting.

"What's up, bro?" I ask him, punching his arm.

It's the first time I've spoken to him in a month, and he looks at me as if I were brainsick and creeps backwards, glancing about the courtyard.

I grab his wrist and pull him back toward me.

"It's okay, I made Second. We can talk!"

I show him the medal Bruce gave me for my promotion. "Integrity," it says.

His face softens and he clutches me against him, and I pat his back awkwardly. It's the first time we've ever hugged each other. After a few seconds, I tighten my grip on him, and the sensation is both comforting and queer. He feels so fragile. My eyes start stinging, and I pull away and punch him again, and he puts his hand on his arm and pretends it hurts, and everything's back to normal.

There's a shush in the courtyard and I look up to see people staring at us.

"So, what's new with you?" I ask loudly.

"Not much." He shrugs, glancing around. "You?"

I shrug back.

"Same old, same old."

We sit at a picnic table grinning at each other. We've got only a few minutes before class, and there's too much to say.

Our classmates sit at the other tables and watch us.

We've both been warned: Mind what you say and do when you're together. No negativity. No cursing. No check topics. If you disobey, we will find out, and we will separate you again.

They fear us because they know we are above The Program's petty narking strategy. We will speak with honesty and won't betray each other for it. We are family. We are indivisible.

After a few days it becomes apparent that we can't talk freely; our classmates see us as a potential gold mine. There's always some kid lurking on the fringes of our conversation, waiting to hear something check so they can tattle on us for points. And keep us apart.

We have to prove that we're not a negative influence on each other by allowing anyone and everyone to listen to us, so we develop a new code to deal with spies.

"Look at that bug!" we'll say when a suspicious character sidles into view, pretending to read with their heads pointed our way. We'll crush the imaginary insect, pointing a shoe in the direction of the intruder, and switch our conversation from secular things to Jesus-approved things, such as the weather or homework or what we ate for breakfast.

Eventually, the intruder will get bored and leave, but the constant fear of getting busted is enough to prevent us from talking about anything meaningful.

Our only hope is for me to make Third Level, so we can volunteer at the village orphanage together. During the thirty-minute walk there and back, we could talk privately.

+   +   +

The rejection was limited to insults and cold shoulders until the summer we were eight, when we were physically attacked.

It happened on a July afternoon when our fifteen-year-old sister Debra escorted us to Kingston Pool. While she slathered herself with coconut oil and slowly toasted under the white glare of the Indiana sky, David and I dunked each other in the pool and did the Nestea plunge. The other kids our age were playing Marco Polo at the other end of the pool, and we longed to join in, but didn't dare ask—they were the same ones who yelled the "N" word at us.

Deb gave us money for slushees and flaky jakes, which we munched sitting side by side on our towels, watching the game. When our bellies were full of sugar, we napped with the sun drying our backs, the shouts and splashes fading to a comforting hum, the summer scents of chlorine and wet concrete thickening the air.

We woke to the lifeguard's whistle burst—the pool was closing—and dragged ourselves to the dank locker rooms to rinse off, reluctant to go home after so much brightness. As usual, we were the last kids to leave.

The Johnsons were waiting for us on the other side of the fence. There were four of them, three boys and a girl, older than us, younger than Deb. They waited until we crossed the clover patch between the pool and playground before jumping us.

"Stay out of our pool, Niggers!" they yelled. "You're polluting it!"

As Debra got into a shouting match with the oldest boy, the three youngest kids bore down on David and me. My ponytail was yanked, ripping hair from my scalp. We scrambled up the monkey bars and perched on top with our backs together, screaming and bawling and kicking at the white hands that tried to grab our ankles and pull us down. Our flip-flops fell into the sand and we continued kicking, bruising our feet on the metal bars.

It ended when a minivan pulled into the parking lot.

"Mom's here!" one of them yelled, and suddenly they had retreated and it was quiet and the sun blazed red and purple on the horizon.

We ran all the way home through the darkening woods, but still got in trouble for being late for supper. Mother had no patience for childish brawls.

Turn the other cheek, she scolded.

PRO-GRESS

"Now inhale and hold it!"

The fumes sear down my windpipe into my lungs, and I count to five before blowing them out of my pursed lips in a blue stream.

"Excellent!" Susan says, as I start to hack. "But you'd best tie your hair back, cuz it about caught afire."

We're in the bathroom, smoking matches. It's Free Time, and everyone else is downstairs, writing letters and listening to the new Keith Green album, *Jesus Commands Us to Go!* If you use your imagination, you can make him sound a little like Paul McCartney. As we listen to the title track, Susan and I slow dance together under the gas lamp:

> *Jesus commands us to go,*
> *but we go the other way.*
> *So He carries the burden alone,*

While His children are busy at play,
Feeling so called to stay.

"What do you think?" Susan asks after the song ends.

She hops up on the bathroom counter.

"I like *The Prodigal Son* better," I say.

She nods her agreement, and lights another match.

They think we're giving ourselves facials, and indeed, we've mixed bowls of sugar water and placed them in the twin sinks, just in case someone checks in on us or wants to use the toilet. As an added precaution, Susan has taken off one of her sneakers and wedged the toe into the gap at the bottom of the door; the only doors with locks in Starr are on the houseparents' and group leader's quarters. At night, we hear them slide their deadbolts shut against us as we lie in our bunks. We are fornicators and druggies and Satan Worshippers and prostitutes, and we outnumber them.

I'm on my third match and Susan's on her tenth. Sulphur smoke hangs in the air. Her skills are superior to mine because she was a smoker in real life—she can do the French Inhaler and blow rings and talk and exhale at the same time. I'm still learning not to gag; it's like learning to give a blow job.

My throat is raw and my mouth tastes foul, but I'm in a rare good mood. Susan and I are friends.

"I need to score a sixty-five tomorrow, or I'm fucked for Third," she says, smoke curling from her mouth. She scowls at the rusted ceiling. "If I don't get out of here by the end of summer, I'll kill myself."

Susan's parents lied and told her she'd only be down here a couple weeks, until the troubles back home blew over; she's been here seven months. It happens to a lot of kids. Parents will say anything to get you on that plane—they know that once you've landed on the island, you're as marooned as Gilligan.

My own parents, for example, told me I'd be going to the beach every weekend and we haven't gone once yet. When I asked Susan about this, she snorted and gave me a pitiful look.

"Nah," she said. "This ain't no beach."

Downstairs, the music stops and we freeze and stare at each other and then at the door. A second later, Keith Green starts up again—someone flipped the tape over—and Susan lights another match.

"Maybe you should try confronting someone," I say with a sly smile. "There's always Jolene."

Confronting is a nice word for narking. Confront someone about their bad attitude or behavior, and you get a 5 in the Being a Helpful and Positive Influence box. But the staff have to see you do it, or it doesn't count. Jolene's an easy target because she still pouts and curses under her breath when she gets angry.

"Oh, you are *too* good," Susan says, exhaling. "Jolene it is."

Footsteps start up the stairs and Susan flicks the match in the toilet and we rake our nails over our faces to make them glow. The door is pushed, then shoved, and Susan's sneaker is dragged inward across the cement.

It's Becky. She looks at us, and then down at the sneaker.

"Becky, Hon, may I please have a Band-Aid? I done got a blister," Susan says without skipping a beat. She lifts her bare foot and rubs the heel. The room is cloudy with smoke; Becky sniffs the air.

"Susan here has got a bad case of diarrhea," I tell her. Everyone uses matches to mask the stench. It's a common courtesy and a plausible explanation for the fumes.

"Okay, I'll get a band-aid," Becky says. "But then it's Bed Time."

"Yes, ma'am," Susan responds in her best southern belle voice. "Straight away." When Becky tucks back out the door, I high-five Susan.

"*We* are too good," I tell her.

Downstairs, we hear chairs shoved across the tile floor and realigned precisely along the edge of the dining room table.

"If dumb was dirt, she'd cover about an acre," Susan whispers.

Right as I'm chugging along toward Third, I hit a snag that threatens my PRO-gress toward freedom.

After Bruce dumps my underwear drawer on the floor for the fourth day in a row without an explanation, I ask him for one.

We're standing beside my bunk bed, my panties scattered like used Kleenex at our feet. He jots a 2 on my score chart, then looks at me to gauge my reaction. I put on my humble face.

"Please, Bruce, will tell me what I've done wrong?" I ask. "Please, just this once?"

He considers this request for a long moment, tapping an index finger against his fat lips, before exhaling sharply and bending to snatch a pair of panties from the floor. He kneels beside the bunk and motions for me to join him.

"Watch carefully," he says, gripping the cotton in his hairy fingers and stretching out the SCHEERES on the inside back waistband. My cheeks burn at seeing my underthings in his woolly grasp, but this is important: I cannot let a pair of panties stand between me and Third Level.

Bruce executes the Escuela Caribe underwear fold on the tile floor: crotch to waist, right side to center, left side to center. When he finishes, he slowly presses his fist over the white square like an iron, the tip of his tongue jutting from his mouth in concentration.

I grab another pair from the floor and mimic his movements, right down to the fist iron and the jutting tongue. When I lay my pair next to his, they look identical.

"Nope," Bruce says, shaking his head.

He taps the pair he folded.

"My panty is tighter than your panty, eh?" he says. "It's tidier. More compressed."

I look at my panty. I look at his panty. They *are* identical.

"You're right, Bruce," I say, shaking my head with feigned amazement.

I must show proper Courtesy and Respect Toward Authority Figures, and part of that is letting authority figures win panty-folding contests. *Yes, Bruce, you do have the tightest panty. You are the Queen of Panty Folders, you Canadian faggot.*

We stand and he gives me a sideways smile, then jots a + after the 2 on my chart. A 2+ doesn't mean squat—I'm punished for any point below a 3. It's suddenly clear to me that this has nothing to do with panties. It has to do with Bruce provoking me to see how I react. If I break and rebel, or if I obediently swallow all his bull crap.

Bruce is taunting me.

He points at the 2+ and looks at me expectantly.

"Thank you, Bruce," I say sweetly. "That's very generous of you."

When he turns to walk downstairs, I flip him off with both hands.

After school, Bruce orders me to move the rock pile uphill even though I'd just finished moving it downhill yesterday. And I know he's just doing it to fuck with me, and I'm tired of being fucked with. As I cradle the dusty rocks in my arms and lumber up the hill, a sewer of dark thoughts churns through me.

I wonder if Bruce hates me, or if he hates all females, or if he hates life in general. I wonder how he expects us girls to be positive when he's always breaking our spirits. He could keep me down here forever, despite superior housework and high grades, just to spite me.

A hot wind sprints up the hillside, blasting dust devils over me and setting palm branches a-chittering at the edge of the property. As I carry a bread loaf–sized rock in my hands, a blister pops on my palm and the rock grinds against the torn flesh. I drop the rock, it lands on my foot, and I sink to my knees howling.

There's a shout, and I look up to see Bruce standing on the patio with his hands on his wide hips.

"Get up!" he yells.

I pull myself off the ground, grit my teeth and pick up the rock, cradling it to my chest. My palm oozes pus and sweat runs into my eyes. As I climb the hill, a snippet of a song floats into my head, and I start to sing it: *I don't care anymore. You hear? I don't care any mo-oh-ore.*

I sing it loud, louder. All I remember is the chorus, which is the only part that matters right now anyhow, and I belt it out, compulsively, angrily, as I dump the rock beside the driveway.

Susan's on the front patio, knifing mud from her hiking boots, and she lifts her head and gives me a queer look.

She's pissy because she got demoted to Second after flunking her English and Geometry midterms. She never got a chance to nark on Jolene, who got wise to Susan tailing her around and threatened to "warp Susan upside the haid" if she didn't leave her alone.

Susan's fallen into a sorry state, not raising her hand when Bruce wants water or laughing at his jokes. She's in serious danger of losing Second Level as well if she keeps this up.

"No way you'll get home by the end of summer with that attitude," I warned her today when I found her sulking against a wall between classes.

"Whatever," she said, and walked away.

She's sore at me, too, because I now outrank her, even though she's been here four months longer than I have.

She glances back at the closed sliding glass door behind her as I dump my rock, now yelling my song. *I don't care anymore. You see, I don't care any mo-oh-ore.*

I know we're not supposed to sing pop songs or even mention the names of bands, because the staff believes secular music leads to all manner of depravity, such as perverted dancing, fornication and drug and alcohol addiction, but right now, I don't care what they think. *I don't any mo-oh-ore. You hear?*

When I return to the driveway, still crooning loudly, Bruce steps out from behind a pillar with an a-ha expression on his face. Susan is gone.

"What's that you're singing?" he demands.

My heart sinks, because I know Susan betrayed me.

"A song," I say, cradling my rock tighter against me.

Bruce takes a step closer.

"A Christian song?"

I chew my bottom lip.

"A, um, radio song."

"A Christian radio song?"

"Well . . ."

"So, a check song!" he shouts. "A secular song!"

I hug the rock to me and look at my feet.

"You just earned yourself a casita, eh? When you finish the pile, start running."

Susan refuses to look at me at supper, and sure enough, when our points are tallied up at the end of the day, she gets a 5 in the Being a Helpful and Positive Influence box and I get a 0.

I was an easy mark, I know, but I thought things were different between us.

David was right: Trust No One.

"Thank you for being a friend," I sing bitterly as we wash up for bed. She towels off her face without looking at me and goes to curl up on her mattress with her back toward the room.

Later, when her muffled sobs rise from the bottom bunk like the gasps of a drowning woman, I'm the one who tells her to shut up and let the rest of us sleep in peace.

We have this thing called "The Weekly Challenge" where we're supposed to come up with some personal defect that we can vanquish in seven days' time, such as zit-picking, or hatred of staff, or forgetting to pray before bed.

On Sundays, we meet individually with Becky to tell her the foible we plan to conquer, and she checks our progress throughout the week.

"How's the Challenge coming?" she'll ask.

"Well, I've got five pimples now, but I haven't touched a one since Tuesday," I'll respond, for example, lifting my bangs to show her the red lumps straining to liberate themselves from my forehead.

"Good girl," she'll say. "Keep striving."

As the weeks have worn on, it's been harder and harder to come up with new material. I've already used my hatred of Bruce (several times), of certain teachers, and of most of the other girls. In a hatred challenge, Becky has us make a special effort to be nice to the person we hate by complimenting them, or giving them a backrub, or helping with their homework or chores. I clean Bruce's shoes a lot.

I've also used forgetting to pray (no way to prove that one), gluttony (mistake—she made me forfeit dessert for an entire week), pride (bigger mistake—she made me switch house jobs with Jolene), envy (she made me write a list every day of ten things I was thankful for), and all the other deadly sins except for lust—which I do often in my bunk as I think of Scott or Tommy and rub the swelling place between my legs with a nail polish bottle. It helps me sleep better.

And I've used zit-picking and forgetting to pray so many times that Becky says they are longer valid challenges.

One Sunday when I keep drawing blanks, I finally tell her that I need to work on my hatred of my brother Jerome. When she asks me why, I stupidly tell her the truth.

The next day, I find myself in the school therapist's office during Work Time, instead of hauling rocks. Susan, Rhonda, and Brenda are also there. We are all, the therapist says, "victims of incest." She makes each of us share our story, but when my turn comes, I can't pull the words from my mouth.

"My brother, but he's not really my brother," is all I can say before a loud buzzing fills my ears. The noise is new since I entered The Program, and it happens during stressful situations, like during two A.M. sessions or when I see staff shoving students around. Sometimes the sound is like a waterfall and other times it's like a thousand tiny bells ringing, but mostly it's just a buzzing, as if a wasp were crawling inside my head. It prevents me from thinking too hard about whatever is happening, and in that way, the noise is soothing.

The other girls were also molested by male relatives living in their households, and this surprises me since they all come from upstanding Christian families. But then again . . . so do I.

During the hourlong session, Marie has us do mental exercises. She gives us a word like "bedroom" or "future" or "vacation" and has us draw pictures with crayons. I know she is looking for disturbing colors and images that signal a disturbed mind, so I draw her flowers and rainbows and baby animals, so she'll know I'm okay. See the cute little puppy? I AM OKAY.

Other times, she'll play a symphony with a heavy drum track and have us write a story to go along with the music. Again, she is looking for violence and despair, and I give her spring rain and fields of poppies. REALLY, I AM.

"Hmmm, interesting," is all she ever says when we turn in our stories and drawings. Afterwards, we're supposed to discuss "feelings."

I find these exercises disturbing. I'd rather haul rocks than haul these memories from my head. Does she really think she can wipe the past clean with crayons and Verdi's "Requiem"? The only way to get over the past is to stop living it. But she won't let us.

And it gets worse.

A few days after I start therapy, David marches over to me during afternoon break. I'm sitting on a bench in the courtyard, cramming for a Spanish quiz. I look up and he just stands there for a second, with an anguished look on his face.

"Did Jerome sexually molest you?" he finally asks.

I'm looking right up at him when he asks this, I'm sitting on a concrete bench with both feet on the ground, and suddenly it seems like I'm tipping over, head-first onto the brick patio. I grab the bench with both hands and the buzzing begins. The *bzzzzzzzz* gets louder and louder until David's face fades and recedes, until the buzzing is all there is. Next thing, I'm stumbling into the empty Spanish class with my textbook smashed open against my chest.

David tries to talk to me in the following days, but I walk away from him again and again. I feel dirty in his presence. I will never look him in the eye again. I wish a jungle creature would leap over the barbed wire fence and kill me.

I ask the therapist why she told him about Jerome, and she says, "Oh, I thought he already knew," and I think, "Oh, you idiot." I tell her I'd rather do Work Time than therapy, and she hesitates before agreeing.

"If you've got the wrong attitude, you'll just waste everyone's time, anyway," she says gruffly.

David sets the letter beside me on the picnic table as I'm finishing lunch. I see his brown hand slide the envelope next to my plate and I stiffen, but he walks away without saying a word.

"Family feud?" asks Tiffany.

I glare at her and stick the envelope in my backpack.

During Free Time, I read it on Starr's patio.

> *Julia,*
> I know that what hapenned is not your fault. Please don't feel bad.
> You are my big sister, and I will always look up to you, no matter what.
> Love,
> your cuddly little bro,
> *Dave*

My heart uncrimps and I gaze up at the crescent moon and the stars and feel peace rain down on me in their soft light. David knows this about me. And he still calls me his big sister.

+   +   +

Family was always crucial to David.

He loved The Brady Bunch *and would convince me to sneak up-stairs with him while Mother napped to watch it in Dad's study. We'd huddle side by side on Dad's swivel chair in front of the small black-and-white television on his desk, the volume low, poised to hit the power but-ton at the slightest noise downstairs.*

The moment the giddy music cued up ("Here's the story . . . of a lovely lady . . .") and the kids and parents started grinning at each other from their little boxes, we entered a trance. Our family was like the Bradys in many ways: We both had three boys and three girls. We both had been thrown together by fate (theirs by remarriage, ours by adop-tion). We both lived in the suburbs. And like Bobby and Cindy, David and I were the youngest.

But the similarities ended there; the Bradys were a happy bunch and we were not.

When the Brady kids got in trouble, their parents didn't hit them or tell them they were counting the days until they moved out. They got grounded, not whupped. They got talked to, not threatened. There were no stomach-churning wait-until-your-father-gets-home pronouncements. And by the end of the show, everyone was back to smiles and hugs as the giddy music cued up again.

In our minds, they were the real family and we were the fakes. We wanted to be the Bradys. We created alternative homes—under the ping-pong table with a blanket draped over it, in piles of leaves we'd raked to-gether, behind the sofa—where we'd reenact scenes from the show.

Years later, when I was the one counting the days until I could move out, David kept his faith that someday, somehow, our family would pull it all off.

CHAPTER 14

RAPTURE

There's not much to do on weekends between church and chores, as we are sick of playing Scrabble and writing letters that don't get answered, and reading books about sinners who find Jesus Christ. We are young and restless, and we crave fresh air and movement. But there's no playground in our barbed wire pen.

Ted Schlund comes up with a solution.

"I miss playing basketball and I'm sure you do too," he announces one Sunday at Vespers. "So I've decided to suspend classes this week so we can build ourselves a decent hoop court."

A hush smothers the chapel. Bugs sizzle and pop in the gas lamps. On the pew next to me, Tiffany grimaces down at her freshly manicured pink nails.

"Let's hear it for basketball!" Ted shouts from the pulpit. He pumps a fist in the air, grunting "Bask-et-ball! Bask-et-ball! Bask-et-ball! Oh-oh-oh!"

The staff applauds politely, and, after a lag, the students join in. We are leery of any change in our routine, which may be harsh but is comforting in its predictability.

The next day, we rise at dawn to begin work. When I slide out of bed, I notice Susan lying unmoving in the bottom bunk, and remember being woken several times to the vile backfiring of her bowels in the bathroom. She's got a bad case of the blues.

Chronic bouts of diarrhea plague everyone at Escuela— there's always someone sprinting to the john with a jagged face, hands clutching their gut, terrified the angry shits will erupt before they can bare their ass over a toilet. It's been known to happen. It's part of the Third World experience, along with three-inch cockroaches and the dire lack of shopping malls.

But the blues also have an upside: weight loss. I once lost eight pounds in a week. You can pork out with impunity when you have chronic diarrhea. Back in Indiana I used Ex-Lax for the same effect, but the blues are much more effective.

Susan's lost so much weight that her ribcage pokes through her nightie. She gazes up at me with glassy eyes, and I give her a dirty look and thrust myself into my clothes. She's neither my friend nor my responsibility. She's a nark. As I join the downstairs stampede to fetch my cleaning utensils, it dawns on me that if she dies, I could nab her foam pad, which is a good two inches thicker than mine.

A half hour later, the entire student body assembles on the lumpy slope southwest of Starr, minus Susan. She's running a temperature, so Bruce took her off points for the day; it's not fair. When we left the house, RuthAnn was crouched beside her bunk, spoon-feeding her lime oatmeal.

The rest of us form a circle in the still-wet field grass. Preacher Stevie steps into the middle of it and the early morning breeze presses his white T-shirt against his meaty shoulders and chest. He extols the virtues of physical exertion, then cracks open his Bible to read from Corinthians.

"What? Know ye not that your body is the temple of the Holy Ghost which is in you, and ye are not your own?" he reads.

He closes the book.

"We're not building this basketball court for ourselves," he says. "We're building it for Jesus Christ."

I think of Jesus doing a lay-up and suppress a giggle.

Next to me, Rhonda flutters to attention, tugging at her hair and puffing out her chest and sighing, and when we join hands to bless the basketball court, her hand is hot with lust for Preacher Stevie. And while there's no denying that Preacher Stevie is a stud who can fill a girl's head with a thousand dirty thoughts when he falls into a frenzy at the pulpit and his muscles start twitching under his tailored shirt and his cheeks flush and he starts breathing heavy, he is still a Man of God, and Rhonda's got no business tossing herself about like the $2 whore she once was.

She's been afire with the Lord ever since she started attending personal devotions. Lots of kids go to these one-on-one meetings with Preacher Stevie hoping to get extra points, but Rhonda is a true convert. She says she can feel the Holy Spirit moving in her during these prayer sessions, and she's taken to starting sentences with "The Bible says this" and "The Bible says that." And I swear that if she "Bibles" me one more time, I'll take an expanded and illustrated King James and cram it down her throat.

As Preacher Stevie's prayer drones on I imagine the things Rhonda's sweaty hand touched while she was hawking her underage pootie on the streets of Oklahoma City. Penises. Carloads of 'em. Dirty, nasty, liverwurst-smelling penises. I jerk my hand from her grasp and wipe it on my jeans.

She gives me a look.

"Itch!" I whisper, before grabbing her fingertips.

When the prayer finally ends, Ted points to a steep chunk of weed-choked terrain, and tells us to start digging.

We grab machetes and shovels and pickaxes and fan out in a row, first scalping the earth, then puncturing it, gouging great holes in the hard soil. Cinnamon-colored dust hangs about us in great lazy clouds, powdering our skin orange and flooding our nostrils with the scent of chalk and old hay.

Behind us, Ted and the other staffers direct our blades, urging us to keep going, keep digging, keep striving. We pry boulders loose from their cavities like giant rotten molars and roll them downhill. Pile smaller stones onto each other's outstretched arms. Shovel dirt into wheelbarrows. Dump everything we dig up in a pile at the bottom of the hill.

As the July sun crawls higher into the cloudless Caribbean sky, so does the temperature. By mid-morning, sweat has glued our jeans and T-shirts to our bodies like sausage casings. I catch David's eye and we exchange a grim look; the hated chore of gardening was cake compared to this.

Nevertheless, everyone smiles at the staff and swings their tools with grunts of enthusiasm. We will absolutely score in the Attitude, Cooperation and Helpful Influence boxes, and we will get out of here that much quicker. Even Boy 0 is acting the good sport, swinging a pickaxe with rigor; he appears to finally have learned that resistance is futile.

Ted leads us in a hymn sing, and we pant out "God Is So Good" and "Just As I am" and "Blessed Reedemer" as we slice and tear the earth. When the sun sucks our throats dry, pitchers of warm Kool-Aid are handed round and we guzzle it directly from the pour spouts, not caring whose lips came before ours or that dust and small insects season our refreshment. Such is our thirst.

At noon we crouch among the dead weeds with dirt-smeared arms and faces and unpack the food baskets prepared by our housemothers. RuthAnn has prepared cheese and lettuce sandwiches and pineapple. We gulp down the sandwiches and suck the pineapple juice from our fingers and ask for more, but there's no more to give. Such is our hunger.

In the mid-afternoon, as the sun blasts overhead in the stagnant sky, smiles and muscles start to falter. Saltwater rolls down my scalp into my eyes, my arms tremble, and blisters form on the pads of my hands.

When the staff's exhortations to *strive harder* fail to speed our progress, a ghetto blaster is called forth, fed six fresh D batteries, and placed on the slope above us. The synthesized guitars and thumping percussion of Petra silence our groans.

> *Caught in the undertow being swept downstream*
> *Going against the flow seems like such a dream*
> *Trying to hold your ground when you start to slide*
> *Pressure to compromise comes from every side*
> *Wise up, rise up*

We work with renewed vigor, as if this were real music and not just Jesus music.

The boys strip off their sweaty T-shirts, and I stop swinging my pickaxe when Tommy tosses his shovel aside and steps back from the growing bank of dirt. He grasps the hem of his red Fear God T-shirt in his hands and slowly peels it over his tan torso, revealing inch by inch his etched stomach and chest, the generous curves of his shoulders and arms.

He balls up the shirt and pitches it into the dead weeds, then swipes his dripping face with the back of his arm and I gasp at his beauty. The heavy drum track of the Jesus music beats something to life inside me, a spark that flares and expands as Tommy picks up his shovel and tosses dirt into a wheelbarrow, his muscles rippling and glistening in the searing light. And I'm not the only one leering at him with awe and admiration; every girl on the hillside has stopped working to witness this carnal perfection. Such is our lust.

I walk past Tommy to a water bucket stationed at the side of the trough and lift it to my face, letting the warm fluid splash into my mouth and over my T-shirt as I drink him in.

My thirst quenched, I stumble over to grab the handles of his wheelbarrow and stand dizzy and dumb in his presence, my shirt sopping and my bra soaked through. His green eyes bore into mine as he slowly spills a shovelful of earth into the wheelbarrow, a corner of his mouth cocked in a knowing smile. I pull back my shoulders and thrust out my breasts the way Susan did that night after Vespers, and his eyes slide over this small offering and linger on my nipples, which poke out like the eraser tips on No. 2 pencils. I feel his steam and smell his yeast and the flame within me leaps and swells as dust swirls around us.

"Julia, dump that load!" Ted bellows over the moaning guitars. His voice jump-starts time, and I rip my eyes from Tommy's and push the wheelbarrow downhill.

As I'm forcing it back up the ragged slope, I notice that the other girls' T-shirts are also pasted to their flesh with splashed bucket water and that the boys' movements are hard and alert, and that the air is thick with more than dust. Male and female shapes heave together, arms caressing, as the earth is groped and pounded, chests grazing as tools exchange. Bold stares. Flushed skin. Panting mouths. Everything in sync to the throbbing Jesus music. A peculiar dance executed by a crazed tribe of mud children.

The staff sense something peculiar in these movements and gather in a circle to press their heads together. I smirk in their direction as I scoop a pickaxe from the ground and, in a delirium of heat and exhaustion and desire, consider how easy it would be for us to turn our blades against our masters.

As I join the writhing line of bodies, there's a whistle blast— a long, terrified scream—and I turn to see Ted standing in the middle of the mass grave we're digging. He motions to the Quemado group leader, who sprints across the dirt and pounces on the jam box, smacking it quiet.

"Everybody stop!" Ted roars.

The white noise of the tropical afternoon washes over the landscape as bodies tumble apart and stand to face Ted, blades in hand. He bends to pick up a discarded spade before speaking.

"Let's take a group break," he says, gripping the spade handle in both hands.

The group leaders post themselves at the four corners of the pit and Becky beckons to us with a downward flick of her hand. We drop our tools and walk to her.

"For modesty's sake, I need you girls wearing light-colored T-shirts to change into darker ones," she chirps in her bird voice. "And please, girls, let's not spill water on ourselves. We don't want to waste this precious resource."

When we reconvene at the work site five minutes later, the ghetto blaster is gone and the boys have covered chests and sullen faces. We're instructed to level the downhill rock pile, which keeps us well away from their agitated presence.

The next five days are a grind of dirt, heat and hymn-sings. I grit my teeth and fantasize about sitting in the coolness of our cement house, reading a book. Any book, even a Jesus one.

The next Sunday during Vespers, Ted congratulates us on our hard work before dropping a bomb:

"There won't be enough funds to pave the court until next year, and by that time I expect every student here to have successfully reintegrated into society," he says.

A hush smothers the chapel. Bugs sizzle and pop in the gas lamps.

"Seriously, folks, your contribution will be appreciated by generations of Escuela Caribe students to come," he says. "I am proud of you. God is proud of you."

I stare open-mouthed at Ted, then turn to look at David, who shakes his head in disbelief. A week of chain gang labor for nothing. A week behind in school. A week behind in our PRO-gress toward freedom.

Ted begins to clap, and the staff join in, and after a lag, so do we. I slap my blisters together and glare at the wooden cross behind Ted's head.

Why do You let these things happen?

Susan doesn't die, but she doesn't get better either. She spent Work Week sprawled on her bed like a wet rag, rising now and again to stink up the bathroom.

When she passes out on the toilet one day, they take her to a clinic in La Vega, a village twenty miles away, and she's found to be a veritable petri dish of the *Salmonella typhi* bacteria, otherwise known as typhoid.

RuthAnn, who used to be a nurse in Canada, tells us you get typhoid by digesting fecal matter, but can't explain how such matter entered Susan's mouth. It serves Susan right I think, for being a nark. *Eat shit and die.*

Susan's quarantined in The Hole to keep her from turning into Typhoid Mary and killing the rest of us, and the next day during lunch, a beat-up Toyota with "Ayuntamiento" painted on the sides rattles through the front gate. A Dominican in a gray suit and a fedora gets out, and Debbie rushes over to greet him.

"He's from the government," Tiffany says, pointing at the car with a forkful of potato salad. "That's what that word "ayuntamiento" means. The mayor's office."

"Like, duh!" I say, glaring at her. I don't know if he's government or not, but I don't like Tiffany thinking she's smarter than the rest of us.

We gawk at the stranger as Debbie ushers him through the courtyard to Ted's office. He's the first outsider we've ever seen on The Property besides the guard and the staff's cook. At the door to Ted's office, the man takes off his fedora and turns to regard the picnic tables with pursed lips. I gnaw on my cold cut sandwich and fantasize that he is our savior. That he's heard we're being held here against our will and has come to shut the school down and send us all home.

Five minutes later, he drives away, and my fantasy goes with him.

But during P.E., he returns. This time the Toyota's crammed full of Dominicans in suits. *Reinforcements. Backups in case the staff resist our liberation.* We're playing dodgeball when the car pulls through the gate and shudders to a stop next to the banyan tree. After Fedora Man gets out, I lose track of him when someone chucks the ball at me and it nearly beans my head.

For many kids, dodgeball isn't a game: It's revenge. It's their chance to settle a score in a legitimate fashion. As I run and duck and cover my face, I watch the Toyota out of the corner of my eye. The suits have gotten out and are leaning against it; there are four of them.

The game comes to a halt when the ball hits Janet in the face and she crumples to the ground, wailing. She sobs in the dirt as the rest of us stand around her with crossed arms, impatiently waiting for her to get up so we can finish the game and get started on our Work Time chores.

Fedora Man reappears with Ted, who hops on a moped and leads the Toyota up the cement drive to the upper reaches of The Property. They wade through the waist-high grass and disappear on the other side of the barbed wire fence.

After Janet drags herself to the losers' area under the banyan tree, the game continues, and when the Toyota rolls back down the hill twenty minutes later, I'm standing next to her in the shade. As the car idles a few feet away from us while Fedora Man talks to the guard, the man in the front passenger seat sticks his head out the window. He's young, handsome, wearing sunglasses and a gold chain that flashes under his open shirt. We regard each other for a moment, and then he sticks out his tongue and flutters the tip up and down in a perverted gesture. I turn my head in shame, and he laughs.

I will think about his tongue later, when I'm alone with my nail polish bottle.

When we return to Starr, Bruce breaks the news: Susan got typhoid from cows. There's a pasture above The Property, and they found a dead cow in the stream that supplies our water, one of those ash-colored Hindu cows, rotting in the shallows and bloated with maggots. Also there's live cows polluting the water supply with manure. In fact, he says, both the dead cow and this fecal matter may be giving everyone the blues.

So we're all eating shit.

We must boil the water we use to clean the dishes and brush our teeth. We're also allowed to help ourselves to Cokes whenever we're thirsty.

And this one small symbol of normality—pop—changes our lives. We're allowed to reach into the fridge and take a green bottle whenever we're thirsty, and I swear I've never been so thirsty in my life. I suck down the cold brown bubbles in five gulps, then reach for another, just because. And when I fetch one for myself, I grab one for Jolene as well, because it makes me happy to see her face light up as she clinks her bottle against mine. Ain't no liquor ever tasted better.

During Free Time, we gather around the supper table to play Scrabble and sip our pop and giggle as if we were normal teenage girls and not fallen women. We piece the Coke jingle together from memory and sing it in a round.

On the ninth round, Bruce pokes his head out of the house-parent quarters to ask us what we're singing, and we tell him it's the Coke song.

"That could be construed as secular," he says. "I don't want you singing it." He sticks Sandi Patti in the cassette player and presses play.

This camaraderie of Coke ends a few days later when the staff locate iodine in a neighboring village, and house pops again become a privilege. The school hires a team of locals armed with machetes to hack up the dead cow and haul it away in garbage bags, and notices are sent to our parents reassuring them that the "water quality issue" has been resolved.

During Free Time, people drift back to their separate corners to write letters or do homework, and once again, Starr becomes a cement box, a place to do time.

Shortly after the typhoid scare, some dark cloud descends upon Preacher Stevie and he starts in with the fire and brimstone.

He'll call a special function after supper, and we'll scoot downhill and file impatiently into the chapel, resentful of losing precious Free Time.

One Wednesday evening, Preacher Stevie seems more perturbed than usual. His muscles spasm beneath his dress shirt and his armpits are damp with sweat. As the wind bursts through the wooden slats covering the chapel windows and the gas lamps flicker, he scowls down at us from the pulpit.

"Some of us here tonight," he says in a smoldering voice, "need to be reminded of the business of Hell."

He drags out the "e" in Hell as if he were choking on it. Heeeeeeell. The word hangs over our heads like a hatchet, setting people to squirm in their pews. We should be used to Preacher Stevie's mood swings by now, but it's still shocking to see him go from Gentle Jesus to Angry God in the lull of an afternoon. I often wonder what sparks this change in him between the time he finishes his one-on-one prayer sessions and the time he rides his moped back to the house in Jarabacoa that he shares with the other single male staffers. Whether it was some student's prayertime confession, or too many hours reading the Old Testament in his windowless office.

". . . and I'm not talking tonight about the Heeeell below," Preacher Stevie continues, his auburn hair aflame in the gas lamp light. "I'm talking Heeeell that will take place right here on Earth."

He's talking Rapture again. I look back at David, and sure enough, he's eyeing me too. We only just heard about this Rapture thing at Escuela, and wonder why Reverend Dykstra never mentioned it back at Lafayette Christian Reformed.

According to the folks down here, one day there'll be a bright flash in the sky and we'll look up to see Jesus hovering in the air above us. He'll spread his arms, and the true believers will float up to meet Him and to be personally escorted into Heaven.

Now, Preacher Stevie says the true believers could be anywhere when The Rapture occurs—driving down the freeway,
mowing their lawn, or sitting on the toilet, when, *poof!* they'll
zoom skyward, slipping through doors and ceilings like Casper
the Friendly Ghost. And even the dead true believers will rise
from their graves, but it won't be gross or scary like in *Dawn of
the Dead*.

The scary things happen to the folks who are Left Behind, to
the unbelievers and Christians who didn't believe hard enough.
Because after the true believers go to Heaven, Satan will take
over the world, Preacher Stevie says. Among other horrible
things, Satan will force everyone who's Left Behind to get 666
tattooed on their foreheads, and he'll set loose an army of
demons that have horse bodies, human faces and scorpion tails
that go around stinging people to death.

"In those days of misery, you will have one last chance to prove
your faith by resisting the Prince of Darkness," he now says, gripping the pulpit and flexing his large bicep muscles. I try not to notice them. "You will experience pain and torment of every form
imaginable. You will cry out to God for mercy, and He will turn
His back on you, just as you turned your back on Him.

"And if you fail this last test of faith, He will banish you to
Hell, where your pain and torment will increase one hundred-
fold and never end."

Hell excites Preacher Stevie. He runs his hands back and forth
over his scalp as he talks, and by the end of the sermon, it's standing on end like a madman's. He pauses to reach down and pull a
Coke from beneath the pulpit, then throws his head back to gulp
from the bottle, his Adam's apple bobbing. I swallow dryly.

"The Rapture's due any day now," he shouts, keeping his eyes
on us as he bends to set the bottle back on the pulpit's hidden
shelf. "The signs of the End Times are here, just like the Book of

Revelation prophesized. We've got nucular bombs and legalized abortion and gay homos on prime-time TV. Evil surrounds us."

I don't recall the Bible mentioning any of those things, but perhaps I wasn't reading it hard enough. Other things confuse me as well. Preacher Stevie says that millions of Christians will be raptured up to Heaven, while John Calvin said only 144,000 souls could fit into Paradise. Maybe God built an addition onto Heaven since John Calvin came up with his figure all those centuries ago, but I don't dare ask; adults think you're smarting off if you pry after such details.

On the pew next to me, Jolene fidgets, peeling off her orange fingernail polish and eating it. On my other side, Rhonda breathes in Preacher Stevie's every word with an open mouth.

"If Jesus appeared in the sky right now, would He take you with Him, or would you be Left Behind?" Preacher Stevie asks us. "If you have any doubt whatsoever, I urge you to rededicate yourself to Him tonight, right here, right now."

He lifts a jam box from the floor and sets it on the pulpit, then jabs the play button. I already know the music he'll play before he turns it on, because he ends each hellfire sermon the same way. The hair on the back of my neck rises as Larry Norman's creepy "I Wish We'd All Been Ready" pours through the speakers, warning of all the evils that befall those who are Left Behind.

I bow my head.

"Please take me with you, Jesus, if you really do appear in the sky," I pray. Better safe than sorry.

When the song ends, the school therapist slides behind the piano and strikes up "Take My Life and Let It Be." One by one, a handful of students walks to the front of the chapel as the rest of the congregation sings, holding hands and swaying queerly.

Rhonda is the first to go. She gets on her knees before Preacher Stevie and gazes up at him.

I wait until the last stanza before dropping Jolene's hand and walking forward. I'm running low on points this week; this might improve my score in the Attitude and Cooperation boxes.

I kneel beside Rhonda, and when I glance over at her, she's crying. Whether her tears are from joy or sorrow, I can't tell; her head is turned toward Preacher Stevie, who's working his way down the line of students, crouching to pray beside each one.

When he gets to Rhonda, she grabs his arm with both hands and pulls him to her, whispering in his ear. He stiffens and says something curt back. She looks scared, he looks angry. They whisper back and forth until the swaying congregation reaches the final chorus, and Preacher Stevie pries his arm from her grasp.

He squats beside me.

"Is it really possible to be one hundred percent pure and free from sin?" he asks in a harsh voice. I turn to him, but he's glowering at the cement floor between us. Before I can respond, he stands. As he gives the benediction, I puzzle over his question, feeling gypped of my personal prayer. Why is he asking *me* if it's possible to be free from sin? Preachers are supposed to give us answers, not questions.

Next to me, Rhonda gawks up at Preacher Stevie like a lovesick puppy, her cheeks wet, her mouth moving.

"Help me, God, oh help me," she wails in a whisper.

God does not help Rhonda.

When she starts complaining of exhaustion and vomiting, she's taken to a clinic in La Vega for a checkup. That afternoon, when we return to Starr from P.E., her things have been cleared out of the dormitory.

"Preacher Stevie and Rhonda are no longer with us," Bruce tells us at the supper table. "They had unfitting corporal contact and have been expelled from Escuela Caribe."

There's a collective gasp—Rhonda's pregnant! And free!—and a couple of snorts—I wasn't the only girl who was suspicious of Rhonda's sudden zealotry. It's now apparent that it wasn't the Holy Spirit she felt moving in her during all those one-on-one prayer sessions, but Preacher Stevie.

Bruce looks at us sternly.

"This is the last time either of their names shall be mentioned, understood?"

"Yes, Bruce," we reply.

Secretly, I admire Rhonda's craftiness. Not only did she manage to get laid, she also escaped The Program. She could always give the baby up for adoption and resume her life afterward. Or she could abort it—I'm sure God would also reject the forbidden fruit of a preacher man and a teenage member of his flock. It would make Him look bad.

Over the next few days, I consider the male staffers I could try to seduce—and I'm sure I'm not the only girl who thinks about this—before shuddering with revulsion; none of them are hot compared to Preacher Stevie, and I'm not that desperate. Yet.

As if to ward off such scheming, the school issues a new policy barring female students and male staff from being alone together.

She whose name shall not be spoken got lucky.

+   +   +

After Jerome was adopted, the violence got worse. Hesitation was rebellion; a question, defiance. Father got into the angry act, beating the boys with a belt in the workshop, making them strip to their underwear and bend over a stepladder. Mother chronicled their iniquities at the supper table, and he disciplined them after reading aloud to us from the Bible. He was the head of the household, the enforcer, the rod and the reproof.

As the violence escalated, David and I began to fight.

Our skirmishes were a way to release the tension festering a scratch beneath the domestic surface. We never knew when our parents would erupt in anger, in a slap or a pinch or a spanking, and it felt better to court violence than to dread its arrival.

We used racial slurs as extra ammo during our brutal kick fights.

"Jungle bunny!" I'd shriek.

"Honkey!" David would yell back.

"Spear chucker!"

"White trash!"

If our mother heard us, she'd make us bite a bar of Ivory. We'd hold it in our mouths while she slowly counted to thirty, the white heat searing our sinuses and knifing tears from our eyes. If, after we'd rinsed our sudsy mouths, she didn't believe we were sufficiently contrite, she'd have us write lines. John 15:12, 100 times:

"This is my commandment, that you love one another as I have loved you."

We'd glare at each other across the dining room table, as repulsed by each other's presence as two magnets with aligned poles, and storm off to our separate corners as soon as we'd finished.

Eventually boredom would precipitate peace, and David would slide a bag of pop rocks under my door, or I'd knock on his with The Ungame tucked under my arm.

We could never hate each other for long.

CHAPTER 15

AGUA DE COCO

Three months after my arrival, I make Third Level. After I recite the required Scriptures and perform the required calisthenics, Bruce gives me a King James Bible with a white plastic cover, an "I ♥ Jesus" T-shirt and a medal that says "Achievement."

None of this moves me.

The only thing that makes the event notable is the fact that David and I are now both on a "trust level" and therefore qualify to volunteer at the orphanage together. Which doesn't necessarily mean they'll let us. They could say no just to mess with our heads. It happens.

We take precautions to make our case stronger. When we meet, as usual, for a few minutes at the end of lunch, we sit in the center of the courtyard and read our Bibles. If someone asks us what we're doing, we tell them we're reading the Scriptures from start to finish to better understand the Holy Word. That we've always wanted to read the Bible straight through, and this is an excellent opportunity to do it, together. Our classmates eye us with suspicion, but the staff nod their approval.

After a week of this display, we work up the courage to knock on Ted's office door and ask permission to volunteer together. I've donned my "I ♥ Jesus" T-shirt for the occasion and David wears "God Rules!" My heart drums at my ribcage when Ted tells us to come in and take a seat.

To our surprise, he says yes right away.

"We're putting a lot of faith in you kids, and we hope you won't disappoint us," he says, leaning back in his chair and crossing his arms. He peers first at David, then at me. "Remember, we can't always watch you, but Jesus can."

He points a finger Heavenward.

"Jesus is always watching and listening and knowing. You can fool us, but you can't fool Jesus."

"Yes, sir," we respond, holding his gaze. "We'll be good."

The next afternoon, when the guard clanks shut the metal gate behind us and we're suddenly alone on the Dominican side of the barbed wire, excitement flares between us. As we walk down the paved drive toward the main road into the village, we don't say a word or even look at one another until The Property slips behind a wall of trees.

And then we start to run. We run leaning away from The Property, leaning so far forward that we're half falling, half flying down the hill, our sneakers catching abruptly on the pavement, the rubber soles slapping in our ears. Once again we are kids, racing each other down the path in the woods behind our old house, giddy with speed.

We continue to race after we turn onto the dirt road into Jarabacoa. We run until our legs are wobbly, and our breath comes out in chunks, and we are beyond everything. David sprints past me and I catch up to him and grab his arm, and we stumble and fall onto the road. We lie on our backs laughing as the jungle whirls around us in a giant green kaleidoscope.

After a while, David staggers to his feet and pulls me up.

"Hot damn," I gasp, my head still spinning. "Holy crap."

"Just remember," David pants, jabbing a finger at the sky and imitating Ted's low voice. "Jesus is always watching and listening and knowing!"

"No sirree," I say. "You can't fool Jesus!"

"And you can't jack off with Him either!"

We fall back into the dirt, howling, and when David pulls me up again, I punch him in the biceps and he clamps his hand over his arm as if it hurt. Just like old times. Just like our old selves.

Two Dominican women appear on the road wearing bright dresses and balancing bundles of twigs on their heads. They give us a sidelong glance, then cross to the far side of the road and hurry past us.

"Come on, I'll take you to this place I know," David says.

We brush the dust from our clothes and continue down the road. The air is dense with the sweet smoke of burning sugar-cane, and the gray clouds that blanketed the valley in the morning have evaporated, leaving a brilliant sapphire sky.

As we walk in the shade of the mango and mamey apple trees arching over the road, emerald green parakeets dart through the branches, live ornaments that twitter and flash. We walk in silence, marveling at this strange land and the fact that we are in it together.

We pass a row of jeweled shanties propped on stilts over a ravine. They are pieced together from plywood and sheet metal and have roofs made of palm fronds. As we walk by, the trapdoor on the bottom of a purple one bangs open and water slops into the ravine. The stench of human waste rolls over us and we squeal and pinch our noses shut and jog up the road.

An ancient VW bus rattles toward us, bouncing hard over potholes. *Gua-guas,* the Dominicans call them. The driver will charge you five centavos to ride anywhere in the village. Dominicans jam the interior and hang off the sides, gripping handles that have been welded onto the exterior. The women gawk at us and the men wolf whistle, turning to stare even after the exhaust fumes envelop us. We shift our eyes to our feet. It's the same as in Indiana—everybody wondering what a business a black boy and a white girl have together.

Up the road, merengue music bounces from a yellow shack with a Coca-Cola sign hanging over its doorway. The primitive two-beat rhythm is everywhere here—blaring from car radios, from shanties, from the jam boxes perched on teenage boys' shoulders like parrots. On weekends, a three-piece band plays live merengue in Jarabacoa's central square as couples sashay over the dirt, their hips pressed together. When we walk by, boys—egged on by their friends and green cans of Presidente beer—ask us to dance, pointing to the gyrating couples before extending a hand.

"Dejame en paz," we tell them. "Leave me alone." It's what Bruce makes us say, and they oblige, shrugging and moving on to someone else. I often wish they'd grab my hand and pull me into the music before Bruce could stop them.

"There," David says, pointing at the yellow shack with his chin, Dominican style. "Let's get something to drink."

I glance at my watch; we have to be back at The Property in an hour and fifteen minutes.

"Come on, we've got time," he says, stepping toward the shack. "The missionaries don't keep track of our comings and goings—they're too busy saving souls to notice."

There's no one inside. The only furnishings are two plastic card tables and plastic chairs. A ghetto blaster playing the merengue music rests on one of them, and we sit at the other, next to an open window. The music is too loud to talk. A girl in a New York Yankees T-shirt walks through a screen door at the back of the shack and lowers the volume before turning to us. David says something to her in slow, struggling Spanish and she nods and walks back through the screen door.

"Did you get me a Coke?" I ask him.

"I ordered coconut juice," he says with a sly smile. "I think."

"But I wanted Coke. I already used all my house pop privileges this week."

He smirks and brushes a fly from his face. "Trust me, you'll like this. If you don't, I'll buy you a Coke. I got enough pesos."

An overloaded *gua-gua* clatters past the window, playing the same merengue song that's on the ghetto blaster. I look at David and smile and then look back out the window as the dust stirred up by the *gua-gua* settles back onto the road. It's weird to suddenly be alone with him like this, to be sitting across a table from each other in a private place. There's too much to talk about, and nowhere good to start.

The waitress returns with two glasses of chalky white liquid, and David hands her some coins.

"To getting out of here as soon possible," I say, raising my drink.

"To going home," he says, clinking his glass against mine.

I look into my glass when he says this to avoid his eyes, then chug half my drink. I notice the metallic taste only after I set my glass down on the table.

"Hey, there's booze in this!" I shout, lifting the glass.

David frowns and sniffs his drink.

"Hey, I think you're right," he says. "Must be my bad Spanish. I'll send them back." He starts to raise his hand to signal the waitress, who's sitting on a stool by the entrance.

"Are you nuts?" I cry.

"But it's against Program policy," he says.

I press my glass against my "I ♥ Jesus" T-shirt protectively, and he cracks up.

"I guess it's not our fault the waitress brought the wrong drinks," he says, grinning. "Although she tends to do it every time I come here: I ask for coconut juice, and she brings a piña colada."

"You are so bad," I say, clinking my glass against his.

He's changed since Indiana, when he'd call me a lush for siphoning Comfort from the pantry. I guess he now understands why people drink. To feel something. To feel nothing. To feel better.

A disc jockey babbles Spanish on the ghetto blaster before the first unmistakable guitar chords of The Police's "Don't Stand So Close to Me" waft from the speakers. I jerk around and stare at the radio; it's my favorite Police song, and the first pop song I've heard in three months.

"Oh my God!" I squeal, turning to look at David. "Can you believe it?"

He nods and smiles slyly again.

"I knew you'd like this place."

We order two more drinks and tap our sneakers against the cement floor and drum our fingers on the table. The waitress sees us grooving and cranks up the volume, smiling. Which is fine by me, because I don't want to discuss The Program, or home, or what will become of us, or anything else. I want to drink, and listen to secular music, and pretend to be normal.

The Police song turns into Joan Jett's "I Love Rock and Roll," and David taps his watch.

When we walk back into the sunshine, the Go-Go's "We Got the Beat" is playing and we're dancing down the dirt road chanting *We got the beat, we got the beat, we got the beat, yea-ah-ah! We got the beat!* over and over like an incantation. A *gua-gua* rolls by and when the passengers gawk and whistle, David waves at them and I flip them off.

We stop at a roadside *colmado* stand to buy peppermint chicles from a wrinkled man and stuff our mouths full of them and arrive at the orphanage light-headed yet minty-fresh.

A little boy, naked but for a pair of torn shorts, opens the gate. He smiles shyly up at David before sprinting back to a small bent slide crowded with children. An old Dominican woman sits on a tree stump behind them, jiggling a baby on her lap.

David turns to me.

"Basically, our job is to keep the little kids busy while the missionaries convert the older ones," he says, pointing at a building beyond the slide; a chorus of high voices sing "The Bible Tells Me So" in the interior. "It's not that hard."

"Beats hauling rocks," I say.

As we walk toward the slide, a throng of kids swarms around David, tugging his arms and shrieking *Daveed! Daveed!* He beams down at them and slings a tiny potbellied boy into his arms. I watch this spectacle of my brother circled by adoring children like some modern-day black Jesus and my heart is warmed by more than rum.

"Aren't you popular!" I say.

He shrugs away my comment, smiling. We spend the next hour playing Duck, Duck Goose and Ring Around the Rosie, and David and I holler as loudly as the other kids. Every once in a while we stop to grin at each other, tipsy and smug with our exploit.

On the way back to The Property, we consider running away. We could catch a bus to La Vega and from there, another to Santo Domingo. But we have only $6 in pesos between us, not enough to cover the fare. We could hitchhike. But even if we reached the capital, we'd have no money for a plane, and they'd find us and haul us back.

"My hair can't get much shorter, but I don't think you'd look so hot with a shaved head," David says.

We trudge back to The Property with deflated spirits, each footstep a step away from freedom. When we reach the gate, I turn to David. His joy is gone, replaced with the same expression of grim wariness that everyone sports at Escuela.

"Maybe they'll let us out again next week," I say, punching him lightly in the arm.

"Just keep your points up," he says.

"You too."

The guard hears us talking and swings open the gate and the German shepherd strains at its leash to sniff us as we enter. When the gate clanks shut behind us, we climb the hill in silence to our separate cement houses and our separate unwanted families.

"See ya around," I say when we reach Starr's driveway.

In the following weeks, a series of events convulse the school and set everyone on edge.

Boy 0 tries to poison David's entire house one night by sticking cat poop into the beef stroganoff. He'd been collecting turds from the TKB house cat, Negro, for several weeks and stashing them under the refrigerator, David said. When the housemother left the kitchen to answer the front door, Boy 0 dumped them into a pot of meat on the stove.

David said the meal didn't taste any worse than usual, and that they noticed it was extra foul only when people started finding bits of fur and cockroach on their plates. Steve, the group leader, found a long turd that Boy 0 had not sufficiently crumbled, and then people noticed he wasn't eating his food and remembered it was his job to clean the cat box.

A minute later, everyone was lined up under the clotheslines behind the house for a communal retch.

Boy 0 hasn't stopped running since. Before school, he does casitas. During lunch, casitas. After school, casitas. When he collapses from exhaustion, the TKB group leader pulls him to his feet and herds him along with his moped. When Boy 0 no longer has energy to stumble up the hill, he's forced to crawl up it. We observe his buglike ascent during lunch from our picnic tables, and afterward, he staggers into Bible class with scraped knees and palms and sits shivering in his chair.

Jolene doesn't poison anyone but herself. She drinks bleach one morning during House Jobs. I was mopping the dormitory when I heard Becky shriek and raced to the bathroom door. Jolene was hunkered down between the toilets, her mouth latched onto the bleach bottle like a baby at a plastic teat. We tried to snatch it away from her, but she kept us at bay with sharp kicks.

"Go on and let me die!" she squalled. "Go on, then, and let me die!"

Bruce charged upstairs, and RuthAnn followed with a glass of milk. Bruce grabbed hold of Jolene's legs and dragged her out and sat on her stomach. Becky pinched her nose shut to force her to open her mouth and RuthAnn poured in the milk. Jolene spit it right back in her face.

She only swallowed when Bruce threatened to send her back to The Hole.

"Suicide is an act of rebellion against God, a sin!" Bruce bellowed at her. "The Father giveth life and only He can taketh it away!"

At this, Jolene changed her story and said she was only trying to sicken herself so she'd get sent home.

"You won't go home until I say you go home," Bruce told her. "Keep up these antics, and I'll keep you down here forever."

Jolene spent the day recuperating in bed, forced to drink liters of milk as she complained of throat and stomach pains.

They still came for her that night. Bruce and Ted barged into the dormitory with flashlights and pulled her, kicking and howling profanities, from her bunk. Back to The Hole. Her screams echoed in my head for hours afterward as I tried to fall back to sleep amid pillow-muffled crying.

Throughout all this wretchedness, a single thought sustains me: David and I will soon be free again, for a few precious hours at least.

Each time Ted grants us permission to volunteer at the orphanage, joy overwhelms us. Each time, he fixes us with a stern look and lectures us on the omnipotence, omniscience and omnipresence of Jesus Christ and each time we hold his gaze and solemnly vow to be good.

The irony of this situation is not lost on us. When we were little, we were often forced to play alone because other kids shunned us, and now these people have made our being alone together a privilege.

Once the gate shuts behind us, we shed our humble demeanor and flee the school full sprint. Our hours together are numbered, and we want to live every second fully.

First we stop at the café to savor *agua de coco* and forbidden music, and then we set out to explore a new corner of the village.

We stumble across a butcher shop where the owner scoops live rabbits from a pen by their hind feet, whacks their heads on a marble counter with a graceful swing, then peels and quarters them. We've never seen something go from animal to food before and couldn't rip our eyes from the flashing blade, from the wet pink carcasses with their bulging eyes. One rabbit, two rabbit, three. The process both fascinates and repels us. When the butcher winks at me, I elbow David and we leave.

We line up behind Dominican kids on the banks of Rio Jimenoa to take turns swinging across the tan water on a tractor tire. The older kids strip down to their underwear and plop into the sluggish river, and the small ones strip naked. David and I just swing back and forth in our jeans and T-shirts, gazing wistfully down at the water. *"Americanos locos!"* the Dominican kids holler

We buy fat mangoes from street vendors and suck out the pulp, flashing each other hairy orange smiles as the fibers lodge between our teeth.

We roam the jungle and stare gape-mouthed at each new discovery: green lizards with red heads, tree trunks as wide as cars, butterflies that glow like rainbow shards as they flit through shafts of sunlight.

Every now and again, I'll catch David's arm.

"Look at us, David!" I'll say when he turns to look at me. "Look at us in the *Dominican Republic!*"

I try to teach David the pop songs that came out after he left, but I've forgotten half the words and get frustrated and hum them instead.

We gripe about The Program. I tell him my letters from home have slowed to a trickle and he tells me this is normal.

"Out of sight, out of mind," he sighs.

I tell him what a pansy Bruce is and how Susan betrayed me and he warns me again to trust no one.

"Except your little brother, of course," he grins.

I thank him for stopping me from slipping into the abyss at Salto de Jimenoa.

"It was nothing," he shrugs.

He tells me that his group leader plays this joke on him whenever they're on a field trip. They'll be walking down a crowded street and Steve will point at David and yell "Haitiano! Haitiano!" and back away from him. *Haitiano. Haitian.*

Dominicans hate Haitians, who are poorer than they are, and dark-skinned like David—African black compared to the Dominicans' wet sand color.

In Cultural Studies class, we learned that Dominicans blame Haitians for everything from their country's poverty to outbreaks of disease; the police routinely round up black people and dump them at the Haitian border.

But they keep coming back because they'll take the one job Dominicans refuse to do: harvesting sugarcane. It's dirty, hot, hard work. I've glimpsed the Haitians as we've driven through the countryside, dark shadows slouching barefoot between cane fields, machetes glinting at their sides.

Calling David "Haitiano" on a crowded street is akin to yelling "nigger" at a KKK rally.

David says the Dominicans glare at him when Bruce does this, and then Steve laughs and thumps David on the back as if it were funny.

"I wish he'd stop," David says, scowling down at the dirt road as we round the corner to the orphanage.

"What a racist pig," I say, shaking my head. "What an asshole!"

That's another thing we do when we're alone—cuss. Neither of us swore much beyond "gosh" and "sperm breath" back in Indiana, but now cursing gives us a *nah-nah-nah-nah-nah-nah* rush of delight. It's another forbidden fruit, another freedom restored.

We cuss, therefore we are. Sometimes we blaspheme all the way to and from the orphanage, inventing new obscenities along the way: "Papaya-fucking goat eater." "Fruity-assed Canadian cunt."

But we never take the Lord's name in vain, because the Bible forbids it. The Good Book doesn't mention those other words, however.

One afternoon in early November, we strike gold.

After passing a high cement wall that runs through the middle of the village, our curiosity overcomes us and we decide to trace it to its opening. We follow it for several blocks and finally reach a large metal door.

It stands ajar. David pushes it open, and it creaks inward to reveal a cemetery so vast that it seems to spill to the horizon in every direction.

"Cool!" David exclaims.

"Fuckin' awesome!" I add.

It's unlike any graveyard we've ever seen. In front of us, row upon row of concrete boxes are laid out like freezers at a President's Day sale. To our right, crosses fashioned from sticks and metal rods sprout from the hard clay. Up to the left, sheds populate a hillock like children's playhouses. All of this is fortified by the high cement wall. It is a walled city of the dead.

David and I stand gawking in the entrance. It is the beginning of the rainy season, and dark clouds swarm over the village, making the ghoulish landscape look doubly ominous, and doubly fun.

"You first," I tell David as the wind lashes my hair about my face.

"Nah, you," he says.

"Scaredy-cat."

"Pussy."

I shove him through the doorway and he turns, laughing, to grab my wrist and pull me after him. We sprint to a concrete box and crouch behind it, glancing about. The only motion we detect are mounds of trash blowing across the barren ground, the only noise a parrot squawking atop an iron cross. We are alone.

We stand to peer down at the lid of the concrete box, which is covered with a fine layer of red dust. David wipes it clean with his hand.

> Mario Agusto Martinez
> Nasio 1 de Oct. de 1921
> Fallesio 25 de Dic. de 1974

"He croaked on Christmas day!" I say, tapping the lid.

"Musta had a heart attack when he didn't get no presents he liked," David says.

"*Any* presents he liked," I correct him. "Stop talking like some hick."

The wind shifts direction, and the air is suddenly tangy and sweet with a stench akin to rotting pineapple.

"Must be all the trash," David says, wrinkling his nose.

We amble about the tombs, reading the dead people's names and making up stories about what killed them. Jorge gorged himself on pinto beans and exploded in an enormous fart. María drowned in shit when she walked under a stilt house and a slop bucket emptied on her head. Rogelio was eaten alive by an army of three-inch cockroaches.

As we walk across the cemetery, I notice the high cement wall is honeycombed with squares, which I recognize as compartments for bodies—Papa Scheeres was sealed in one after he died of cancer a couple of years ago. But some of the squares are fringed with cement shards, as if they'd been busted open. *Weird.*

"This one says Elsa Gómez Gómez," David says, squatting before a spray-painted cement block inscribed with nothing more than the name. I creep away from him to hide behind a jaguar palm. "Gómez Gómez. Sounds an awful lot like kissing cousins, don't it?"

He chuckles.

"Julia? Where you at?"

I peek around the palm to see him dusting off another cement box and tiptoe behind him. When he leans down to read it, I jump on his back. It's an old trick, one we used to scare our friends at Grandview Cemetery in Lafayette. His shriek ricochets off the high cement wall, and then he whips around and starts after me.

We swerve, whooping and laughing, past the legions of bodies crammed into their cement freezers and holes and compartments. *Look at us, we are still alive!*

After a while, his footsteps fall silent behind me and I turn; he's gone.

"You can't scare me! I see where you're at!" I yell.

It's a lie that sometimes works, but this time elicits no response.

After a few minutes of pussyfooting about, whirling around every few seconds to check my back, I get bored and wander up the hill to the cement playhouses and walk down a paved lane between them. The metal grate entrances are secured with chains and padlocks and I press my face between the bars to study their interiors.

From the murky light cast by a small window at the back of each shed, I make out shelves attached to the side walls, and on these shelves are coffins. Most of the sheds have a stand under the window that holds saint candles and decaying flowers and photographs pinned to corkboard.

I reach a shed that is chained but not padlocked, and swing the grate open.

There's only one coffin, on the lower right shelf. I glance nervously behind me before entering, imagining David slamming the grate shut and trapping me alone with this dead person. This one has a lot of pictures, but it's hard to see them, so I feel around on the stand at the back and find a book of matches, then light several saint candles.

It's a girl. In one photograph, she poses in an elegant red gown and sparkling earrings, her long brown hair piled atop her head. In another, she stands with her arms flung around two friends, beaming mid-laugh at the camera. In another, she's a little girl taking a bubble bath.

She's lovely and I covet her beauty, even in death. I lean down, lit match in hand, to read the metal plaque on her coffin:

> Gloria Hilda Váldez Martínez
> Nacio el 8 de Julio 1963
> Fallecio el 2 de Abril 1982

She was ninteen, just two years older than us. *What killed you, Gloria?*

"Whoa, she's hot!"

I jump. David's beside me, eyeballing the pictures. I elbow him in the ribs.

"Have some respect for the dead."

He glances at his watch, then pulls my arm.

"Come on, I wanna show you something."

"What?"

"You'll see."

I blow out the candles, and we leave Gloria's and walk along the cemetery wall past a section of busted-open honeycombs.

"Looks like they unburied someone," I say, motioning at the wall.

"A whole lot of someones," he responds. "Maybe they weren't dead yet."

He leads me to a back corner of the cemetery that is vacant but for large sheets of plywood lying on the clay ground. Here the stench of rotting pineapple is strong, and I plug my nose.

"It stinks," I say in my plugged-nose voice.

"Just help me out a second," David says, kneeling beside a board.

"Help you do what?"

He grabs the edge of a board.

"Move this."

"Why?"

"Because I want to see what's underneath," he says.

I unplug my nose and kneel beside him. We both push the board, grunting with effort, and it skids over the ground, revealing a deep pit. We sit back on our haunches and squint down into it, but it's too dark to see anything.

David gets on his belly and lowers his head into the hole.

"I see something! . . . like a branch or something," he says.

He scoots forward until his shoulders are underneath the plywood and I grab him by the waistband of his jeans as he wiggles around.

"Got it!" he shouts.

I stand to get out of his way as he drags himself backward from the pit. He leaps to his feet, holding his arm triumphantly over his head. In his hand is a human femur. A thighbone. I recognize it from Biology class at Harrison. Only the Harrison one belonged to a white plastic skeleton that hung in a corner next to the chalkboard, and this one is dark and cracked and wet like an old dog bone. Only that one was fake, and this one is real. I scream.

David lowers his arm and stares at the bone for a horrified second before heaving it away; it clatters onto a piece of plywood.

He scrubs his hands on his jeans, over his own femur. "Get off! Get off!"

"David, let's go! Let's get out of here!" I yell.

He's too busy erasing death from his hands to hear me, so I grab his arm and yank him toward the cemetery exit.

As we wind through the tombs, we pass a young couple standing next to a tiny cement box. A child's grave. They are dressed in black, and the woman holds a single white rose in her hand.

She lifts her head as we sprint by, and in the moment our eyes meet, I glimpse a desolation that chills me to the core. Although her dark eyes look directly into mine, they see nothing beyond the hell at her feet.

At least the dead no longer suffer.

The next day during kickball, when Susan stubs her toe and the P.E. teacher calls a time-out, David saunters up to me. A few kids look in our direction, but they're too far away to eavesdrop.

"I know where that leg came from," David says, pretending to tie his shoe. "Those wall spaces are rented, and if your family falls behind on the payments, the cemetery owner busts you out and throws you into that hole to rot alongside the other people who can't afford it."

Down the field, Susan limps back and forth in front of the P.E. teacher, who frowns and crosses his arms. People are always faking injuries so they can sit out the game and rest.

"And what makes you so smart?" I say, still watching Susan's lame performance. Her limp has no rhythm; she's totally faking it. *Wuss*.

David stands.

"Sam told me."

Sam's a fourth ranker in David's house. He's standing in the middle of the field right now, chewing on a piece of grass and gazing up at a bank of dark clouds rolling into the valley.

I whip around to face David.

"What'd you tell him for?" I ask loudly.

A couple of kids glance in our direction and David waves at them.

"Shhh . . . ," he says. "Sam's my bud."

"Your *friend?*" I struggle to contain my voice. "What happened to 'trust no one'? You know what Susan did to me."

The P.E. teacher shakes his head at Susan, and she slowly walks back onto the playing field, limp gone. David looks at Sam still staring up at the sky, and grins.

"Shoot, Sam won't tell no one. He's my friend."

The P.E. teacher blows his whistle.

"Friend indeed," I say, before turning to rejoin my team.

Ted's waiting for us at the edge of the field when P.E. ends. While the other kids murmur and shoot glances at his looming presence, Sam bounces the kickball off his knee, pointedly ignoring him. *Fucker*. I give David the stink eye when Ted calls our names.

As we follow his wide back through the courtyard, David worries his bottom lip, his face contorted with panic and confusion and disbelief. Despite everything, he still believes in the goodness of humankind, that our parents will someday welcome him home with open arms, that his friends will not betray him. That's the fundamental difference between us. He needs to trust, and I don't. I narrow my eyes at the back of his head as we walk into Ted's office. *Life would be a lot easier for you, David, if you stopped being so damn optimistic.*

"So, I hear we had quite the adventure yesterday," Ted says once he's got us alone. He leans back in his chair with his hands behind his head and grins as if he were in on a joke. "Let's talk about it."

He doesn't invite us to sit on the metal chairs in front of his desk today, so we stand stiffly behind them. Sweat trickles down my ribcage under my T-shirt, tickling my skin, but I keep my eyes locked on Ted's; adults tend to believe you if you look them in the eyes while you lie.

But my lie pours out in a squeaky gush.

"We tried to teach those kids 'Take Time to Be Holy,' but the lyrics were too hard for them, so instead we . . ."

"That's not what I'm talking about!" Ted roars.

He drums his fingernails on the metal desktop and glowers at me, and then at David, before swiveling around to a tall book-case behind him. I turn to glare at David—*this is all your fault*—and he frowns at the floor and chews his lip.

Ted pulls several thick books from the bookcase, then walks around the desk and stands in front of David.

"Hold your arms up at your sides," Ted commands, towering over him.

David glances at me before slowly raising his arms.

"Palms up," Ted says.

He places a World History textbook and a Child Psychology manual on David's right forearm and a Teen Devotional Bible and a Spanish-English dictionary on his left forearm. David curls his fingers over the covers to keep them from falling, his head listing to the side with the effort. He looks like some modern art project: *Black Jesus, Crucified with Books*.

I can't see the names of the books Ted piles on my arms, but I can sure feel them. I press my elbows into my hipbones to counteract their weight and Ted barks at me to straighten my arms.

"You're going to hold those books until someone tells the truth," he says. "Drop them, and it's back to Level 0 for both of you."

When Ted turns to sit back down, I curse David with my eyes and he apologizes with his. Ted drums his fingernails on the desk and watches us with a bored expression.

After a couple of minutes, I can no longer stand the pain screeching up and down my shaking arms and I gasp sharply. The books on my left arm shift and I dig my fingernails into them, but still feel them slipping in slow motion.

"Yes, Julia?" Ted asks.

Bitter tears dribble down my cheeks and my face burns with shame at them. I shake my head at Ted and blink at the green felt banner hanging over his head. On it, two hands clutch a red bowl. "I am the Potter and You are the Clay" it says in gold letters beneath the hands.

"It's not her fault!" David suddenly cries. "It was all my idea!"

I turn to him; his face is also glazed with sweat, his arms also shake.

"David, don't . . ."

"Silence!" Ted bellows. "Let him talk."

"She didn't want to go," David continues, panting out the words. "But I convinced her."

David looks at me, and his face is so full of bravery that I begin to sob. My arms collapse and the books bang to the floor, their crisp pages crushed against the cement. I bend to pick them up.

"Get out of here, Julia," Ted says. "I'll deal with you later."

I take one last look at David before backing out the door. He's trembling under the weight of the books, but his eyes shine with determination. He gives me a tight smile. *Everything's fine.* I sprint uphill to Starr and don't speak to anyone for the rest of the afternoon.

I know that if I open my mouth, there will be no way to stop the venom pooling in my mind from spilling out.

My punishment: a week scrubbing floors. I spend every evening on my hands and knees scouring tiles during Free Time.

David's punishment: He's booted back to Level 0. This despite telling Ted the truth.

And once again, we are forbidden from communicating.

Unable to use words, David and I hold entire conversations with our eyes. In a glance, he tells me the state of his mental health, and I reassure him that we'll be okay. I tell him that I will always be his big sister and take care of him and love him. I tell him these things with my eyes that I've never told him with my mouth.

But as the days wear on, I watch hope fade from his warm brown eyes. He's no closer to leaving The Program now than he was when he entered it, a year ago. He's the lowest ranker at the school, outranked even by Boy 0.

I cringe when I see him slumped in a doorway waiting for permission to move, or hunched over the TKB picnic table waiting for scraps as Sam stuffs his face across from him, enjoying his recent promotion to high ranker.

I should be on 0, too, but once again, I'm the privileged one, the white one. The white daughter who sleeps upstairs while the black sons share a room in the basement. The white student who slips unnoticed through the halls of her new high school while the new black student is assaulted. The white girl who breaks a rule and is slapped on the wrist while the black boy who commits the same transgression is shoved back to the starting line.

What am I supposed to do about it? Hate myself for being the same color as the people who hurt him? I can't help being white.

Sometimes when no one's looking—as I run past him in P.E. or skirt his picnic table at lunch—I sneak out a hand to touch him, in an attempt to reignite some fire in him. But he won't react, won't even look at me. And it makes me wonder if he hates my whiteness and if I can be a true sister to him without sharing the trauma of his skin color. If we can ever be more than black and white, more than the surface of our skin.

The Sunday David starts his second week on Level 0, I obtain Fourth Level, becoming Starr's second-highest ranker. Janet reached Fifth and was sent home, so only Tiffany ranks higher than me now.

Some of the other girls are mad because I've only been here four months and have ascended so quickly. But I've worked hard to get where I am, fronting my ass off and getting good grades. And I haven't stooped to narking on anyone. I'm going to get the fuck out of here as soon as possible and nobody will stand in my way.

Except David.

How can I leave him alone down here?

I can't.

This becomes perfectly clear to me one afternoon after yet another Group spent kneeling before abortion posters. I'm trudging back up the hill with the rest of Starr when there's a commotion behind the school. I turn and see David. Jay, the economics teacher, is screeching in his face. Jay's got his back to me, but it's clear that he's worked himself into a frenzy; his arms thrash at his sides and his hands are balled into fists.

I stop walking.

I can't quite make out the harsh torrent of words spewed from Jay's mouth, but I know they are wicked from David's bowed head. Jay is notorious for hissy fits. For the slightest perceived offense—an "irreverent" look or attitude—he'll have you doing suicides while he lectures you about respecting authority. Escuela Caribe is full of his type: adults who seem to hate teenagers and enjoy making them suffer.

As Jay vomits evil at my brother, I stand and bear witness. Jay seems to be demanding some kind of answer from David, who remains bent and mute, his hands hanging limply at his sides like small dead animals.

His numbness, his refusal to accept what is happening by refusing to react—all this is familiar. Things are done to you and you can't do anything back. And so you play dead. Because if you don't acknowledge something, it isn't real. It doesn't happen.

But this is happening, it's happening to my brother.

Becky falls back to where I've halted and says something I can't hear. My eyes, ears and every fiber of my being are pointed to what's happening to my brother. The words "idiot!" and "now!" slap into my ears and I wince as Jay shoves David; he staggers backward and continues to stare at the ground, frozen. When Jay slams his fist into my brother's stomach, my own breath is punched from me.

I stumble forward, and Becky yanks on my arm.

"NO!" I bellow.

David looks up from his doubled-over position and feebly lifts a hand, palm out, everything's fine. *No, it's not!*

Jay turns toward the road with his fists on his hips and I bare my teeth at him. *How dare you?*

I let Becky drag me up the hill backwards, her words as blurred as the cement road, the dried weeds beside it, the dark clouds churning overhead. I hold David's eyes for as long as I can and promise him that someday, we'll be free. Free and happy. Free together.

According to the Escuela Caribe doctrine, situations that push your ability to cope beyond the realm of everyday experience "build character." These situations include being rousted for two A.M. sessions, spending Free Days on your knees scrubbing floors, and apparently, watching your brother get sucker-punched in the stomach. The fact that Jay hit my brother in public makes me wonder what horrible things are done to him behind closed doors.

After having a staffer tell me for the umpteenth time that such-and-such hardship will help me "build character," I look up "character" in the Starr dictionary, because I'm no longer sure what it means.

Character: 1. the qualities that distinguish one person from another. 2. a distinguishing feature or attribute. 3. moral or ethical strength. 4. reputation. 5. an eccentric person.

I figure it must be the third sense of the word because it's got the words "moral" and "ethical" in it. But in my experience, making people suffer doesn't make them more virtuous, it just makes them despise you.

The numbness that sheltered me from Jerome's nighttime fumbling has become my sanctuary at Escuela Caribe. I don't get excited by my advances in The Program or disappointed by my setbacks, because such emotions are simply manifestations of the staff's control over my mind. Happiness, anguish, fear—these are all fake emotions here, products of their manipulation. It's better to be numb and prepared for the next "opportunity" to build character than to get your hopes dashed repeatedly.

Anger is now the only emotion I allow myself. Anger and hatred, which is simply anger boiled down to its core element. I hate this place and I hate these people and I hate the God that allows these things to happen. I go through The Program like a circus tiger, obeying commands and concealing my true nature. Knowing that someday, my fangs and claws shall be useful once more.

But every now and again, some whispered reminder of Freedom weakens my resolve. The fresh perfume of crushed green grass. A love song hurled over the barbed wire from a passing car. A warm breeze that lifts my hair and caresses on my neck. These things make me bite my lip and dig my nails into the scarred grooves in my palms. These things ache. These things can wound you.

+   +   +

Jerome shook off Father's beatings with a sneer and a curse, but they chipped at David's soul bit by bit.

I tried to be a good big sister to him. When he returned from the workshop or pole barn with fresh welts on his back, I'd sit beside him on his bed while he curled into a ball and stuffed a fist in his mouth. I'd sit there in silence, not touching him, not knowing what to say, what to do, who to tell.

There was a 1-800 number printed on the inside cover of the phone directory to report child abuse, but belting your kid was hardly considered abuse in that time and place; students were spanked in principals' offices across the Midwest. There was no 1-800 number to report emotional injury.

All I could do was bear witness as his body shuddered and tears seeped out under his long lashes. When he reopened his eyes, I wanted to be the first thing he saw. Me, gazing down at him with a fragile smile. Asking if he'd like a glass of water.

CHAPTER 16

THE PASTOR

Another preacher arrives a few weeks after Preacher Stevie departs, only this one is referred to as "The Pastor" with a capital T and P. He's Gordon Blossom, the man who started this place.

The Pastor—as we're repeatedly told to call him—founded New Horizons Youth Ministries in 1971, when he began sending teens from his church on summer mission trips to separate them from the "negative influence" of American culture. The strategy proved so successful that he built Escuela Caribe, a place where disgruntled parents could dump their kids year-round if they had enough money. Eventually, The Pastor's reform school empire grew to include Escuela Caribe, a sister institution in Marion, Indiana, and a survival camp in Canada, where teens are sent into the wilderness to tough it out alone.

I didn't know about the Indiana school—a mere two hours from Lafayette—until I was already down here. My parents must have deemed it was too close to home.

One morning during chapel we are informed that The Pastor will be dropping in for a visit that evening, and the campus is turned upside down in preparation. The unexpected news makes the staff jittery, which makes us kids doubly so, because we bear the brunt of their mood swings.

Class is canceled and the student body is divided into regiments to spit-shine The Property. One group is handed machetes to mow the "lawn." Another is armed with bleach to scour the classrooms. A third tromps up the hill with brooms and mops to clean "The Pastor's Place," a small house tucked behind a screen of trees at the top of The Property. I long to glimpse its interior, but am assigned the school toilets instead.

After a day of frenzied cleaning, we don our Sunday finery to reconvene in the chapel after supper. Ted steps behind the pulpit and the school therapist strikes up "Onward Christian Soldiers" on the piano. As Ted's gaze scrapes over us, we quit slouching and magically transform into redeemable teenagers, our faces bright, our hymnals high, singing our lungs out for Jesus Christ.

Halfway through the fourth stanza, a tall man in a tan suit marches up the center aisle, and excitement ripples through the room. It's The Pastor. Ted shakes his hand, then cedes the pulpit.

The Pastor joins in the hymn, his scarecrow body bobbing to the beat. He looks like any old churchman you'd see back home: 60s, gray hair greased over a large bald spot, bifocals, abbreviated Hitler mustache. Wattle spilling over shirt collar. Dried out and severe. The reason we're all here.

At the hymn's refrain—*ON-ward CHRIST-ian SOLD-iers, MARCH-ing as to WAR*—The Pastor jerks his arms up and down like a manic choir director, bifocals flashing like strobe lights. I twist round to look at David and we goggle at each other, our mouths twitching with swallowed laughter. Surely, this is a man possessed.

After belting out the last stanza, we remain standing until the piano strings cease their vibrations before folding ourselves back onto the wooden pews. The room falls silent except for the low hiss of the flickering gas lamps and a palm branch scratching at the metal roof in the breeze.

The Pastor stands as erect as a general. I stare at The Pastor's mustache, which is thick and black and reminds me of the marker that conceals the sex in Scott's letters. He sweeps his eyes over us, pausing on every face; I look down when his eyes land on mine. When he speaks, his voice is as low and gravelly as a smoker's.

"When I was a child, I spake as a child, I understood as a child, I thought as a child: but when I became a man, I put away childish things."

He peers down at us through the bottoms of his bifocals.

"You kids were sent to Escuela Caribe to put away childish things," he says, his voice rising and falling in preacher speak. "To put away your rebellion and come clean with the Lord. To surrender to Jesus Christ and become his faithful servants. To humble yourselves before God."

He bangs his fist on the pulpit and I jump.

"You kids don't know how good you have it!" he shouts. "You should be on your knees right now, thanking God Almighty for the opportunity to be here! For the loving parents who made the financial sacrifice to send you here! For the dedicated staff who see beyond your filth to your true potential!"

He leans back, gripping the pulpit with long fingers and sucking in his cheeks. Heads droop before The Pastor's fiery gaze like wilting flowers.

"Do you know why I started New Horizons? Let me tell you. Because I, too, was a filthy sinner! Caught up in the pleasures of the flesh! Of sex and drugs and rock 'n' roll! But places like Escuela Caribe didn't exist when I was young, oh no!

"I did *hard* time. My body was beaten into submission, but my soul remained depraved. And when I finally found Jesus, I promised Him I'd do better. I vowed to build Him a place where dirty sinner kids would be cured by discipline, hard work, *and* the Blood of the Lamb!"

The Pastor again pounds the pulpit.

"Hallelujah!" cries a female voice behind me. I turn to see Debbie standing in a back pew, slowly swaying in a pink sundress with her arms over her head and her eyes closed, as if she were listening to music only she could hear.

The Pastor nods at her and continues in his loud hypnotic voice.

"The Lord Jesus brought you here! To rescue you! To save your souls!"

"Amen!" yells another voice, male, this time. I turn. It's Steve, TKB's group leader. He's also popped up from his pew and is swaying with raised arms. David, seated next to him, looks at him with open-mouthed astonishment, as if he'd just dropped naked from the sky. People don't do such things in church back home.

"Will you continue through life as filthy little sinners? Or will you choose God? Which is it, Satan or Jesus?! Eternal Life or Eternal Damnation?!"

One by one, staff and students rise from their pews as The Pastor sermonizes with upheld arms and sway like seaweed tugged by an ocean current. Many of the teachers' upturned faces are split in grins of ecstasy, while most of the students look down, their arms hung limply overhead as if someone were forcing them down a dark alley at gunpoint.

The collective exuberance has made the chapel's temperature rise, and the bitter smell of sweat clouds the stagnant air.

The Pastor barks from the pulpit and the voices yelp back.

"Jesus died for you!"

"Amen!"

"Jesus will make you clean!"

"Yes, Jesus!"

"Jesus forgives you!"

"Hallelujah!"

"Jesus wants you!"

"Praise God!"

I've heard tell of such caterwauling and carrying-on by Pentecostals, but such behavior would be considered obscene at Lafayette Christian Reformed, where standing to recite the Apostle's Creed is as exciting as it gets. I smirk, wondering what Mother would say if she knew we'd been exiled with a bunch of "Holy Rollers."

I turn to see my amazement reflected on my brother's face. We're the only two people still sitting; this is not good. I slowly rise, and so does David. Stick my arms in the air, and so does he. I turn to face the front of the chapel, close my eyes, and lightly bump against the bodies on either side of me in the sultry heat.

It's been a long time since I had touching like this, soft and gentle, and my mind wanders back to Scott. I remember how he'd skim his hand over my stomach and breasts, barely grazing me. My skin would become electrified, every nerve standing on end, craving contact. He'd skim me until I could no longer stand it and arched my back against the mattress, thrusting myself into his hand.

All this soft bumping reminds me of my arching desire, even as The Pastor continues to bark from the pulpit.

"Come to Jesus!"

"Yes, Lord!"

"Surrender to Jesus!"

"Glory be!"

"Give yourself to Jesus!"

"Amen!"

I squeeze my eyes shut tighter and try focus on his words, but the image that comes to me is not of Jesus nailed to the Cross or kneeling in a field surrounded by multicolored children. It is of Scott, stripped naked and walking toward me as I lie in my bed at home, his stiff penis wagging back and forth like a chiding finger. I fling open my eyes and gaze about in terror. But no one has seen my thoughts; the bodies around me continue to groan and sway.

I close my eyes again, and Scott kneels between my legs, then lowers himself into me. His hot tongue swishes into my mouth and I grab his butt and pull him deeper. His curved brown shoulders dip and rise in the slanted lamp light, his eager skin bumps mine. His salt taste and beef bouillon smell, they envelop me. His heat and his desire, they comfort me. I shall not want.

A spark flares in me and swells into a flame, and I sweat and sway and whisper "Yes, Jesus."

Suddenly, there's a commotion and I'm shoved aside. I open my eyes to see Jolene rushing toward The Pastor.

"I want to be saved!" she yells, throwing herself into his arms. He catches her and lowers her to her knees on the cement floor.

"Praise the Lahd!" Becky shouts beside me.

And then other kids are rushing the pulpit. The Pastor lays a hand on each one as they kneel before him. The school therapist strikes up "Have Thine Own Way, Lord" on the piano and we open our hymnals to page 68, still swaying. Some of the kneeling kids are stone faced and others cry hysterically. I consider going to boost my points, but am too full of Scott to fake it right now.

When he finishes praying over these questionable converts, The Pastor dabs his face and neck with a white hanky.

"What we've witnessed here tonight is nothing short of a miracle," he says, the kids still bowed before him. "Our Lord moves in mysterious ways. He has shown love and compassion even unto these filthy sinners, and has accepted them into His fold. It is now our duty as fellow Christians to keep them steadfast in their journey toward Heaven."

He nods at the therapist, who launches into "Just As I Am, Without One Plea." The new believers stand with their heads bent piously and their hands clasped and filter back to their pews. When Jolene walks by me, she raises her head and smirks at me. She's finally gotten with The Program.

Later, when I'm lying in my bunk surrounded by the mute shapes of sleeping girls, I reach under the sheet with a bottle of nail polish, spread my legs, and slide the fat glass bottom over my panties. Over the place where, earlier, the flame grew, then flickered out.

I think of Scott and his musk and his meat and how I'd shudder with pleasure when he sank into me. Slow, soft. Fast, hard. When the wave of fire crashes through me, I bite one hand and clamp the other over my swollen flesh, trying to keep it in.

Sweet Jesus.

+   +   +

A school van pulls into Starr's driveway during supper the next evening and Ted Schlund gets out. Bruce walks out to meet him on the patio with his napkin still tucked in his collar like a bib, and they confer in hushed tones before Bruce turns to call my name.

"The Pastor wants to speak with you and David," Bruce says after I excuse myself from the table and join them. I glance back at my half-eaten plate of tuna and carrot bake. I'm hungry, as usual, and won't have another chance to eat until tomorrow.

"You can finish your food when you get back," Bruce assures me.

I follow Ted to the van; David's already inside. When I look at him, he shrugs. He doesn't know what this is about either.

As we speed downhill, my hunger is replaced by fear. *Maybe something happened to Debra! . . . Or Laura! . . . Maybe our parents want us back!* Fat chance.

The school is dark except for a light streaming from Ted's office.

The door is open, and The Pastor is sitting behind Ted's desk, leafing through a three-ring binder. He doesn't look up when we enter.

Ted leaves, closing the door behind him.

David and I exchange nervous glances as The Pastor takes his time reading a handwritten page in the binder, grunting now and then and shaking his head.

After a few minutes, he closes the binder with a swipe of his hand. JULIA SCHEERES is written on the cover. I gulp nervously.

He raises his head and looks at us.

"Good evening," he says, sliding his bifocals up his long nose.

"Good evening," we mumble back.

"You have been summoned here tonight because I have a message for you," he says in his preacher voice, his eyes latched somewhere above our heads. "A message from Dr. and Mrs. Jacob Scheeres, your parents."

He pauses. A giant green bug slaps against the window behind his head, trying to reach the gas lamp on the opposite wall.

"And that message is this: Your brother, Jerome, is in prison."

He tilts his head and regards us as we sit frozen, waiting for more. But he doesn't speak.

"What'd he do?" David finally blurts out.

"He was charged with corruption of minors."

"With what?" I ask.

"He inducted a group of minors into the life of crime."

David and I exchange a blank look.

"Um, what does that mean, exactly?" I ask.

"They burglarized a business or something," he says, flicking away my question with his hand. "You'll have to get the details from your parents. What's important is that he's paying for his sins. Six years in the state pen."

David gasps and falls against the back of his chair. Part of me is shocked, too, but the other part knows Jerome's whole life has been leading up to prison. I look down and count the years on my fingers: Jerome will be locked up until he's twenty-four.

"I have personally assured your parents that you two kids will NOT follow in your brother's footsteps," The Pastor says, his voice rising. "And by the Grace of God, I intend to keep that promise!"

He slams his fist on the desk again, but this time I don't jump.

"I intend to keep you both in The Program until I'm convinced you've turned your lives around. Until you're eighteen, or older, if need be. Do I make myself perfectly clear?"

Anger washes over me and I glare at The Pastor while David gazes into his lap. Why does he think Jerome is someone we'd want to imitate? And they can't keep us down here once we're legally adults! No way.

"You can't . . ." I start to say.

"Can't what?" The Pastor interjects, leaning forward. "I can do anything I want. It's *my* program."

The buzzing starts in my ears. They could imprison us down here forever if they wanted; we have no money to leave. I watch the tapping green bug, insane with its desire to fly into the gas lamp, where it will burst into flames. I so want to open the window and let it in.

David traces a finger down the ladder of scars he cut into his forearm last Christmas. I nudge his leg with my knee, and he shifts away from me.

"And now, young man, I'd like a word with your sister," The Pastor says, smiling broadly at me.

David gets up and shuffles out of the room like a sleepwalker, leaving the door open.

The Pastor gets up to close it, then perches on the desk in front of me.

"I once knew a girl like you, a real smart aleck," he says. "Only fifteen years old, and already a whore, fornicating left and right. Her daddy was dead, so her mother called me for help. Would you like to know what I did to her?"

He bores into me with his steel gray eyes and I want to shake my head "no," but know he'll tell me anyway. I look at the bug, at the felt banner over the desk. *I am the Potter and You are the Clay*. If I look at him, something bad will happen. If you stare down a growling dog, it will bite you.

The Pastor leans forward until his face is a few inches from mine, blocking out the rest of the room. His breath smells of boiled cabbage. I stare at the stubble on his chin. Some of it white, some of it gray.

"I took that little whore, and I stripped her naked and I beat her black and blue," The Pastor says, his voice a hoarse whisper.

"Beat the Devil right out of her. And believe you me, I would not hesitate to do it again."

He straightens and pulls a hanky from his breast pocket. Takes off his glasses, huffs on them, and rubs slow circles into the lenses, and all the while his eyes boring into mine. A thousand tiny bells start to chime in my ears and I watch him from my numb space as if he were a television commercial that would segue into the regular program at any second. Blip off the screen so *The Waltons* can continue. *He's not real.*

He puts his glasses back on, walks around the desk, sits down.

"You are dismissed," he says, opening the binder with my name on it.

Outside, David sits on a concrete bench in the middle of the courtyard. I sit next to him, shaking and concealing my anguish from him until Ted pulls up to drive us back to our residences.

In the van's dark interior, I wrap my fingers around David's thin wrist. Through his warm skin I can feel the steady tap of his pulse, and I focus on his heartbeat, taking deep breaths until my own heart slows to match his beat for beat. This comforts me. I am not alone; I have my brother. And he will not forsake me.

I'm one of the girls chosen to clean The Pastor's house when he leaves, although I no longer consider this an honor. We lug our cleaning supplies to the top of The Property and enter the foyer quietly, as if we were entering a house of worship. His residence is much nicer than ours, with tall windows peering over the valley and normal living room furniture instead of metal chairs. It's a lot of space and comfort for one person.

Becky assigns me The Pastor's bedroom and I climb the stairs with heavy feet, not wanting to be alone in the private space of the man who threatened me with unthinkable things.

His bedroom is large, with paintings of tropical beaches and waterfalls on the walls and an overstuffed chair under a picture window, and I feel a flash of envy as I think of the dark cramped space down the hill where I sleep every night.

I walk to the window and crank it open to drive out the real or imagined boiled cabbage smell and any evil spirits The Pastor might have left behind.

As I rip the dirty sheets off the bed, I notice the mattress is real as well. A thick, soft, normal mattress of the kind used in the United States, not the three-inch foam pad on my bunk at Starr. I contemplate stretching out on it for a moment just to remember what a real mattress feels like, but then imagine The Pastor lying on it in his soiled old-man pajamas and resolve instead to finish my chore as quickly as possible and wash my hands in bleach once I'm done.

As I shove a broom underneath the box springs, a bottle rolls out and clinks to a stop against the opposite wall, a urine-colored liquid swaying in the bottom. I pick it up. Ron Bermudez, the label reads. Bermudez Rum. I stare at it for a long moment and consider taking it downstairs to show Becky, but chuck it out the window instead. It sinks soundlessly into the jungle carpet, where it will never be discovered. What good would it do?

It's *his* program.

+   +   +

Confronted with racism, David and Jerome had opposite reactions. Jerome was tall, muscular and mean, and kids didn't dare insult him to his face. David was slight and mild-mannered, hunched with insecurity. He was an easy target.

While Jerome's response to adversity was "beat 'em," David's—for a period of time—was "join 'em," and he excelled at self-denigration.

In junior high, David had this friend who called him monkey. "Hey, monkey! Wanna play ball?" the boy would yell across the gym.

David would lope across the polished wood floor, swinging his arms and grunting like an orangutan, and everyone would whoop with laughter. When I saw him do this, and I'd fight an urge to run over and knock him to the ground.

He'd also entertain our classmates by performing tricks with his face. He'd distort his African features, pushing out his full lips, flaring his nostrils and bugging out his eyes and rolling them around. A black boy in black face. They watched, laughed, asked for more. And he gave it to them.

It took him a while to figure out that gaining an audience was not the same thing as gaining friends.

CHAPTER 17

TURKEY

Thanksgiving morning breaks dark and wet. Raindrops drill Starr's metal roof with the force of marbles, and I lie on my back watching rivulets of rusty water run down the metal slab a few feet from my face.

The dormitory is sour with mildew. Nothing dries since rainy season began; our clothes are stained with webs of green mold that even bleach can't erase and our clean towels smell like sweaty socks. The rain has driven hordes of cockroaches and tiny black ants into the house, where they lurk in the hampers and closets and between our sheets.

Thanksgiving. My mind reels back to this day last year. Jerome in the pole barn, hungry and shivering in his nest of rags, trying to thaw a bowl of dog food. Now he's in his prison and we're in ours, and our parents will eat Thanksgiving dinner at the MCL Cafeteria. Mother will be thankful that she doesn't have to play-act the part of the happy mom and housewife for the guests and the camera. God is her only family now, just like she always wanted.

Becky unlocks her door and lights the gas lamp. Light floods the room.

"Happy Thanksgiving!" she shouts over the drilling rain.

"Can't we just sleep today?" someone shouts.

"It's Thanksgiving!" Becky shouts back. "We must celebrate!"

"Celebrate what?" someone else shouts. Becky doesn't respond.

After Room Jobs, Breakfast Time and House Jobs, we change into our Sunday best for the "Annual Escuela Caribe Thanksgiving Holiday and Worship Celebration." The rain has stopped, but the sky swirls with dark clouds and bursts of wind tug at our dresses. We walk down the hill hunched over, our hems gathered in one hand, to avoid getting our points docked for immodesty.

The boys have formed a circle by the banyan tree and I spot David across the grass in a light blue suit. In the tumult of the wind and our arrival, I venture a quick smile at him, and to my surprise, he smiles back. And for this small gift I am thankful.

Yesterday afternoon he forgot his Spanish book on the TKB picnic table and I managed to slip a note into it. I'd watched him get permission to stand, walk, and enter his next class then spotted it on the bench.

REMEMBER FLORIDA I'd scrawled in my notebook, drawing a heart beneath the words. I ripped the page out and stuck it in his textbook when no one was looking.

I think we both realize that the chance of us moving to Florida together at this point is slim. I've decided to go to college to become a social worker and David wants to become an actor and work on TV.

But I wrote REMEMBER FLORIDA anyway, because for years, it's what we've done when things get tough. Anymore,

Florida is not a place, it's a concept. It's freedom and happiness and being in control of your own life. Remember Florida: Remember there's a better place than this.

Ted walks into the circle and reads passages from the Bible that contain the words "thanksgiving" and "thanks" and compares us kids to the Pilgrims because we "also have voyaged from afar to be free in Jesus Christ."

When he finishes preaching, Ted instructs us to join hands and share something we are thankful for. And while the other kids dutifully thank The Program for a "second chance in life" and for "saving them from Hell" and even Boy 0—who's now on First Level—thanks the staff for "curing his rebellion," I refuse to engage in such bullshit.

When my turn comes, I look directly across the circle at David.

"I'm thankful for my brother," I say in a loud voice. "Because in the end, family is all you got."

I hear the kids around me scoff with disdain because family is what got them into this hellhole, and out of the corner of my eye, I see Bruce scrutinizing me to figure out whether my words could be construed as communication with my brother. I don't pay him any mind. I stay focused on David, and David on me. We know our truth.

After everyone says their bit, we sing "Now Thank We All Our God" and then Ted steps forward with a big grin on his face.

"I do believe there's something missing from this Thanksgiving celebration," he says. He lifts his whistle and blows into it and a moment later the Dominican guard jogs into the circle with a large package under his arm. He sets the package on the ground and it unfolds into a turkey the size of a coonhound. Everyone applauds with delight as the massive bird flops about in a circle with its bald red head listing to one side as if it were concussed.

Ted motions at the Dominican, who pulls his machete from his waistband and hands it to him.

"Jesus said the first shall be last, and the last shall be first," Ted says, striding across the circle. He stops in front David and hands him the sword and David accepts it with bugged-out eyes. Everyone laughs. Ted points at the turkey and David's actor side kicks in. He raises the machete over his head and charges the gobbler with big loping steps as the bird screeches and runs in larger circles, flapping its useless black wings. David stops and pants when the bird stops, and shambles forward when it moves, like some retarded detective. Everyone howls. But he keeps the blade raised over his head, and it's clear he has no intention of harming this animal, but is merely performing his clown act.

The turkey darts against the fence of our legs trying to escape, and the girls squeal and the boys kick it. And everyone's hee-hawing, and dang if this ain't the most fun ever been had at Escuela. When the bird lowers its warty head and tries to penetrate the space below my dress, I knee its dirty feathers and it yelps and careens away.

After a while, Ted grows tired of these antics and motions to the guard, who shouts in Spanish and tackles the bird. He struggles to his feet with his hands clenching the turkey's neck and holds it aloft like a trophy as it claws his chest and everyone titters. The Dominican jabbers in his language and grins, but the bird is silent because he is choking it. Ted drags a tree stump into the middle of the circle and the guard stretches the bird's long neck over it.

"David!" Ted calls, beckoning with his arm.

My brother throws me a look of doubt and apprehension before trudging over to Ted with the machete drooping at his side. They consult over the prostrate bird, with Ted pointing down at it and murmuring and David standing stock-still. And then Ted barks "now!" and the Dominican leaps away and David raises the machete and turns his head and slams down the blade.

There's silence.

And then there's pandemonium.

For the turkey is yet alive.

It lurches to its feet with half its head dangling to the side and blood spurting from its neck like some demonic fountain. As it flails about in a blind bloody circle, there's a communal screeching and several girls erupt into tears and a boy shouts "holy shit!" and Susan collapses into Becky's arms.

David stands in gaping horror before this monster he has created, his blue suit splattered red. The Dominican yanks the machete from his hand and swings it at the bird like a baseball bat; its head and a piece of neck soar through the air and ricochet off the trunk of the banyan tree before falling back onto the field. The Dominican kicks the headless body over then stomps on the neck until the bird stops convulsing.

By the time the Annual Escuela Caribe Thanksgiving Holiday and Worship Celebration has ended, the other girls are clutched into a bawling knot and a boy is horking into the dirt. Yep, best darn fun ever.

We eat it in the courtyard. A couple of kids suggest that they'd rather scrub toilets or haul rocks or do anything else besides participate, but Ted will have no such nonsense.

"Waste not, want not,'" he lectures them.

We sit at our picnic tables and the bird reappears on a platter, fat and brown and naked. Ted carves it to pieces and makes sure everyone forks a slab onto their plate and I exchange a grim look with David, who's changed into a clean tan suit.

After he blesses the food, Ted turns to a jam box set on a cement bench and presses the play button. The high girly voices of the Vienna Boys' Choir rise from the speakers.

The turkey flesh is pink and spongy and tastes slightly of soap. I hold my breath while I chew, and down the table Susan chews with tears running down her face as Becky rubs her back. Ted gets up and cranks up the volume on the jam box.

The late-afternoon air is damp with the gathering rain and a chill wind rips through the courtyard. I press my goosebumped legs together under the picnic table and shovel the spongy pink flesh into my mouth, chewing as little as possible before swallowing as the queer girly voices scream "Edelweiss" in my ears.

+ + +

The staff make it clear that I won't get Fifth until I:

Break up with Scott.

Apologize to my parents.

They don't say these things outright. Rather, Bruce tells me that he's concerned about my PRO-gress. He says my parents feel I haven't internalized The Program's values and worry that I'm still "under the influence" of a certain young man back in Indiana.

Okay. It's true that I wrote my parents a letter telling them my sex life was none of their business. But that was back on Level 1, before I'd fully realized what I was doing. We haven't broached the subject of my deflowering again, either in letters or in my one parental phone call (a five-minute conversation over a buzzing and echoing phone line at Ted's house where he sat across the table from me, and my mother updated me on the goings-on at Lafayette Christian Reformed and I yelled "what?" periodically for lack of anything better to say).

After Bruce tells me his concerns about my PRO-gess, I sit down immediately at the dining room table to write two letters. One to Scott ("I think there was, like, way too much fornication in our relationship") and another to my parents. This is the hard one. What, exactly, should I apologize for?

"Dear parents," I write, before grabbing the pen in my fist and carving a black hole in the page. I rip it from my notebook, crumple it into a ball, and stare down at the blank new sheet.

When I was little and teachers had us make Mother's Day cards in art class and told us to write "I love you" inside, I'd write "no" somewhere near the phrase. I no love you because I know you no love me.

Is it wrong to dislike your parents? What if they disliked you first?

I scrawl words on the fresh page before I think too hard about them.

> Dear parents,
> I recognize that I haven't done the best job in the past, but I've been working hard during the past six months to become a better daughter and Christian and human being. I have ended things with Scott and hope things can be better for us. Sorry for everything.

I bite my lip and sign "Love, Julia" at the end, instead of my customary "bye, Julia."

Bruce and Becky read the letters before I seal them in their envelopes and Bruce nods and Becky pats my back and I look down at the table. This isn't defeat. This is survival.

I become Starr high ranker the next Sunday, setting a school record for reaching Fifth Level in the minimum amount of time. I stand before Bruce and quote the required Scriptures, then lower myself before him to do the required calisthenics. When he pins the Leadership medal onto my T-shirt, I beam at the sour faces of the other girls. *Losers.*

Tiffany is especially pissy about my promotion; she recently failed to make Fifth when Becky caught her smoking matches in the bathroom because she'd forgotten to jam shut the door.

That evening, while we are luxuriating in the hot shower that is the foremost high-ranker privilege, I catch a whiff of rank coffee and look over to see her standing with her legs apart, massaging her neck and pissing a dark yellow stream onto the tiles. Her urine merges with the water flowing over my feet to the drain.

"Hey!" I shout.

"Hey what?" Tiffany shouts back, still massaging her shoulders.

"Quit pissing on me!"

She grabs the shampoo bottle from the ledge between us.

"You're insane!" she says in a dismissive voice.

I turn to face her.

"Don't do it again," I say. "Or else."

"Or else what?" she asks, finally looking at me.

She squeezes shampoo onto her head without another word and I rush to finish my shower. As I rinse off, I glance at her and she's got a smug smile on her face that I'm tempted to slap off. Instead I grit my teeth and leave the bathroom. I'm too close to winning the game to fuck up now.

The Christmas tree is a branch, painted white. We try to gussy it up with popcorn and ribbons, but ultimately, it's just a dead tree branch.

Starr is in a mournful state, with everyone struggling to adjust to the dead branch and the fact that they are not going home. Part of the deal for most kids was that if they agreed to attend Escuela Caribe, they'd be home for the holidays. And although they may be hardened reform school kids, it still breaks their hearts that their parents lied to them.

At Starr, there are a lot of red eyes at the supper table and a lot of sniveling after lights-out.

The pain of not being home for the Great Family Holiday is especially sharp for David. Although he's made First Level again, on many days during P.E. he doesn't even bother chasing the ball, and now I'm the one urging him on with pleading eyes.

During Free Time, I often see him doing casitas, his thin body pushing slowly uphill, then stumbling down it. I watch him from Starr's patio, silently cheering him on. *Don't give up, David. Remember Florida.*

On a joint parental phone call, our parents shout their plans for us over the crackling phone line at Ted's. We are still forbidden from communicating, so I repeat everything our parents say *(What? I'm flying back in June?)* so David knows what's happening, and he does the same.

After I graduate Escuela Caribe, they're sending me to Portugal for the summer with a group called Teen Missions to help build a missionary compound. In the fall, I'll attend a Christian college in Upland, Indiana. I'll be home for the shortest time possible between these events to "avoid problems," they say.

David—who's almost a year behind in his studies—will transfer to the sister school of Escuela Caribe in Marion, Indiana, in January. No, he can't go back to Harrison or live at home, they say when he asks. It's Marion or the Dominican Republic. He picks Marion.

By the time we hang up, it's abundantly clear that neither of us will ever again return home to live. We're on our own.

This news doesn't surprise me, but it harms David. On the way back to The Property, he stares out the van window with a wooden face, and doesn't look at me once. He's finally realized that his Brady Bunch dream will never come true. He'll always be the outsider, seeking to belong. To family, to society, to something. I sense his sorrow and long to reach across the seat to grab his arm and remind him who I am—his sister, always—but Ted's wife is sitting behind us, scrutinizing.

On Christmas Day, we gather in the chapel during a rainstorm to listen to Ted tell us that God gave the world the gift of His Only Son and that our parents gave us the gift of Escuela Caribe, and how both these gifts will redeem us.

Candles are passed around and we sing carols with our faces illuminated by the dancing flames. I can't see David because he's sitting behind me, and this frustrates me.

We exchanged gifts through Debbie earlier in the afternoon. I gave him a blue dress shirt and he gave me a hat to replace the one Bruce ruined. It's a man's fedora, dark brown. It sunk to my eyebrows when I put it on, but made me smile all the same.

"Tell him 'Merry Christmas,'" I said to Debbie when she dropped it off at Starr. "And 'Happy New Year,' too."

In the flickering chapel, the therapist plays "Silent Night, Holy Night" on the piano, and Susan and Janet, seated on either side of me, start to cry. I get a lump in my throat and hastily blow out my candle, splashing hot wax on my dress. Susan looks at me with a wet face and raised eyebrows. I give her a dirty look, and she turns away.

I set my candle on the pew beside me and dig my fingernails into their grooves, staring in silence at the wooden cross at the front of the chapel. *You will not break me.*

+ + +

During the summer of 1983, when we were sixteen and still a few months away from the time when everything started to fall apart, David's favorite song was "Our House" by Madness.

He bought the single and played it over and over again on his cassette player. The song is about a large, boisterous family doing routine domestic things like getting ready for work and school and a mother who sends her kids off each morning with a small kiss. It's about a nostalgia for this blissful mundanity, about a family that manages to stay joyful despite daily pressures. It's about the family David longed for.

CHAPTER 18

FLORIDA

We are given a parting gift a few days before David returns to Indiana.

A weekend trip to the beach, accompanied by the P.E. teacher, Peter, and his wife, Marie, the therapist.

Ted calls us into his office one afternoon to announce this surprise and to give us permission to communicate again. He skips his usual "Jesus is watching and listening and knowing" speech and simply tells us to have fun.

"You're practically adults now," he says, shrugging and lifting the palms of his hands in a helpless gesture. "There's not much more The Program can do for you."

We leave The Property late on a Friday afternoon in an Escuela Caribe van, bumping down the mud-and-rock roads of the mountains to the sandy flatlands of the coast. During the three-hour ride, the Madsens play jazz instead of Sandi Patti, and

David and I sit behind them, jiggling our knees and pointing out at curiosities in the passing landscape.

We arrive in Sosua, a fishing village on the island's north shore, as the sun melts golden orange into the ocean. Our hotel is on the beach, a stucco block building with rickety metal balconies. The therapist and I stay in one room, David and the P.E. teacher in another.

There are cigarette holes burned into the bed sheets, but the mattresses are thick and lush, and when Marie goes into the bathroom, I take off my shoes and bounce on mine silently to celebrate.

The four of us eat a supper of fried plantains and pinto beans in the dingy hotel dining room, then play Concentration with a beat-up pack of cards we find in the lobby, and go to bed early. I fall asleep instantly on the soft mattress, lulled by the swish of waves, and, for once in a very long time, am not woken by the cries of nightmaring girls.

On Saturday morning, the four of us line up our beach towels and read through a box of American magazines that were left at the hotel. They are months old and filled with information that was sometimes reported back to us, and sometimes not.

We knew, for example, that President Reagan had been reelected and that a new edition of the New International Version of the Bible had been released. We did not know that Duran Duran had released a new album or that *Three's Company* ended its seven-year run. Important moments in history have passed us by, and it dismays us.

David and I don't want to abuse the privilege of being together, so we stick close to our chaperones. We wade in the ocean when they do, buy conch fritters and coconut popsicles from street vendors when they do, return to our towels when they do.

After supper, *Tootsie* is playing on a tiny black-and-white television in the hotel lobby, and the Madsens let us watch it despite the sex and the profanity and the man in a dress. The screen keeps dissolving into rolling gray static, but David and I sit in rapt attention—it's the first TV we've seen since we left the States. The Madsens laugh at the funny parts as hard as we do.

"Don't tell Ted," Pete says, winking.

Saturday night, I lie awake for hours on the soft mattress, watching the salty breeze billow the balcony curtain, listening to the waves, and thinking about David.

Tomorrow is our last day together. The last day of our childhood, really. We're about to take separate paths in life, and don't know when we'll see each other again.

Maybe we'll meet up in the fall, when I start college and David's finishing high school in Marion, fifteen miles away. But he'll be eighteen in June, and why would he stay in reform school when he's not marooned on an island or obligated by law? As he says, you don't need a diploma to be an actor.

What will become of him? Of us?

After surviving Escuela Caribe together, I cannot imagine life without the daily comfort of his presence. Nobody knows me as well as he does. Who will be with me when life grows unbearable, and force me to laugh despite myself? And how will I know he's okay if I can't read his eyes? These are the thoughts that keep me awake as the sea breeze billows the curtains.

"Why don't you two go off and spend the day together?" Marie suggests at the breakfast table the next morning. "I'm sure you'll want to catch up before David leaves."

We exchange a wide-eyed look before shrugging and looking nonchalant. If we show our excitement, they might change their minds.

"Okay," I say.

"We'll meet you back here later," Pete says.

"What time, six?" David asks.

"Make it eight," Marie says.

We walk barefoot into the sunshine and cross the empty white sand beach to the end of the horseshoe-shaped bay, following the lapping waves to a small rise where we could see the Madsens coming if they tried to sneak up on us. Better safe than sorry.

We unfurl our towels and sit down.

The ocean spreads turquoise before us, and seagulls swoop and cry over pastel-covered fishing boats rocking in the center of the bay. Somewhere beyond the horizon lies Florida, and the United States, and our future.

We sit in our swimsuits staring at the bay and contemplating all this in silence. The sun beams down on us, already tingling hot at ten o'clock. This is an important day, and we both know it. The knowledge juts awkwardly between us, and I almost wish the Madsens were here to distracts us.

I scoop up a palmful of sand and let it rain through my fingers and David draws up his knees and hooks his arms around them.

We watch a pelican dive-bomb the water and surface with a flash of silver in its beak. It tosses its head back and the fish tumbles into the leather bag of its gullet, snap, snap, swallow.

Where to begin talking? How to begin sorting out everything we've been through? Jay's punch and The Pastor's dirty threat and Indiana before that, the shameful times I turned my back on him, and the time he kicked me in the stomach and when he sliced his wrist and when Dad broke his arm. It is not our habit to talk about such things. We don't know how to do it.

I unzip my backpack and take out a *Glamour* and a *Sports Illustrated*.

"Something to read," I say, handing David the sports magazine.

He frowns down at the cover photograph of a black baseball player named Darryl Strawberry. "The Straw That Stirs the Mets," it says.

"I'm not into sports," he says. "Only Purdue."

"I know, but it's all they had."

He lays the magazine on the sand and goes back to staring at the water as I flip through *Glamour*. It's the September 1984 issue, five months old. Last fall, mismatched socks were in, side ponytails were out, and men still wanted women to be virgins in public and whores in private.

"Wanna go in?" David asks.

I look up and he points at the ocean with his chin.

"Okay," I say, returning the magazine to my backpack, just in case the Madsens come by.

We stand and David takes off his glasses and flings them onto his towel.

He turns to me, and grins.

"Last one in is a mango-assed redneck!" he shouts.

We take off thumping over the hot sand, our feet sinking in, scrambling toward the water. David reaches it first and thrashes through the foam before diving into an oncoming wave.

He's a fast runner, but I'm a faster swimmer. I chase him through the bathtub-warm water, grab the hard knob of his ankle, and yank it backward before plunging his shoulders underwater.

He comes up sputtering and laughing as I race away.

"Just you wait, Ju-la-la!" he yells.

I stop swimming and turn to him.

"Wait for what? For Jesus Christ to appear, hovering in the sky?"

I shield my eyes with a hand and scan the sapphire heavens, and when I look back, he's sharking toward me beneath the waves and then already dunking me.

"Truce," he says when I rise.

I nod, gasping for air.

"Truce."

When he turns to wade to the beach, I launch after him again, chasing him amid swells of waves and laughter. I catch him and knock him underwater again before flaring away and running up the sand to flop belly-down on my towel.

He climbs the rise and lays down.

"I let you do that," he says, putting his glasses on.

"I know you did," I say.

A marshy breeze blows over us and ruffles the mopheads of the palm trees arched over the shoreline. The fishing boats are trailing out of the bay to the open sea, and the gulls now soar in lazy circles over us.

"It's like Florida," David says, taking it all in.

"Better," I say.

He takes a corner of his towel and wipes his gleaming forehead.

"Remember how we were going to move down there?" he asks.

"Yeah. We talked about it for years."

"Guess this is as close as we'll get," he says, sighing.

I watch a wave rear up celery green and collapse *shhhhhhh* onto the sand before turning to him.

"Let's pretend this is our Florida. Today."

He crosses his arms in front of him on the towel and rests his chin on them, smiling.

"Okay," he says, closing his eyes.

"Let's pretend that everything turns out fine. We're living on the beach, and we're happy."

"I *am* happy right now," he says. "I only wish it would stay like this."

"Shh," I reply, seeing his forehead crease. "We're fine."

I wake when a seagull lands in a flurry a few feet from our heads. David lies facing me, glasses askew, breathing deeply. The beach is dotted with people now, and vendors carrying coolers and baskets move between them. A Dominican shouldering a blue cooler walks toward us. I sit up and nudge David awake. He blinks up at the high noon sun.

The Dominican sets the cooler in the sand and lifts the lid. Inside float cans of Coke, Pepsi, *Presidente*.

I fish out a green can.

"I always did want to try one of these," I say, grinning at David. "And now we got ourselves a special occasion."

David peers up and down the beach—no sign of the Madsens—before shrugging and reaching into the cooler to grab a green can as well.

"To Florida," he says, after the man leaves, tapping his beer against mine.

"To Florida," I repeat.

As we drink, a young boy lumbers up with a basket of ice and sets it down before us. He plucks a corrugated shell from the ice and cracks it open with a paring knife before holding it out to us.

"Ostras," the boy says.

"Oysters," David says.

"Duh," I say.

The meat is large and slimy in the pearl interior, and the boy squeezes a slice of lemon over it.

"Try," he says to me. I look at David and he grimaces.

"When in Florida . . ." I say, shrugging and taking the shell from the boy.

As David watches with big eyes, I slide the oyster into my mouth and bite down. It explodes in my mouth, bitter and gritty. Nasty. I swallow it whole, trying not to think too hard about its internal organs, then take a swig of beer.

"Yum-my!" I say, wiping my mouth with my hand.

David wrinkles his nose.

"Serious?"

"Serious. But make sure you chew it up real good before you swallow."

The boy's already got one prepared, and David takes it and slides it into his mouth and chomps on it and makes a face.

"Keep chewing!"

He grimaces and keeps chomping and I'm busting up because the oyster exploded on him, too.

"No! No!" the boy says, wagging his finger at David. He says something in Spanish and points to his mouth before lifting an oyster to his lips, slurping it in, and immediately swallowing it.

"Guess you're not supposed to chew," I say. "Otherwise the guts squirt out."

David gives me an impish grin.

"Bet I can eat more than you can," David says.

"Is that a challenge?"

"It's a fact."

We devour oysters as fast as the boy can shuck them, and David beats me fifteen to twelve. Afterward we lie on our backs under the hot sun, groaning, our heads pleasant with alcohol.

"I can feel them swimming inside me," he says, rubbing his stomach.

"Be quiet."

In the afternoon we go body surfing, then build a scale model of Escuela Caribe in the sand. As we're stomping it into oblivion, a merengue trio sets up under a clump of palm trees in the middle of the beach and starts to play.

"Let's dance!" I shout at David.

He starts to protest, but I grab his wrist and drag him over the sand and he rolls his eyes and lets himself be dragged.

Brown and white bodies move to the two-beat rhythm in the fringed shade, Dominicans and tourists, adults and children. We sprint toward them, and as the music grows louder, I feel a surge of elation at finally being able to join in the dance.

The musicians, three old men, sit in a circle on rickety wooden chairs. One scrapes a fork against a cheese grater, another squeezes the lung of an accordion, a third slaps his palms against a drum made from a rum barrel.

David and I try to mimic the Dominican couples, jerking our hips side to side and keeping our shoulders stiff, but after a while we give up and make up our own moves, spinning and twisting and jumping and laughing at each other.

When he lifts my hand to twirl me like a ballerina, I catch a light in his eyes that's been missing for months. Impossible not to rejoice in that light, in this moment, in us. Impossible not to feel the sunshine inside and out and notice sparkling ocean and feel the soft sand between our toes. We spin and twist and grin like idiots and don't give a damn who scrutinizes us.

We are young, and we have our entire lives ahead of us. Together, we have survived racism and religion. Together, we are strong. Together, we can do anything.

Life may not be fair, but when you have someone to believe in, life can be managed, and sometimes, even miraculous.

After everything else falls away, we shall remain brother and sister. *Family*.

EPILOGUE

The summer we were twenty, David died in car crash on his way to see me.

A few days earlier, he'd bought a black Plymouth Turismo 2.2 with a red racing stripe down the side, and he wanted to show it off. He took a corner too fast, careening into an empty field, and when he tried to swerve back onto the road, he collided with an oak tree instead.

He died four miles away from home.

David's death was senseless in too many ways. He was just pulling his life together. After running away from the Marion boarding school two years earlier—complaining of verbal and physical abuse—he'd joined the 113th medical battalion of the Indiana National Guard and was studying to get his GED.

And then there was the accident itself. Between the place he drove off the road and the oak tree there was a hundred yards of open space—if he'd turned the steering wheel a moment earlier, he'd still be alive. Ditto if he'd been wearing a safety belt.

I went to see his car at the junkyard after the crash and found a list of items he was planning to purchase for it in the glove box, including fuzzy dice for the rearview mirror, a pine tree–shaped air freshener. It was his first car, and he was proud of it.

I wasn't home on his final day, Saturday, August 1, 1987. I was in Indianapolis at a Latin American exposition with my mother and sister Laura, preparing to spend the fall semester of my sophomore year at the University of Costa Rica. Escuela Caribe had inadvertently given me an appreciation for Latin culture— whose passionate exuberance was the welcome antithesis of my Teutonic background—and I was majoring in Spanish.

We were driving back to Lafayette when David crashed into that oak tree, and I immediately knew something terrible had happened. I was sprawled in the backseat of my mother's car watching cornfields tick by when I was seized by panic. My heart crimped painfully and I sat up to ask my sister Laura the time. She was too busy talking to respond, so I reached over the seat to twist her arm around—over her strident protests—and look at her watch. It was almost 6:30 P.M.: the time later established by the coroner as the moment of David's accident.

When we turned into the driveway of our house, a fretful neighbor drove up with a message to call my father's surgical partner (Dad was out of the country), and as Laura and I stood next to her at the kitchen counter, Mother dialed the number.

She gasped, before turning to us, phone still in hand.

"David's dead," she said flatly, before returning the receiver to her ear.

"No, he's not," was my scornful reply.

I stood there holding trinkets from the expo—a small Nicaraguan flag, a postcard of a Mayan temple—in my hands. A few days before, we'd talked of him flying to Costa Rica on a discounted military flight to visit me. We were going to explore the country together.

Even after the preacher and police officer dropped by to make it official, I refused to believe he was dead. Their polite condolences angered me.

"Prove it," I told them. "Take me to the morgue. Show him to me."

They wouldn't, of course.

I still refused to believe it when I saw him in a casket a few days later. The mortician had used gray foundation to hide the disfigurement caused by his head injuries, and the face in the casket looked nothing like my brother's. Apparently, the funeral home didn't have the right makeup palette for colored skin, given the limited number of dark-skinned people in our town, and the result was surreal.

Even when I bent to kiss his cold gray forehead, my eyes saw, but my brain refused to believe. The twenty-one-gun salute at the funeral, the bugler playing taps, the friends and acquaintances lining up to squeeze my hand with sheepish pity—none of it seemed real.

David and I were finally starting the part of our lives we'd been so impatient to reach during all those years—decades of adventure awaited us—and in the turn of a steering wheel it was gone. It was unthinkable.

I went on to tell my classmates in Costa Rica all about my twin brother David who was planning to visit. After I returned to the States, I transferred to a new college and told my classmates there the same thing.

"He's a real goofball," I'd say. "He'll crack you up."

It took me more than a year to admit the truth, which I blurted out to astonished friends in a Valium and peach schnapps–induced haze.

But admitting the truth didn't mitigate the horror of it. I developed chronic migraines and stomachaches for which I took a host of prescription drugs and followed special diets. At the same time, I dulled my heartache with booze.

All this culminated one icy January night as I sat alone with a pint of cheap scotch and photographs of our childhood, blowing smoke rings and listening to The Smiths' "There Is a Light That Never Goes Out" ("to die by your side, is such a heavenly way to die") again and again. I tried to stifle my mental agony for a few moments with physical pain by stamping out a cigarette on my arm.

It didn't work, of course, and I still bear the scar.

After David's funeral, I found a green notebook among his things that contained excerpts from his life story. He was writing about growing up black in a white family, about racism and Escuela Caribe.

His notebook has been one of the few constants in my life— I've toted it with me from country to country and relationship to relationship. Reading his cramped handwriting on the yellowing pages is by turns both painful and entertaining. David kept his unwhippable sense of humor despite the difficulties in his life, and he loved to spin a good yarn.

Jesus Land was inspired by his manuscript.

I chose to tell my brother's story as a memoir because in many ways, our story is the same. David is etched into my earliest and most vivid memories. I remember the first time I saw him, when I was three. I remember the last time I saw him, on a scorching afternoon in late July, a week before he died. Concerned about his diet, I force-fed him a plate of pan-fried zucchini and accidentally poked his tonsils with the fork in my maternal zeal.

"You perforated me!" he hollered, and we laughed so hard we cried. Such horseplay was common between us—it refreshed our souls and renewed our bond. I've never laughed harder with anyone else.

It took me ten years to work up the courage to stand over his gravestone, as we'd stood together over so many others, and read the words.

> David W. Scheeres
> June 2 1967-
> Aug. 1 1987

Even then, it didn't seem real. It was just a stone, just words. It wasn't my brother.

I believe my parents had good intentions when they adopted my brothers, but good intentions go awry, as with missionaries bent on saving souls who obliterate entire tribal cultures in the process. Or former juvenile delinquents who find Jesus and decide to start reform schools.

I thank my parents for bringing me David, but not for the life they gave us.

"Figures he wasn't wearing a seat belt—rebellious to the end," was my father's sole comment to me on his death.

My mother told me she suspected David suffered from the attachment disorder syndrome prevalent among children adopted from Dickensian orphanages in Russia and Eastern Europe. For that reason, he'd "failed to bond with our family," she confided.

I know this is not true.

In 2001, I returned to Escuela Caribe to gather information for this book. I walked over the basketball court David and I dug in the hillside (which had since been paved) and stopped by Starr. It was a Saturday afternoon, and the girls were on their hands and knees like so many Cinderellas, scrubbing the same tile floors I'd spent so much time polishing sixteen years earlier. They'd failed house inspection and were spending their free day cleaning. I recognized the despair in their faces and longed to offer them some words of encouragement—"After surviving this hellhole, you'll survive anything"—but the housefather lurked at my shoulder and I wasn't able.

The staff considered me an outstanding alumna—I'd gone on to get an M.A. in Journalism and had worked for the *Los Angeles Times*—and introduced me around.

"What's the most important lesson you learned at Escuela Caribe?" one of them asked me with a smug smile.

"To not trust people," I answered without hesitation.

They changed the subject before I could tell them the other important lessons The Program had taught me, but perhaps they'll read them here:

—To believe in people over dogmas.

—To not turn the other cheek, but to master and subvert the rules of the game.

—To strive to find small joys even in the bleakest of circumstances.

If The Pastor were still alive, I'm sure he'd still consider me a filthy little sinner. But I can no longer have blind faith in creeds, because I am no longer blind. As Bruce used to scold, I've learned to "pay attention, really *think* about what I'm doing."

It's taken me twenty years to grasp the truth of what happened in Jesus Land, as well as losing my brother, excommunication from my church, and leaving the Midwest for good.

David continues to accompany me in dreams. In the years following his death, I'd have recurring dreams where I tried to save him from plummeting glass elevators and other dangers, or where I dug his grave alone as people streamed by me, indifferent to my anguish. There was also a repeated and macabre dream where I was in the car with him during his final seconds; we held hands and smiled serenely at each other as our heads shattered the windshield.

Nowadays when David appears in my dreams, it's to comfort me. I'll be standing in line to register at a new college, friendless and anxioius, and he'll materialize out of the crowd to give me a bear hug before walking away. Or I'll be stressing over a story deadline, and he'll appear in the newsroom as a colleague and offer to make some phone calls.

Sometimes when I see a picture of a black man with glasses who has David's same features in a newspaper or magazine, I'll cut it out and put it in a box with his photographs. I like to imagine what he would have looked like at the ripe old age of thirty-eight, and what he'd be like. I bet he'd still have his slapstick sense of humor. I know he'd be a great uncle, or dad.

I wonder what it would be like to walk with him down the streets of my adopted hometown of San Francisco, California. If we'd finally fit in here, in this mix-raced metropolis, or if we'd still draw stares.

Most of all, however, I'd like the chance to sit down with my brother and talk everything through, to go to a bar and say "remember when" over glasses of *agua de coco*. Then I'd finally be able to say all the things I wasn't brave enough to tell him when he was alive.

David, I love you.

ACKNOWLEDGMENTS

My big sister Debra, a stellar Catholic who listens without passing judgment and plays angelic flute music.

Laura, my middle big sister, a persevering friend who shares an appreciation for *Pee Wee's Big Adventure*.

Tim Rose, for knowing best how to calm me down and for sticking by me on the machete-sharpening days. I love you.

Joe Loya, bank robber extraordinaire-cum-author extraordinaire, my primary cheerleader for this book. *¿Quiubo huevon?*

Colleen Morton Busch, fellow Hoosier and writer, for her critiques and mountain bike riding tips.

Planned Parenthood, for its tireless crusade to protect women's reproductive freedom.

My editor, Megan Hustad, and my agent, Sam Stoloff, for getting this thing published.